THE
GREEK
PHOENIX

To
the memory of my friend
Reginald Turnor

Contents

Preface

At the outset this story of the centuries-long Turkish enslavement and eventual liberation of the Greek people called for certain decisions. It appeared to me obvious that with a panorama of past history so vast—stretching from 1453 to 1833—there would need to be a fairly drastic personal selection of material. Furthermore, the Greek War of Independence, if it was to be depicted in its proper historical setting (even more so than the events which preceded it), both politically and inherently presented a very complex problem. To over-simplify would be to distort facts away from the truth. On the other hand, the details of much fighting remain the same; so that to plod through every minor battle would be to invite boredom from the reader.

A compromise, therefore, seemed necessary, concentrating upon those aspects and highlights of the drama which struck me as most significant. But, above all, I have aimed at reproducing the colour and atmosphere of the scenes chosen and also tried to reveal the principal characters as living men and women. For both these purposes, and for the sake of authenticity and verisimilitude, I have been obliged to employ a certain amount of quotation; for nobody can contradict an eye-witness. For example, I would justify on this account such quotations as the extracts from Byron's long letter to his mother describing his sojourn with Ali Pasha, the pieces from the *Memoirs* of General Makriyannis, the Captain Fellowes's report for Admiral Codrington of the incident which started the Battle of Navarino. Of the splendours and disasters of the war, the cruelties, the heroism, the historic facts must speak for themselves.

Among some of the classic authors, listed in the Bibliography, which I have consulted, I have relied chiefly upon George Finlay, Thomas Gordon, Alison Phillips and the distinguished contemporary philhellene Colonel C. M. Woodhouse, to all of whom, perhaps particularly to the last, I am deeply indebted. I would like to express my personal appreciation to those Greek friends who have so kindly helped me by their conversation about the war, notably to Mrs. V. A. Zannos of Kifisia who also showed me documents relating to the struggle and who sent me the photo-print copy of Admiral Miaoulis's letter; to Mr. John Collas of Corfu; to Mr. Michael Peraticos and Mr. Geoffrey Allibone for some valuable introductions. Also my most grateful thanks are due to the National Tourist Organisation of Greece, for their practical help in arranging for me to visit the main sites of the fighting both in the Peloponnese and in continental Greece; and to the patient encouragement of my wife, Muriel, which was invaluable. Finally, I would like to thank the London Library, Tonbridge Public Library, Tunbridge Wells Public Library and Lewes County Library for their unfailing courtesy and always prompt assistance.

JOSEPH BRADDOCK

THE
GREEK
PHOENIX

From Makriyannis: The Memoirs of General Makriyannis, *Oxford University Press*

Greece at the time of the War of Independence

PART I

FROM LONG DARKNESS TO DAWN

CHAPTER I

The Fall of Constantinople

The fall of Constantinople on Tuesday, the 29th of May, 1453, was an historical event of dramatic magnitude and of long-enduring consequence. Although the siege had high moments of suspense, the catastrophe had long been foreseen by many percipient people as inevitable. A thousand years of history was about to terminate; to the West the downfall of this magnificent oriental, though Christian, holy city seemed at first a cosmic disaster. The last days, the final tragic hours, suggest some purple passage of painting, a lurid diorama depicting the splendour of the East, whereon both the casual bravery of the Turks and the undaunted resignation to death of the Christians share an equal importance.

When the Emperor Constantine I built Constantinople on the 900-year-old site of a Greek city-state named Byzantium as the Eastern capital of the Roman Empire, he could hardly have chosen a more favourable or impregnable position for ensuring his Christian city's prosperity. Situated around the narrowest sea-crossing between Europe and the great land routes to Asia, it soon became a centre of commerce for the known and the almost unknown world. Products poured into its markets from countries as far separated as China, Iceland, Russia and Ethiopia. There were fertile regions to the west and it possessed a magnificent harbour and outstanding natural defences. A city also of incomparable beauty that had materialized like some vision from the Arabian Nights, a centre of Graeco-Roman and Christian civilization, Constantinople attracted travellers from all parts of the known world. The sea was dominant, caressing the wooded shores of the Bosphorus. Apart from mosques and minarets, it is easy to praise

"Stamboul"; perhaps first of all the harbour, for, as in Venice, the sea comes directly close, home into the city. If from your hotel you would reach the bazaars, you must pass the broad blue pathway of the Golden Horn with its manifold shipping. In past centuries the sea was the slave of each Sultan: "She comes to his feet with the treasures of the world—she lifts his armed navies to the very gates of his garden."[1]

From the beginning the population of the Eastern Roman Empire had been cosmopolitan and grew progressively more so in the capital. The Greek language was the current speech of the thirty-two million inhabitants of the Empire and after a few centuries replaced Latin as the official language of the administration. Besides Constantine's Roman nobles, there were pure Greeks, Hellenized Greeks, Arabs, Egyptians, Syrians, even Goths, and a plentiful mixture of races from Asia Minor. Those who were Hellenized formed the chief military, commercial and intellectual core of the State. There was hardly any racial prejudice. Provided he was Orthodox and spoke Greek, even a negro was welcome as an equal citizen.

By the fifteenth century the cosmopolitan metropolis, with its bazaars and shops, forums and the hippodrome, had added to its population Venetians, Genoese, Cretans, Armenians, Jews, Catalans, pilgrims from Russia who came to visit the churches and relics, and Slav or Moslem merchants. The glorious city attracted travellers and pilgrims from all over the known world. The Greeks have always loved city life; their first famous metropolis had been Alexandria founded five hundred years earlier by Alexander the Great in 332 B.C. The Greeks were always, and still are, a gregarious people with no word in their language for privacy, loving to gossip, and relishing such social activities as eating in restaurants, carnivals, circuses, watching jugglers and strolling musicians. The Byzantine Greeks were also addicted to sports such as chariot-racing which was highly organized.

However, the real key to this complex amalgam of people was the Greek Orthodox faith. The symbols of Christianity were to be seen everywhere; for, under the Cross, the Byzantines believed themselves to be chosen of God and the Emperor who ruled by divine right, ruled in the name of Christ the Ruler of All. So that in Christ all men and women were politically and socially equal; and therefore any inhabitant of the Empire, without distinction of sex or class, whether bondsman or free, could rise to the highest office in the State, even that of Emperor. An exception was made of those who were physically blemished, such as eunuchs and the blind. Two women, Zoë and Theodora, sat upon the imperial throne. The Byzantines were besides evangelists whose foreign policy, although its main purpose was defence against the barbarians, sought to convert the heathen and were successful in spreading Christianity to Slavs and Russians, Ethiopians and Egyptians and to many others. So Constantinople had become not only the mother city of a world empire, but also of more than half Christendom, a city under divine protection.

Although it was this perfervid Orthodoxy that so provoked the contempt of Edward Gibbon in *The Decline and Fall of the Roman Empire*—he conceived the whole pious atmosphere as little more than bigoted religiosity—it was nevertheless true that this Christian society was theologically orientated. Theology certainly was an obsessive, and to the modern mind a slightly absurd, subject of conversation among the ordinary humble citizens of Byzantium. St. Gregory of Nyssa recorded that when he went to the capital he had to listen to unending and unintelligible theological argument:

> The whole city is full of it, the squares, the market-places, the cross-roads, the alleyways; old-clothes men, money-changers, food-sellers: they are all busy arguing. If you ask someone to give you change, he philosophises about the Begotten and the Unbegotten; if you enquire the price of a loaf, you are told by way of reply that the Father is greater and the Son inferior; if you ask "is my bath ready?" the attendant answers that the Son was made out of nothing.

On the other hand, it should always be kept in mind that to most people in Byzantium correct thinking on such vital matters seemed crucial to the life or death of their souls.

By the sixth century, under Justinian, the Byzantine Empire had achieved its largest extent. It stretched from the Danube, across the Black Sea to the Euphrates, to Mt. Sinai, Alexandria, Gibraltar and Milan. During the fourteenth and fifteenth centuries it had shrunk to a travesty of its former self. The contraction had been long and slow and piecemeal. At the beginning of the fifteenth century there were only two important cities left, Constantinople and Thessalonica, together with a few lesser Aegean islands, a town or two along the Marmora coast of Thrace, and some land in the Peloponnese. Everywhere else the Turks had conquered. The Sultan's armies had penetrated ever further into Europe and reached the Danube. So that Constantinople was completely encircled by the Sultan's dominions. Yet by a curious caprice of history these years of political and territorial decline co-existed with a cultural life which was more vital and creative than had flourished at any other period of Byzantine history.

The "Queen of Cities" had been besieged before. The Eastern Empire had never really recovered from the attack of the Fourth Crusade in 1204, when, weakened by a century and a half's resistance to the Asian hordes, it was unable to withstand the Venetians and Crusaders. This brutal sack and ruthless plunder had never been forgotten, nor had the enormous loss of wealth and treasure to the Latin West. But the final fall of Constantinople was postponed for half a century by the Mongol conqueror Tamerlaine's (Timúr the Lame) onslaught on the Turks from the East, when Sultan Bayezit was defeated and taken prisoner at the battle of Angora in 1402. Many Byzantines believed the remnants of their dying Empire saved. Manuel II Palaeologus, hearing that the Sultan was ready to march against Constantinople, hurried home from the West where he had gone to seek aid of the Pope, to find his capital indeed saved. However, the Turkish power was only scotched; yet dynastic quarrels damped down Turkish aggression for another two decades. When in June 1422 Sultan Murad II had invested Constantinople, he was forced to raise the siege almost at once because of threats of family dissention and rumours of rebellion.

But long before the year 1453 it must have become obvious to any dispassionate observer that Byzantium was doomed. As her hour of destruction approached a strange fatalism and pessimism took hold of the city. To Western humanist historians it must have appeared suicidal for Byzantium to reject union with the heretic West. Yet in a religious age the Byzantines thought less of their material safety than of their immortal souls and of the everlasting life to come. A final catastrophe might well be God's punishment for their sins. In the humid, often depressing climate of the Bosphorus the natural high spirits of the volatile Greeks grew somewhat sober. Prophecies had been whispered in the greatest days of the Empire, that even an Empire which had endured longer than any other in recorded history would not last for ever. The reign of anti-Christ might come. Perhaps the Empire which began with Constantine would end with Constantine.

Those who now believed that God would never allow the holy city of Byzantium to fall to the infidel were few in number. But union with the heretic West would neither bring salvation, nor alter fate. Too many people bore in mind the comparatively short-lived Latin Empire and how, when the cream of Christian chivalry had become the Lords of the East, they had pillaged, raped, tortured, and destroyed everything in the name of Christ, revealing themselves as illiterate thugs, rapacious robber-barons who showed only cruelty and avarice. When the Venetian Doge Dandolo had stormed Constantinople, incalculable damage was done to the Imperial palaces which the Venetians robbed of their art treasures. It was at this time that the famous bronze horses of Lysippus were removed and sent to adorn the portico of St. Mark's in Venice. The Latin Empire survived until 1261, when Michael Palaeologus recaptured the city and the Byzantine Empire was restored. But Christendom was divided against Christendom. Yet even if Christendom had been united, the West could not have sent sufficient practical help to offset the abundant organized military power of the Turks. Besides, union would have mortally offended the Greeks, who had striven to preserve their Orthodoxy against the Franks, and only caused a further schism. To underline a somewhat paradoxical position: to join with Rome could easily lose the Greek Patriarch more than three-quarters of his bishops; therefore the most hopeful chance of reuniting the Greek Church and the Greek people could lie in the acceptance of Turkish bondage. By this means alone it might be possible sufficiently to preserve the Orthodox Greek nation, until, with the passing of time, it was strong enough to cast off the yoke of the Infidel and recreate Byzantium.

There may have been more to be said for this apparently outrageous argument than at first appears plausible. Gibbon, writing of the winter before the Turkish conquest, when a service attended by ecclesiastics representing both Greek and Latin rites was held in the Church of the Holy Wisdom, comments:

> No sooner had the church of St. Sophia been polluted by the Latin sacrifice than it was deserted as a Jewish synagogue, or a heathen temple by the clergy and people; and a vast and gloomy silence prevailed in that venerable dome, which had so often smoked with a cloud of incense, blazed with innumerable lights, and resounded with the voice of prayer and thanksgiving. The Latins were the most odious of heretics and infidels; and the first minister of the empire, the great duke,* was heard to declare that he had rather behold in Constantinople the turban of Mohammed than the pope's tiara or a cardinal's hat.

The Emperor John VIII Palaeologus survived for nine personally unhappy years after his return from Italy. He did his best to keep the peace between his quarrelling brothers in the Peloponnese; also to parry the intrigues in his distressed and divided capital. But his most wise and prudent act was to use all the money the state could afford on strengthening the massive land walls and giant rounded keeps of the city so that they might hope to withstand the inevitable and imminent Turkish attack. He died on the last day of October 1448.

It will be helpful at this point to take a look at the character and personal appearance of Sultan Mehmet II, who earned for himself the proud sobriquet of the "Conqueror". Born the son of Murad

* Lucas Notaras, the last great minister of Byzantium.

8

II and quite probably of a Turkish slave-girl, he was only nineteen when he became Sultan. But in order to impress both his Turkish and Greek subjects he lent support to the belief that his family stemmed from a prince of the Imperial house of Comnenus, who in Konya had become a convert to Islam and married a Seljuk princess. What is positive is that as a result of his early education his sentiments were those of a devout Moslem; for example, when he talked with an infidel he purified his hands and face by the legal rites of ablution. And the dream of his boyhood had always been to capture Constantinople. By the time he came of age, under the tuition of the best masters he had become one of the most highly educated men of his period, speaking, if we include Arabic, five languages, Persian, Hebrew, Latin and Greek. This would prove of great advantage to him in understanding and dealing with people over whom he was ambitious to reign.

There exist two characteristic portraits of Mehmet II, the best-known being the one by Gentile Bellini in the National Gallery, London; the other is a drawing in profile in the collection of the Seraglio Library, Constantinople, by an unknown artist which has been attributed both to Gentile Bellini and Constanza da Ferrara. The first depicts the Sultan in his prime, white-turbaned, his dangerous, sharp black eyes glowing beneath arched eyebrows, with a neatly coiffured black beard and a thin acquiline nose that overhangs his sensual red lips. In the profile drawing he is much older, the beard reduced to scarcely more than scrubby shading, with the nose that reminded Turks of the beak of a parrot "about to eat ripe cherries". In his prime Mehmet was a powerfully built, handsome man of average height. His manner was generally dignified—unless he had been impious and drinking too much—and aloof; yet he could be cordial to scholars whose work he appreciated and to artists whose company he enjoyed. But he was notoriously secretive, for his life had taught him to trust no one. Though people could admire and respect him for his determination, he was not a man to make himself beloved. He had never shown any desire for popularity; nor could his will be deflected from the task upon which he had set his mind. His one obsessive objective was the conquest of Constantinople. In the years before the siege began, he had talked peace when war was in his heart.

Unfortunately Mehmet had inherited—along with some of their not inconsiderable virtues—the brutal vices of his ancestors. He possessed plenty of animal courage, but he was also a prey to violent and unnatural lusts. Of his ancestors Bayezit I had been the first sultan to indulge in alcohol, a pleasure forbidden to devout Moslems by the Koran. In an admittedly licentious age, the gross orgies and crude bestialities of his court had scandalized Europe. Mehmet had always remained at heart a lonely man, full of strange contradictions; suspicious yet judicial, promoting men when he found merit in them but punishing weakness or failure with ruthless savagery. His policy made him treat all men coldly as mere pawns in his game of world conquest.

It is quite likely that these contradictions in Mehmet's character, his double life, owed something to the non-Turkish blood in his veins. The Hamlet-like student "sicklied o'er with the pale cast of thought", interested in philosophy, theology, science and art, was extremely un-Turk-like. On the other hand, he frequently revealed himself as a bloodthirsty tyrant indifferent to human slaughter, who took a sadistic pleasure in human suffering. Yet, his two contradictory lives were curiously blended. He would revert from study to slaughter, and after indulging in torture would show signs of pity for the agonies of his victims.

To understand the last tragic days of the siege of Constantinople, it is necessary to keep in mind the Moslem attitude towards the infidel. The dichotomy in the Turkish character has been neatly summarized:

The unbeliever is any enemy of God and of Mahomet, and it is a sacred duty when he is fighting against the Moslem to slay him. Those who are at war against Islam must be utterly destroyed, root and branch, unless indeed they will accept the faith. Men, women, and children must alike suffer the penalty. But when no religious sentiment obscures the natural feelings of humanity, the same Turk is good-natured and kindly . . . . Mahomet II both in his cruelty towards his enemies and in his spasmodic kindness was a not unfair representative of his race.[2]

By the autumn of 1452 Mehmet, who by now had managed to dominate the Bosphorus, was in a strong position to isolate Constantinople by imposing a total blockade. In the spring (with the help of a thousand masons) work had begun on building a formidable fortress, Rumeli Hisar, some five miles from the Greek metropolis and almost opposite the castle of Anadolu Hisar on the Asiatic shore of the Bosphorus which had been built by his grandfather Bayezit. Rumeli Hisar was finished on the last day of August.

But as autumn and then winter advanced, even Mehmet's own ministers remained uncertain of his intentions. With control of the Bosphorus, would he wait, without fighting, until the city for lack of provisions was obliged to surrender? He had plans for an opulent new palace at Adrianople. His Vizier Halil—whom some supposed to be in the pay of the Greeks—disliked the idea of a siege and much hoped that Mehmet would instead transfer his court and government to Adrianople. A siege would be very costly; and should it fail, the damage to Ottoman prestige would be both humiliating and irrevocable.

The Sultan during these months of indecision spent many sleepless nights brooding over his prospects. He walked the streets of Adrianople dressed as a common soldier. Anybody who recognized him and saluted was immediately put to death. One night Mehmet suddenly ordered Halil to come before him. The old Vizier, fearing dismissal, trembled and brought with him a bowl filled with gold coins as a gift for his master. Mehmet brushed the gift aside. He had no use for such conventional gestures. "Only one thing I want," he cried. "Give me Constantinople." He then informed Halil that his mind was made up, he would attack the city as soon as this was practicable.

Within doomed Byzantium "amidst hope and fear, the fears of the wise and the hopes of the credulous, the winter rolled away."[3] From the Turkish standpoint, the task they faced was immense; for the defences of the town were enormously strong. From as far back as the fourth century, various Emperors had strengthened the fortifications. The historian Critobulus describes the land enclosed as more of a fortified town than a fort:

The walls and towers still remain and form the most picturesque object which the traveller sees on his passage through the Bosphorus. Each of two peaks is crowned with a strong tower. These are connected by a long high wall interrupted with smaller towers, and from the two largest towers similar walls at right angles to the long wall connect them with great towers on the shore at the end of another line of walls parallel to the channel. Small guns or bombards enabled the enclosure to be defended against any attack by land. On the sea shore and under the protection of the walls were stationed large cannon which threw heavy stone balls and commanded the passage.[4]

All through the winter of 1452 both Greeks and Turks prepared for the siege. The Emperor did what was possible to repair and reinforce the now decidedly dilapidated walls of his capital. To placate the Holy See, he had belatedly agreed to the Union of the Greek and Latin Churches; but this move had led to fierce dissension within the city. So that Constantine also lacked funds, because the wealthy Greek churches, angered at his heresy, refused to disgorge their treasure to help finance the defence. A few hundred Genoese under a soldier of fortune, Giustiniani, with the addition of some Spanish and Italian mercenaries, were all the help that Constantine could get from Europe. He was barely able to muster in all 7,000 men, an inadequate number to hold the walls.

Mehmet, on the other hand, had collected at Adrianople a formidable army of eighty thousand soldiers, besides hordes of irregulars. He had always taken a keen interest in the latest machine-products of science and was a convinced believer in the use of modern artillery in siege warfare. Therefore he had commissioned (at a huge salary) a Hungarian engineer named Urban to construct a cannon which, the man boasted, "would blast the walls of Babylon itself." And this cannon had already sunk a Venetian ship which was trying to run the blockade. In the foundry at Adrianople Urban now cast one twice the size of the first, much to Mehmet's delight. The length of the barrel was twenty-six feet and eight inches, and the balls weighed twelve hundredweight. The road that led to Constantinople was levelled and the bridges strengthened, and in March 1453 the cannon commenced its long and difficult journey, drawn by sixty oxen, with two hundred men marching alongside to steady the gun-carriage.

In early April Mehmet arrived before Constantinople, vowing that he would either add it to his Empire, or lose both. His army was enthusiastic at the thought of a promised three days' sack. Even the humblest trooper could dream of a life of wealth and ease, following the division of the spoils, the treasures of the churches and palaces, and the sale of the people as slaves. Women and boys in plenty awaited their lustful desires. And any Moslem soldier who died in battle would be rewarded with a Paradise of even greater sensual delights. For the holy book of Islam, the *Alkoran of Mohammed* gave some promising pictures of the Moslem paradise:

> As for the righteous, they shall surely triumph. Theirs shall be gardens and vineyards, and high-bosomed maidens for companions: a truly overflowing cup.
> They shall recline on couches ranged in rows. To dark-eyed houris We shall wed them.
> Fruits We shall give them, and such meats as they desire. They will pass from hand to hand a cup inspiring no idle talk, no sinful urge; and there shall wait on them young boys of their own as fair as virgin pearls.

Meanwhile from the walls of the city the Turkish fleet could be seen cruising in the Sea of Marmora; while the Sultan's army, with Urban's monster cannon, moved up towards a favourable position against the fourteen miles of walls. The Byzantines were superstitious and inclined to believe in omens. One or two minor earthquakes, accompanied by torrential rain, had been taken by the inhabitants as evil signs. Men and women remembered ancient prophecies foretelling the doom of the Empire and the coming of Anti-Christ. Yet, while they despaired in their hearts, all showed courage and joined unitedly in preparations for the defence. The hope of help from abroad was unreliable. A promised Venetian flotilla procrastinated, then was further delayed by adverse winds, so that when at last it sailed from Venice Constantinople had already endured blockade and bombardment for a fortnight. Constantine had sent for his secretary Phrantzes and asked him to make a census of every available man in the city, including monks, who were able to bear arms. The odds against the Byzantines, as noted, were so uneven and the Emperor so appalled, that he told Phrantzes to suppress the figures.

As the days passed, for the Orthodox Greeks the conflict had its unexpected moments of triumph, of hope even. Yet on that first of April, 1453, which happened to be Easter Sunday, there can have been no joy or real hope in the hearts of the Christians. But at least they were permitted to celebrate the rites of Holy Week and Christ's resurrection in peace. Nature, of course, was indifferent to their plight: ironic spring had returned to the Bosphorus in all its heart-breaking beauty; fruit-trees were coming into bloom, nightingales were preparing to sing, and storks to build their nests on the roof-tops. But a vast hostile army was on the move, and by the fifth of April was encamped outside the walls, with Sultan Mehmet himself in command. The defenders also took up their positions.

Following the law of Islam, at the outset of the siege the Sultan had sent a last message to the beleaguered town promising to spare the citizens and leave their families and property unharmed if they would voluntarily surrender. Failing this, no mercy would be shown. But the Greeks of Byzantium had no faith in such promises; nor would they desert their Emperor. Constantine therefore caused some thousand Venetian sailors, whose costumes were distinctive, to parade the length of the walls so that Mehmet should believe that the Venetians were present among his enemies. It is believed that Constantine made several attempts to negotiate, that embassies passed between the camp and the city; if so it was without success. Though Mehmet would have liked to spare the blood of his soldiers, provided he could secure for himself the Byzantine treasures, his terms remained unchanged. And nobody trusted his clemency. So, probably after some fruitless parleying, the Sultan was finally resolved. He would find either a throne or death under the walls of Constantinople.

Throughout the nearly two months gruelling siege the Christians had their successes, notably the victory of their ships over the Sultan's hasty and deficient navy. On April 20th three Genoese galleys which had been hired by the Pope, loaded with both arms and food—they were later joined by an Imperial transport crammed with corn—were observed by the watchers on the sea-walls to be approaching. The Turks had seen them too. The Turkish Admiral Baltoghlu was commanded to capture or sink these ships. Should he fail in preventing them bringing relief to the city, he was not to return alive. In the event, the result proved a very encouraging triumph for the Christians; for the discipline on their ships was splendid. The Genoese wore adequate armour, and had ample water aboard their galleys to extinguish fires; also they used their axes dexterously to chop off the hands and heads of boarding-parties. The Imperial transport was stocked with barrels of inflammable liquid known as "Greek Fire", a weapon that had saved Constantinople in many previous sea-fights. The Christians used it with a stunning and decisive effect, and in all ways showed the superiority of their seamanship.

Sultan Mehmet, who was watching on horseback from the shore, kept urging his animal into the shallow water as if he himself would have liked to take part in the fighting. Not properly understanding the art of seamanship, he was mortified and grew enraged at his defeat and by the knowledge that Constantinople had been reinforced with arms, and also with wheat, oil, wine and vegetables.

Although Admiral Baltoghlu by common consent had fought with the utmost courage, in spite of the handicap of a painful wound in the eye, harrying the Imperial transport until his position had grown hopeless, he was utterly discredited and disgraced and only escaped death because his officers bore unanimous witness to his personal bravery. He was deprived of his offices and private possessions, bastinadoed, then exiled to spend his remaining days poor and obscure. Gibbon sardonically describes his punishment "in the royal presence, the captain bashaw was extended on the ground by four slaves, and received one hundred strokes with a golden rod . . . and he adored the clemency of the Sultan."[5]

The Christians in their great delight at such a heartening victory boasted that ten or twelve thousand Turks had perished in the sea-fight and not one Christian, although several sailors died of their wounds later. But this was a preposterous exaggeration.

At one moment the Turks almost raised the siege in despair, in spite of their irresistible advantage in numbers. But after seven weeks of continuous bombardment by the Sultan's new devastating artillery, including Urban's monstrous masterpiece, the land-walls had been broken in three places, most seriously at the gate of St. Romanus where a wide breach had been made. The magnificent defences were at last crumbling; by the end of May a majority of the defenders realized that fate could no longer be averted and that the holy city's last hour had come.

During these final days, under cover of darkness, a brigantine reached the city with the news that no Christian help could be expected in the fight for Christendom. The Emperor had wept on hearing this, but then stoically observed that all Constantinople could do now was to put its faith in Christ and Mary and in Saint Constantine its founder. Also fighting for the honour of God and of all Christendom was a group of Venetian sailors, a contingent of Genoese volunteers under their gallant leader Giustiniani, and in addition some philhellene Castilians, Catalans, Germans, Hungarians and Serbs, with even a few renegade Turks.

The Christians required all their faith, because signs in Heaven pointed to destruction. Constantine to Constantine: people remembered prophecies that the Empire would perish. A superstition existed that the city would be safe under a waxing moon; but the moon (oldest symbol of Byzantium) was full on the 24th of May, with an eclipse and a three-hours darkness. When, as a last desperate intercession to the Mother of God, Mary's holiest ikon was being carried through the streets, it slipped from its platform and was only replaced in position with much effort. Next, a violent thunderstorm broke, accompanied by hail and torrents of rain of such force that the procession had to be abandoned. The following day the town was obscured by a thick fog, unprecedented in late May when the roses were blooming. That same night the fog dispersed to reveal an unusual light playing round the cupola of the Church of the Holy Wisdom. The Turks saw it too, but interpreted this astonishing phenomenon with a difference. The Sultan's soothsayers assured him that the light signified that the light of the True Faith would shortly shine in the infidel building. The Emperor Constantine was urged by his ministers to escape in time and lead the defence of Christendom from a safer place. Worn out and weary, he fainted while they were speaking. When he came to, he had one answer. He could not desert his people; he would die with them in Byzantium.

Mehmet had faith in the science of astrology. This granted the defenders a brief respite since the fortunate day for the Turks had been indicated as the 29th of May. Two evenings previously the Sultan had issued final orders to his military chiefs. He warned and menaced any would-be fugitives or deserters in true Oriental style: had they the wings of a bird, they would not escape his inexorable justice. The Moslems were bidden to cleanse their minds with prayer and their bodies with the seven ablutions, and to eat no food until the close of the following day. Dervishes visited the soldiers' tents to whip them up to a relish for martyrdom, and to assure those who would die in battle of an immortal youth to be spent in Paradise in the arms of black-eyed virgins. But Mehmet himself believed in more temporal and earthly rewards.

A double pay was promised to the victorious troops; "The city and the buildings," said Mohammed, "are mine; but I resign to your valour the captives and the spoil, the treasures of gold and beauty; be rich and be happy. Many are the provinces of my empire: the intrepid soldier who first ascends the walls of Constantinople shall be rewarded with the government of the fairest and most wealthy; and my gratitude shall accumulate his honours and fortunes above the measure of his own hopes."[6]

Within the city walls men listened to the sounds of jubilation coming from the Turkish camp. The Sultan's proclamation, according to Islamic tradition, had promised his hordes of soldiers a three days uninterrupted pillage. The Moslems were impatient for action. Their shouts re-echoed tumultuously: "There is no

God but God, and Mohammed is His Prophet." All night they continued with their preparation, singing and shouting, urged on by fifes and trumpets, and both sea and land were illuminated by their lurid nocturnal fires. The Christians, hearing, waiting, could only kneel and pray.

On Monday the 28th of May Constantine told his Greek subjects that the decisive assault was imminent. Silence had fallen on the Turkish camp; by contrast in Constantinople the bells of the churches rang, gongs were beaten as relics and ikons were borne upon the shoulders of the defenders to bless those places where damage, and therefore danger, seemed likeliest. Everybody, Orthodox and Catholic, sang hymns and recited the Kyrie Eleison. Each man was resigned and ready to die for his religion, his Emperor, his country and his family. Constantine reminded them that they were the descendants of the ancient Greek and Roman heroes, exhorting them to be worthy of their ancestors. Let them lift up their hearts, with God's help they would win victory yet. But though the Byzantines assured the Emperor of their total devotion, they embraced one another as men who were expecting to die.

The same evening the moment of truth was realized in a brilliant, moving last service of intercession in the Church of the Holy Wisdom. All futile past bitterness was forgotten. At this eleventh hour ecclesiastics of both the Orthodox and Latin persuasion had buried their centuries old antagonism. Priests, who previously would have considered union with Rome a mortal sin, now served at the altar with their Roman brothers. The Cardinal was present, standing next to bishops who before would not have acknowledged his authority. And the crowd who confessed and took communion were indifferent as to which persuasion administered it. Italians and Catalans mixed with the Greeks. The golden wall-mosaics of Christ and His Saints, the images of the Emperors and Empresses of Byzantium, shone beneath the beams of a myriad lamps and candles. And through this glittering, subdued effulgence the priests in their gorgeous vestments acted out the sacred rhythm of the Liturgy. At last there was union in the Church of Byzantium.

On the order of the Sultan the grand assault started at about half-past one in the morning of Tuesday, the 29th of May. The previous afternoon the Turks in their thousands had sprung into feverish activity, bringing forward war-engines, and filling up the foss. The sinking sun had almost blinded the defenders on the walls but there was little they could have done to stop the progress of the preparation.

The attack was launched in darkness, and the noise from the advancing Turks, screaming blood-curdling battle-cries, accompanied by drums, trumpets, fifes, was deafening. The Christians waited in a tense silence; but directly the men on the watchtowers gave the alarm the belfry of every church in Byzantium clanged out its warning. Each Christian soldier took up his post, while helpers on the walls included women, even nuns and children, who brought water to sustain the troops. Many—the infirm, the very old and very young—sought sanctuary in the churches, hoping against hope that somehow the angels and the saints would deliver them. Tuesday was the feast-day of Saint Theodosia and her church by the Golden Horn had been decorated with roses from the gardens. Many people repaired to the great cathedral of the Holy Wisdom, recalling a prophecy that, although the enemy might infest the city, at the last moment the Angel of the Lord would come with his flaming sword and drive the infidel back to perdition. Through the long hours until dawn the helpless multitude watched and prayed.

At daybreak, with no warning gun, the full Turkish onslaught swept against the town by sea and by land. Mehmet had planned cunningly, for he respected his adversary. First, he was prepared to sacrifice his irregulars, the Bashi-bazouks, a motley host of many thousands of mercenaries recruited from every land and race (Christians as well as Turks), to draw the Greek fire and exhaust his enemy. But these undisciplined troops—motivated by greed and the allurements of the "rapine of an hour"—were unreliable, excellent for an initial charge, yet quickly discouraged if unsuccessful. So Mehmet had placed behind them a line of military police, who wielded maces and whips to flog any waverers forward. The Bashi-bazouks attacked on a wide front, and there was fierce fighting. But the walls were still too strong and the defenders desperately resolute. At first neither the Bashi-bazouks, nor later the waves of Anatolian light infantry who followed them, were able to breach the walls. Stones hurled down by the defenders killed many men at a time and any Turks halfway up the ladders attached against the walls were disposed of before they could reach the top by the indomitable Giustiniani and his Italian and Greek supporters. After two hours fighting, Mehmet called off the attack; but, although his troops had been repulsed, they had sapped much of the energy of the defenders.

And then, fresh and vigorous and regarded as invincible, the Sultan's *corps d'élite*, the Janissaries were waiting. Mehmet on horseback directed their charge, and could judge their valour. He had promised a noble prize to the first soldier who should penetrade the stockade and he hoped that it might be one of his favourite "Praetorian guard". The Christians had hardly had time to make more than a few hasty repairs to the stockade when, under a shower of mixed missiles, the Janissaries were upon them. These crack troops, advancing at the double, made no wild rushes such as the Bashi-bazouks and the Anatolians had done, but came on at a controlled unhurried pace in perfectly disciplined order. Martial music supported them, loud enough to be heard, above the thunder of the cannon, across the Bosphorus. Mehmet stood by the foss, shouting his exhortations as the troops swarmed past him. Magnificently armoured, they arrived in waves and reached the stockade which they proceeded to tear down, hack at, and dismantle. They placed their scaling ladders firmly where they would be difficult to dislodge. Wave after wave of Janissaries made way for its successor. The Christians had been fighting for over four hours and were exhausted; but each one of them knew that to weaken now in the slightest degree would mean the end.

Now, to prevent the risk of desertions, the gates of the outer wall had been shut behind the garrison; so that all they could do was to die fighting. And the issue still remained hotly contested. The immediate loss of the city was hastened by a close-range shot from a culverin that pierced the armour of the Genoese captain Giustiniani, who up to this point had been the inspired soul of the defence. Now, bleeding profusely and in terrible pain, he asked to be carried off the battle-field, although the Emperor himself pleaded with him to stay at his post. However, he insisted on flight. His troops, noticing his body being carried into the city and then down to the harbour, assumed that the battle was lost. The nerve of the Italian contingents was broken. The Greeks and their Emperor were left to fight alone. Never had the Greeks fought more tenaciously, persisting in a quite hopeless defence until walls, suburbs and the centre of the city had in turn been overrun by the Janissaries. Constantine XI, as soon as he knew that the Empire was lost, no longer wished to survive. There is evidence that, after discarding his imperial uniform and insignia so as to be less easily recognizable, he returned to the fighting and fell at his post. He was never seen alive again.

At one moment during the Greeks' last desperate stand the cry had gone up: "The city is taken." Then wailing shouts of "the city is lost!" re-echoed through the streets. From the Golden Horn both Turks and Christians could see the Turkish flags flying from the towers of Blackernae, where only minutes before had flown the standards of the Lion of Saint Mark and the proud Imperial Eagle. Signals of the break through the walls and the entry were flashed to the whole Turkish army, as the Turkish hordes swept into the city, and began a merciless and indiscriminate massacre.

For many hours before this Sultan Mehmet had been in no doubt about the issue. He exulted that at last the great oriental metropolis was his. At dawn, with a now waning moon "hung aloft the night", he had gone to examine the breach through which his Janissaries had stormed in triumph. But he would wait until the afternoon before he made his own triumphal entry into Byzantium; for by then the first excesses of rape and pillage would be over. He would restore order and prevent a continuing and wholesale massacre, because he had no wish to see the entire population exterminated. Mehmet was well pleased. The Emperor was surely dead. He himself was now the conqueror, possessor, and heir of the ancient Roman Empire.

CHAPTER II

Aftermath

According to the laws of Islamic tradition a city which voluntarily surrenders to the conqueror must not be pillaged; although a heavy indemnity will no doubt be extracted. The Christian or Jewish population may keep their places of worship, with few imposed regulations. But the inhabitants of a town that has finally been stormed are left without any rights whatsoever. The victorious army is allowed three days of unrestricted licence. Churches, and all other buildings, belong to the conqueror to be stripped of their treasures and disposed of as desired.

Mehmet had promised his soldiers this three days of pillage. The regiments had marched into the city with some discipline, to music and with flying colours. Soon after, all was chaos, brutality, and a mad scramble for loot. Men, women and children were slaughtered indiscriminately without pity. The Church of Saint Mary of the Mongols came to be known by the Turks as "the Church of Blood", because of the blood that streamed past it in rivers from the heights of Petra towards the Golden Horn. Notwithstanding, gradually the lust for slaughter spent itself, as it dawned on the licentious soldiery that captives and the loot of treasure might bring them more profit.

Nobody will suppose that a Turkish massacre has ever been anything but frightful. Critobulus records that the Turks, having been taunted by the besieged about their long inability to take the city, were outraged at the sufferings they had undergone. As the Turkish historian Sa'ad ed-Din himself makes clear, "having received permission to loot, they thronged into the city with joyous heart, and there, seizing their possessions and families, they made the wretched misbelievers weep. They acted in accordance with the precept, 'Slaughter their aged and capture their youth.' "[1] So the savage killing went on until midday.

While of course it is possible that eye-witnesses of such violent scenes—and even the evidence of contemporary historians—may choose to pile on the colour, there are certain images which carry an inherent conviction of their own. For example, Phrantzes says "that in some places the earth could no longer be seen on account of the multitude of dead bodies," and Barbaro more originally and graphically observes "the number of heads of dead Christians and Turks in the Golden Horn and the Marmora being so great as to remind him of melons floating in his own Venetian canals, and of the waters being coloured with blood." Also, so sinister was the reputation of the Turk for cruelty, that it is more than probable that many nuns and chaste women threw themselves into wells, or committed suicide by other means—as did their heroic successors in the Greek War of Independence and in the still later Armenian massacres of 1895–6—rather than fall into the hands of the Turk.

The systematic plundering went on all that day. Churches, monasteries, convents, private houses were all completely plundered, the private houses ransacked so thoroughly that the Turks left little flags outside to indicate that they were empty of everything. The wretched people were taken away captive with their possessions. In the Cathedral of Santa Sophia the Christians had prayed once more with desperation, but prayed in vain. As the huge bronze doors were battered down, they found themselves trapped. The crazed Turks fought each other for the possession of the most beautiful women. Veils and rich garments were torn from the victims to be used as ropes; masters and mistresses were bound to their servants, and high church dignitaries to the humblest peasants.

On the cultural side, many famous Byzantine libraries, both monastic and civic, were looted and most of the books burnt; unless, that is, they happened to be seen by some knowledgeable Turk as being of marketable value. But a majority of the infidel books were sold not for their price so much as in a spirit of mockery and only for a few pence. Similarly, mocking ribald scenes took place in the churches, precious crucifixes being borne away in sham solemnity, perhaps crowned by a Janissary's cap. From the libraries "one hundred and twenty thousand manuscripts are said to have disappeared; ten volumes might be purchased for a single ducat; and the same ignominious price, too high perhaps for a shelf of theology, including the whole works of Aristotle and Homer, the noblest productions of the science and literature of ancient Greece."[2]

In the late afternoon Sultan Mehmet entered the city in triumph accompanied by a crack detachment of his Janissary Guards, "each of whom [says a Byzantine historian] was robust as Hercules, dexterous as Apollo, and equal in battle to any ten of the race of ordinary mortals." The conqueror looked in wonder and with satisfaction at the unfamiliar, though glorious, appearance of the palaces and domes, so different from the style of Oriental architecture. His viziers and pashas followed. Slowly he rode through the sad and empty streets to Hagia Sophia, which he entered. Observing a Turk prizing out a piece of marble from the pavement, the Sultan angrily asked the man why he was damaging the building. "It is only a building of the infidels," pleaded the Turk. Mehmet threatened him with his scimitar, telling him that permission to loot did not include damage to the buildings which now belonged to him. The Sultan allowed some Greeks, who had been hiding, to go in peace to their homes. A few priests too he sent away under his protection. Then he gave orders that Hagia Sophia should instantly become a mosque. An *imam* ascended the pulpit forthwith to declare the Mohammedan faith that there was no God but Allah. From that moment until it was secularized by Kemal Ataturk in 1934 the Church of the Holy Wisdom remained a Mohammedan mosque.

As he rode through the desolation of the silent ruined streets, the Sultan had been moved to tears. "What a city we have given over to plunder and destruction," he sighed. Within the partly-destroyed Imperial palace of the Palaeologi he grew more philosophical, repeating a neat well-known distich of Persian poetry (Firdusi) on the mutability of human greatness:

The spider spins his web in the Palace of the Caesars
And the owl keeps watch on the Tower of Afrisiab.[3]

But Mehmet was a clever man; not least when he appointed the
scholar, George Scholarius Gennadius, Patriarch of Constantinople, because this underlined both his own succession to the
Byzantine throne and also his decision to govern his new Christian subjects through their own Patriarch.

During the year following Mehmet's conquest of Constantinople
he built a palace on the Third Hill; and then between 1459 and
1465 a larger palace, which superseded it, on the First Hill. The
original palace was now known as *Eski Serai* (Old Serai), while the
later and bigger one was called *Yeni Serai* (New Serai); though
most European writers referred to it simply as the Grand Seraglio.[4]
This palace consisted of an impressive collection of buildings used
for different purposes, and stood half concealed in a vast park of
cypresses, plane trees, and odoriferous shrubs, on the hill of
Seraglio Point, the site of the ancient Byzantine acropolis overlooking the Bosphorus. The first court of the palace became celebrated to Europeans as the Court of the Janissaries, where the
Yeni Cheri (New Troops) had their barracks.

The date of the origin of the Janissaries has been disputed between scholars. While allowing that the creation of this famous
military institution has generally been attributed to Sultan Orkhan
(1326–59), N. M. Penzer in his scholarly book *The Harēm* main-
tains, with others, that this date is too early. About that time
certainly it was the habit of Sultans to keep a personal bodyguard
recruited from the sons of conquered Christians. However, it
appears more likely that the Corps of the Janissaries was organized
by Orkhan's successor Murad I and further developed during the
rule of Mehmet II and beyond. Broadly speaking then the Turkey
of the Janissaries lasted just five hundred years, that is from 1326
to 1826. At the beginning their numbers were few, until the close
of the fifteenth century no more than about 2,000. During the
sixteenth century the figure increased, reaching 12,000 under
Suleiman the Magnificent. By the end of the eighteenth century

the number of Janissaries had swollen to 100,000. The advantage of such a body of troops lay in the fact that, with no family ties and because of the privileged conditions of their training, they remained in the early periods fanatically devoted and loyal to the person of the Sultan.

From the fourteenth to the end of the seventeenth century the Turks were in an almost constant state of war with the Christian countries of Western Europe; so the Ottoman law decreed that, instead of paying a tribute in money or kind, the conquered peoples, Greeks, Albanians, Serbs, Bulgars, and so on, should provide a thousand boys a year between the ages of ten and twelve. A man was obliged to relinquish one in five of his sons, and very naturally the healthiest, strongest and most intelligent boys were chosen and forcibly converted to the Moslem faith. After six years of Spartan training the boys were drafted into the Janissary corps and, not being permitted to marry or own property, they belonged exclusively to the regiment. The boys were torn by press-gangs from their parents and this *devshirmé*, child-tribute, fell as a heavy burden on the Christians. The corps was chiefly recruited from among the subject races of the Balkan Peninsula, with a majority of Greeks and Albanians. For the Janissaries themselves there were copious privileges and membership came to be much sought after. The excitement and triumphs of fighting relieved the hardship and monotony of barrack-room life. Loot rewarded victory; generous pensions comforted age or illness; valour plus intelligence could raise a man to the highest posts in the Empire. The Janissaries soon became the most dreaded and famous body of troops in Europe.

Unfortunately, with the passage of time, under the later Sultans the Janissaries were no longer "the flower of the Ottoman army". As their numbers increased rules began to be ignored; the hereditary principle was introduced so that the sons of Janissaries could join the Corps. There developed a sad falling off in discipline. By the seventeenth century this once almost invincible body of soldiery had degenerated into something like an ill-disciplined rabble who were even prepared to blackmail the Sultan and his Government for higher pay, unreasonable bonuses, and more and more privileges. There were frequent mutinies when Sultans were

actually dethroned, grand viziers and ministers alternately promoted and unseated, with all manner of other excesses. A time
came even when the Janissaries showed themselves reluctant to
take the field. They preferred the soft-living of the capital to the
hazards and dangers of war, until the point was reached when an
unpopular order could provoke a mutiny.

The end, though it was long delayed, came in June 1826 when
Sultan Mahmud II massacred the Janissaries who had mutinied
against his military reforms. The once arrogant praetorians, now
dwindled to little more than a disorderly mob, were mown down
by Mahmud's new field guns in the Hippodrome at Constantinople.

In Byzantium the first few days of brutal licence were over. Yet for
certain Greek captives there were further heartbreaking miseries
and dark atrocities to come. One may enumerate a few. Many
Greek families found themselves divided, never to be reunited.
Several historical reports agree in maintaining that Mehmet made
gifts of four hundred Greek children to each of three contemporary
potentates, the Sultan of Egypt, the King of Tunis and the King of
Grenada. The kindness Mehmet had first shown to the Emperor's
late ministers soon cooled. He behaved equivocally and treacher-
ously towards them. He had let it be known that he might make
Lucas Notaras governor of the city; but his advisers warned him
against trusting the Emperor's great minister and so Mehmet's
first impulse of generosity was turned to suspicion. At a banquet
given five days after the fall of the city, he had the opportunity of
putting Notaras's loyalty to the test. Mehmet was flushed with
wine when somebody told him that Notaras's son was a fourteen-
year-old boy of ravishing beauty. The Sultan immediately sent a
eunuch to command Notaras to deliver the boy to him for his
pleasure. Notaras, who had had two elder sons killed in the fighting, bravely refused this infamous command. Police were at once
dispatched to fetch Notaras and his son and his young son-in-law
before the Sultan. But when Notaras still defied him, Mehmet
ordered his instant decapitation, with that of the two boys:
Notaras demanded that they should be killed before him, lest

watching his death should cause them to waver. When they had both died he offered his neck to the executioner.

The historian George Phrantzes, who had been Constantine's faithful secretary and friend, suffered in the common tragedy. He (with his wife and children) endured eighteen months' hardship as a slave in the household of the Sultan's Master of the Horse, a man who had purchased many other ladies belonging to the Greek nobility. After recovering his freedom Phrantzes was allowed to ransom his wife; but his two children, both god-children of the Emperor Constantine, while still "in the flower of youth and beauty" had been reserved for the use of Mehmet himself. The girl Thamar, who was only fourteen years old, soon died in the Seraglio, possibly still a virgin. The boy John, in his fifteenth year, was stabbed to death by the Sultan for refusing to submit to his demands.

And yet, parallel with such sporadic outbreaks of cruelty, Sultan Mehmet had revealed his native political shrewdness, and a considerable gift for statesmanship, when he appointed the most eminent surviving Greek churchman Patriarch of the Greek Church, offering Gennadius also his royal friendship, together with all the perquisites and privileges of his predecessors. Many fanatical muftis and beys would have preferred a wholesale Christian massacre; but Mehmet displayed a long-sighted tolerance which was missing in his Christian contemporaries. So the churches of Constantinople were shared between the two religions; their limits were defined and for more than sixty years the Greeks enjoyed the benefit of this equal partition.

Mehmet, too, had at once grasped the fact that it was necessary to repopulate the now desolate former capital of the world with far more able, clever and sophisticated people than his own rough shepherd soldiers. So he would need to conciliate the Greeks. He may even have felt some genuine pity for the sufferings of his captives. With this purpose he attempted to quiet the fears of the Greek community by transporting large numbers of Greek Christians from the Morea (the Peloponnese) and the islands of the Aegean, and encouraging them to settle within the various areas of his conquests. Certain noble families were given houses on the slope towards the Golden Horn, and from these he selected boys to become Janissaries; or, if they had enjoyed a superior education, he might take them for his pages. By the end of Mehmet's long reign Constantinople was far richer and more flourishing than it had been under the last of the Palaeologi. Until he died Mehmet was concerned with the forcible or persuasive repeopling of his capital.

Although the capture of Constantinople had initially been felt as a catastrophic shock throughout Europe, the Turkish occupation of Greece in actual fact involved no wounding blow to Greek national pride, because at that time the Greeks did not think of themselves as a nation. The word ἔθνος—which today means nation—to the Byzantines meant nothing more than a race or tribe not yet assimilated into the multiracial peoples of the Empire. What they resented most was that the Turks treated them as second-class citizens, as *rayah*, cattle, making it difficult for them to live and still harder to progress.

Certainly the enslaved Greeks suffered many tribulations and some intolerable penalties. For example, they were obliged to pay a head-tax (*kharaj*), quite literally to keep their heads upon their shoulders! They lived under military law, their lives and property at the mercy of the arbitrary whims of the commanders. Then they were required to hand over a portion of their produce and had to "pay double taxes on imports and exports. In return for taxes they received nothing, neither services nor even security. They could not bear arms, ride horses, build houses higher than those of the Turks, or copy Turkish dress."[5] Also, perhaps worst of all, there was the child-tribute.

And yet, on the other hand, the Greeks could rely on certain advantages—religious toleration for instance, since the Turks never had any desire to proselytize the Christians, and a Greek always remained free to become a Moslem if he wished to do so. Essentially the Turks were first of all a military and nomadic race who, driven west out of their Asiatic homeland by the Mongols, were permanently organized for wars, and much more interested in expanding into other countries and living off the land than in fortifying themselves behind frontiers. Therefore they wanted to have as little to do with the conquered *rayah* as possible. As a result of this the Greeks in the villages were permitted to rule themselves, electing their own councillors, just as they had done in the past days of Byzantium. Much of the Peloponnese was self-ruled by Greeks, frequently by ruthless Greek adventurers using the Turkish title of bey, who had been successful in acquiring money and power. In fact, from the fifteenth to the seventeenth century the Greek peasant under Turkish rule was most probably in a better position than his brother in Western Europe because he had lived for eleven hundred years under the Byzantine theocracy, and in effect still did so, and had never known freedom as the nineteenth century came to understand it.

Though the Greeks were without a doubt, subjugated and oppressed, their chief advantage lay in the fact that the Turks' principal interest and panache was for war. Despising all trade and commerce as vulgar and beneath their military dignity, they were ready, indeed eager, to make use of the keener business acumen of the Greek, Jew or Armenian. So the cleverer Greeks managed to flourish by commercial enterprise in spite of the disadvantage that they must pay double taxes on exports and imports. Unless they were recruited into the corps of the Janissaries, there was no military service; on the other hand they might be pressed to man the oars in the galleys of the Ottoman navy. Many Greeks, whose feelings were somewhat neutral towards the Turks, preferred them to other foreigners. Ironically, the religiously tolerant Turk for a period was regarded as the protector of the Greek Orthodox Christians, against the Catholic Venetians for example. The truth was that the Catholic West presented a danger to the Turks, which Greek Orthodoxy did not.

The early Sultans had enough common sense not to persecute or suppress Greeks of exceptional ability, but preferred to promote them in order to profit by them. Many superior Byzantines, outstanding, highly educated Greeks of good family, lived in the quarter of Constantinople known as the Phanar (near the lighthouse and close to the residence of the Patriarch) and came to be known as Phanariotes. Far ahead in the distant future their descendants, still called Phanariotes, were to play a prominent part in the Greek War of Independence. Now, a class of men who were rich, either by inheritance or by successful business enterprise, they held important positions and functioned as the brains of the Ottoman Empire. Members of this class, by working in the service of their conquerors, could rise to the four highest offices of the State, which by the eighteenth century had come to be regarded as almost exclusively their privilege.

These offices were Dragoman of the Ports and Dragoman of the Fleet (private secretaries to the Grand Vizier and to the naval commander-in-chief, the Capitan Pasha), and the two governors (Hospodar or Voivode) of the trans-Danubian provinces of Moldavia and Wallachia, which are today parts of modern Roumania. In these provinces the administration was allowed to be Christian. The Turks were prepared to permit the Greeks to carry on with their local self-government and not to interfere with the centuries-old Greek municipal system. The organization was plain. The territories fell under the jurisdiction of the "lord of lords" who lived at Sofia, and after 1470 were divided into seven *sandjaks* or provinces. About a century later the *sandjaks* were rearranged with seven or more insular *sandjaks* added, which included Lemnos, Lesbos, Chios and Rhodes. The Capitan Pasha ruled as "lord of lords" of the sea. The *sandjaks* were divided into sub-districts, administered by a lesser magnate who was himself assisted by a judge or *cadi*. Most of these minor officials were Greeks. Also many of the Mohammedan names in the Turkish administration served to hide the identity of converted Greeks. The curious paradox was that it was to the advantage of the Phanariotes and all leading Greek families to support the Ottoman Empire so that they might inherit it whole.

Here it may be well to consider what permanent effect those long centuries of Byzantine history had on the Greek soul. This can hardly be exaggerated. Edward Gibbon, writing in a century of rationalism whose overall atmosphere was hostile to Christianity, has perpetuated a biased pejorative account of Byzantine civilization. Voltaire, too, saw in Byzantine history only "a worthless repertory of declamation and miracles, disgraceful to the human mind". But surely there is greater truth in Sir Steven Runciman's charitable encomium:

For eleven hundred years there had stood on the Bosphorus a city where the intellect was admired and the learning and letters of the Classical past were studied and preserved. Without the help of Byzantine commentators and scribes there is little that we would know today about the literature of ancient Greece. It was, too, a city whose rulers down the centuries had inspired and encouraged a school of art unparalleled in human history, an art that arose from an ever varying blend of the cool cerebral Greek sense of the fitness of things and a deep religious sense that saw in works of art the incarnation of the Divine and the sanctification of matter. It was, too, a great cosmopolitan city, where along with merchandise ideas were freely exchanged and whose citizens saw themselves not as a racial unit but as the heirs of the Christian faith.[6]

All this the Greeks had inherited.

CHAPTER III

The Rise and Decline of
Ottoman Power

Who were the Greeks? During the early years of the nineteenth century it was actually disputed whether such a people even existed. Could their origin have been the little known Pelasgians, "sea-people" as the archaeologists vaguely call them? Were they the direct descendants of Homer's proud Achaeans? Had they inherited the Aeolian tradition of song from Sappho's Lesbos? And was their line of inheritance clearly drawn through the golden age of Pericles, the Empire of Alexander the Great, the Pax Romana, up to the Christian Byzantine Empire? However imponderable such questions may be, the very likely answer is that at the time of the "Turkish Night" the Greeks, at any rate in their race memories, were an uncertain amalgam of all these periods.

And Greece herself as a country? Perhaps she has always been more of an idea than a geographical reality, a luminous indestructible ideal at the core of civilization which, through many vicissitudes, has kept a burning power of energy in the hearts of all Greek people. From the beginning the shores of Greece have been as changing in shape as Proteus. The map of Greece has been re-drawn almost with each new generation. Although one is conscious of a successively fluid racial admixture, Renan's "the Greek miracle" remains valid; for the phrase bears witness to the continuity of a flame that was never quite extinguished. If we regard history as having no sharp dividing lines, a continuum flowing relentlessly with no certain beginning and no imagined end, then Greece's search for independence started long before 1821 and only reached an approximate completion long after 1829. Also it was not until a few decades before the initial risings of the War of Independence that the Greeks began to think of themselves as a "nation" in the modern sense of the word.

The Moslem races, which included the Turks, called the Eastern Roman Empire *"Rūm"*; and when Byzantium fell the Greek inhabitants of the city (with the other subject races of the Ottoman Empire) were known during the centuries of subjugation as *Rūmis* (a corruption of Romans) and later as *"Romioi"*. It was only after the Greeks had regained their freedom that the old name of "Hellene" was revived, the word *"Romios"* passing out of fashion partly because by then it had acquired a pejorative connotation, linked with the often unscrupulous cunning by which the Greeks had learnt to outsmart their masters. The distinction is clear:

> "Hellene" is the glory of ancient Greece; "Romaic" the splendours and sorrows of Byzantium, above all, the sorrows. "Hellenism" is symbolised by the columns of the Parthenon; Byzantium, the imperial golden age of Christian Greece, by the great dome of St. Sophia.[1]

As early as the thirteenth and fourteenth centuries, the Byzantines, though many of them had cherished the classical Greek authors, must have doubted whether there was much left of the original Hellene either on the mainland or the islands. A majority in the city were fervent Christians who neither lived nor thought as the ancient Greeks had done. Indeed, by now the word "Hellene" roughly corresponded to "pagan". Yet there were doubters; not everybody was prepared to accept the Orthodox supra-nationalism of Byzantine belief. For example, the Platonic scholar George Gemistos Pletho told the Emperor Manuel II:

> We over whom you rule are Hellenes by race, as is demonstrated by our language and ancestral education. And for Hellenes there is no more proper and peculiar land to be found than the Peloponnese, together with the neighbouring part of Europe and the islands that lie near to it. For it appears that this land has always been inhabited by the same Hellenes, as far as the memory of man reaches back: none lived here before them, nor

34

have immigrants occupied it and expelled the others, later to be expelled themselves in the same way. No, on the contrary, the Hellenes themselves appear always to have been its possessors and never to have left it.

Pletho wanted the Peloponnese to be fortified and made racially self-sufficient. Unfortunately he was more of a Platonist than a Christian and his version of history remains questionable. But when in 1450 he died in the Peloponnese, his body was taken to be buried in Florence as a mark of respect for his teaching and valuable service to the Greek language. Pletho's theories may have been false, but they proved of considerable importance nearly four hundred years later when the War of Independence first broke out in the Peloponnese. For Pletho had initiated the myth that the inhabitants of the territories of ancient Greece were the direct descendants of the classical Greeks, and that only through the thought and culture of their illustrious ancestors could a modern Hellenic nation be regenerated.

Although by the fifteenth century—and still more by the beginning of the nineteenth—much of the original Greek stock must have been vitiated during the various phases of past history, as well as by migration and intermarriage, two factors of supreme importance kept the Greeks united during their silent crucifixion under the Ottoman Turks. These were the irresistible bonds of language and religion. Never throughout the centuries of Turkish domination did these bonds fail to remain intact. So it was in fact a combination of the tenacity of the Greek religious character and the indestructible resilience of the lovely Greek language (with its enduring alphabet) which so greatly helped to win for the Greeks national independence and preserved for the world the spiritual and concrete advantages of Greek culture.

The Dark Age of Greece endured up to about the beginning of the nineteenth century; for until that period the idea of Greece as a separate nation had scarcely occurred to the consciousness of Europe. During all this time the proud Greeks, through being treated by the Turks as *rayah*, cattle, were degraded and humiliated.

Furthermore, lasting at least up to the end of the seventeenth century, two popular misconceptions about both Greeks and Turks were currently rife among the nations of Western Europe and must be challenged.

First, as to the Turks who lived in an almost perpetual state of war with the non-Moslem world: the Ottoman Empire's victorious army and navy had for so long driven such universal terror and pessimism into the Europeans that they had grown incapable of regarding their enemy with an unbiased eye. To a majority the Turks were simply fanatical, uncivilized barbarians who left a trail of havoc, blood and atrocity wherever they went. Michael Drayton (1563–1631) in his poem "To Master George Sandys", while mourning the eclipse of Greece, had denigrated the Turks as barbarian and unlettered:

> Th' unlettered *Turk* and rude *Barbarian* trades
> Where Homer sang his lofty *Iliads*.

But much of this was prejudice founded upon a total ignorance of oriental culture. For the Osmanlis were not the Mongol hordes of Jenghis Khan, nor the Tartars of Tamerlane, and they by no means wholly devastated the countries they conquered—"witness the numerous Byzantine monuments of Constantinople, Nicaea, Pontus, Thessaloniki and Mount Athos, the Gothic churches of Cyprus, and even the classical monuments of Ancient Greece, most of which survived the Ottoman conquest intact, save for the white-washing and small structural changes entailed by the conversion of the churches into mosques."[2] As for Michael Drayton's other charge "Th' unlettered *Turk*", Alexander Pallis refutes this convincingly:

The Osmanli Turks, given their origin and religion, naturally came under the influence of Arabic and Persian, as opposed to Greco-Latin culture, which was the common heritage of the Christian peoples. Although the former's contributions to world-literature were never of the first order, they nevertheless cultivated with intensity all the forms of literary expression and in this respect may be compared with the Byzantine Greeks. Just as Italian society in the fourteenth and fifteenth centuries amused itself with listening to the tales of Boccaccio, the sonnets of Petrarch and the epics of Ariosto . . . in just the same way the cultured Osmanlis of that period enjoyed nothing so much as listening to the recitation of the works of the classical Persian poets—the *Shahnâme* of Firdûsî, the *Gulistân* of Sáadî, and the *gházals* (sonnets) of Hâfiz. . . . No branch of poetry, whether epic, lyric, satirical, philosophic or religious, was left un-cultivated.[3]

Just as surprising perhaps is the second misconception which arose in the eyes of Europe, a "bad image" of the enslaved Greeks. During the first hundred years of Greek subjection the sentiment in Europe was far more anti-Turk than pro-Greek. Yet a some-what odd notion told in favour of the Turks, to the detriment of the Greeks, namely a surviving medieval, almost legendary belief that the Turks were remotely descended from the Trojans. This may sound curious; but in the fifteenth and sixteenth centuries the theory that the present hapless fate of Greece was in some sort a revenge for the Grecian burning of Troy two thousand five hundred years ago, was attractive to a great many people. After all, it was not so difficult to identify the Turks as descendants of the Trojans who had ruled powerfully in Asia Minor for a long time. The name for the Trojans, *Teucri*, was widely familiar to scholars through Virgil; so it was a comparatively easy step to *Turcae* in later Latin or *Turchi* in Italian. And the fact that the Greeks seemed so apathetic in bondage helped the belief that their plight might well be a just punishment for the Trojan War, thus acting as a balm to the bad conscience of Christian Europe for abandoning them to the infidel.

Less than ten years after the fall of Constantinople nearly all the remnants of Greek independence had gone. The Turkish conquest of the mainland, as of the islands of the archipelago, had pro-ceeded quickly, piecemeal: in 1456 the Duchy of Athens; in 1459 the islands of Imbros, Tenedos, Lemnos; in 1460 Corinth and

Mistra; and by the autumn of the same year the whole of the peninsula of the Peloponnese, although at the close of the seventeenth century it was largely reconquered by the self-assertion of Venice. In 1461 Trebizond, the last capital of the Greeks, surrendered; and then in 1462 Lesbos was taken, which had been ruled so long by the benevolent Genoese family of Gateluzzi. During the sixteenth century Rhodes, besieged by Sultan Suleiman the Magnificent, fell in 1522, to be followed by Patmos, Scyros and Paros in 1537, and by Chios in 1566. Cyprus was wrested from the Venetians, the heretical champions of Christendom, in 1571. Only in the Morea, as the Peloponnese was then called, some traces of independence were able to survive, especially in the scattered remote southern villages of the Mani, whose daunting mountains not even "those hellish Turks, horseleeches of Christian blood", cared to penetrate. So were preserved pockets of freedom, a gleam of liberty. But it was the finish of the free Greek world.

The "bad image" of the Greeks arose from a variety of causes. Some Europeans no doubt felt that the Greeks had behaved too apathetically under the Turkish yoke. But from the beginning there was a general ignorance about the circumstances of their enslaved condition. Knowledge of Greece increased only very slowly between 1500 and 1800; for, while the Turk was still powerful, journeys to those lands he occupied remained not only difficult but hazardous for travellers. So hazardous indeed were the risks to be expected—perils from disease, shipwreck, above all from pirates—that the rates of life-insurance *against* safe return were usually between three-to-one and five-to-one. Shakespeare in *The Tempest* uses the phrase "putter-out of five for one" as a circumlocution for a traveller from a remote country. During the sixteenth century English trade with the Levant had been growing; but it was not until the foundation of the Levant Company in 1581 that it became practical for ordinary people to visit Greece and so gain some knowledge of the country, although the risks were still very great. But, from its inception in 1581 until its dissolution by Parliament in 1825, the Levant Company played a most important part in bringing the English to Greece, the merchants first, then the more adventurous sons of noble families, to be followed later by scholars and men of letters. However, what the English saw of the Greeks by no means always pleased them. So the growth of philhellenism advanced at tortoise pace; for it was not until after Islam had ceased to be a menace to Christianity that interest in Greece could make any real headway.

Not that England at this time felt herself to be in any imminent danger from the Turks. Nevertheless it was the Turk more than the Greek who inhabited the imagination of the Elizabethan, if he or she thought at all about happenings in the Levant. Although for most of the sixteenth century the heretical Venetians still acted as the champions of Christendom against the Turks (later to be joined by the, also heretical, Austrians), Venice could only just hold her own. She remained master of both Cyprus and Crete, and of most of the Ionian islands, besides some other islands in the Aegean. Nevertheless the European powers had learnt to recognize the Ottoman Empire as an equal, for it had made stupendous conquests: apart from territories as far distantly divided as Hungary, the Crimea, Mesopotamia and North Africa, both the Black Sea and the Red Sea, as well as the eastern Mediterranean, were in effect Turkish lakes. Literate Englishmen, although they were not afraid, were fully conscious of the Ottoman peril.

To the Elizabethan imagination the Turk was a source of fascination as well as of concern and repulsion. This vast, powerful, but distant heathen civilization, with its secluded seraglios, its eunuchs and concubines, its fantastic splendour co-existent with shocking cruelty, appeared from far-off exotic and romantic. When at last Cyprus was captured by the Turks in 1571, Shakespeare was a boy of seven years old; but as one reads *Othello* (written probably in 1604), it is hard to miss a throb of excitement whenever "the general enemy Ottoman" is mentioned. There are several more pejorative references to the "Turk" in Shakespeare's plays which no doubt had been used for a long time as current words of opprobrium. The terrible glamour of the Turks had also fascinated the mighty poetic imagination of Marlowe who, in his *Tamburlaine*, told of the downfall of Sultan Bayezit I in terms of his own daydreams of ruthless power and glory. Thomas Kyd, his fellow dramatist, if he was the author of *The Tragedy of Solyman and Perseda*, brought Suleiman the Magnificent upon the stage. All this interest in the Turks, however, worked towards an almost complete lack of curiosity about the Greeks in Elizabethan and Jacobean minds. Few cultured Greeks travelled in those days as far as England who, if they had done so, might well have spread some interest in the virtues of their race and country. So, as things were, the undeservedly lightweight image of the Greek character persisted in Western Europe up to the turn of the eighteenth and nineteenth centuries.

Erasmus himself had incorporated some of these prejudices into his *Adagia*: "Every schoolboy could learn to sneer at the Greeks. . . . First, the word 'greek', generally preceded by an epithet like 'gay', 'mad', or 'merry', became an ordinary conversational expression meaning a person of loose and lively habits, a boon companion, a fast liver." Shakespeare's Cressida, hearing of Helen's wanton behaviour, says of her, "Then she's a merry Greek indeed." The truth was that for a very long time the Greeks had been forced to suffer the contemptuous denigration of Western Europe, accused unkindly of licentiousness, drunkenness and general voluptuousness; also, of deviousness and double-dealing, of the wiles of the confidence-trickster and cheat. The sixteenth century saw the nadir of this humiliation of Greece when she who had once been so glorious, skilled in the finest arts of living, famed for an ennobling culture, was cast down, degraded and oppressed. Europe appeared blind, completely indifferent to her Christian brothers' plight, which could hardly be exaggerated. The changeover to a widespread philhellenism was slow and long in coming. It was to the credit of individual writers and travellers, notably Englishmen, that the attitude towards the Greeks gradually improved.

A little after the middle of the sixteenth century some noble words, which helped towards both the conception and progress of philhellenism, were addressed to Europe by the Flemish writer and diplomat Busbecq, who had twice served as ambassador from Ferdinand I to Sultan Suleiman the Magnificent. In them are to be found sympathy as well as knowledge, combined with an admirable sense of Europe's indebtedness towards the unfortunate Greeks.

But it is more deeply afflicting that Greece, the home of the nymphs, the land of the muses, should be crushed into servitude. She longs for Christian care and culture. . . . She was once the creator of all the ennobling arts of life, all liberal culture; and now she seems to be begging back from the Europe she has civilized something of the humanity which she has bequeathed to us. She appeals to all those things which in common we hold sacred, and implores our help against the Scythian barbarian which oppresses her. But it is all in vain; the Princes of Christendom have their minds set on quite different things.[4]

Before the century was out, one or two Englishmen had helped to change the general attitude, conspicuously Sir Anthony Sherley and his brother Sir Thomas. Embarking at Venice for Aleppo in May, 1599, Sir Anthony visited Greek territory on his way, including Candia (Crete) and Cyprus. He found Cyprus "a most ruinated place" under the Turks' government. Elsewhere in the account of his travels Sir Anthony thought that with courage, arms, and provided that "the Princes Christian had but a compassionate eye turned upon the miserable calamity of a place so near them . . . I do not see . . . but the redemption of that place were most facile." Of the isle of Candia (unsubjected to the Turks) Sir Anthony was able to write of the Greeks with approval, if not exactly with flattery:

There we were royally used, but especially by one of the governors, which was a Greek, for there are two governors, the one a Greek, the other an Italian. The city of Candia is a town of garrison, which hath to the number of one thousand five hundred soldiers continually there; this governor, being a Greek, caused four proclamations to be made, which was, that we should have free liberty, both day and night, to pass quietly by their court of guard and sentinels, without any let, which was a very great favour: we were kindly used amongst the citizens, but especially by the gentlewomen, who oftentimes did make us banquets in their gardens, with music and dancing. They may well be called merry Greeks, for in the evenings, commonly after they leave work, they will dance up and down the streets, both men and women.[5]

Sir Anthony Sherley's brother Sir Thomas, who was gifted with keen powers of observation and with the ability to extract accurate information on contemporary events, knew the Turks well. He had been in Constantinople from 1603 until 1606 and spent a part of that time in prison. On his release he had remained in the city to begin writing his valuable *Discours of the Turkes*, which he completed in April 1607, following his return to England. He observes that the Turk, being in a small minority within all the occupied countries, should his military power ever be relaxed or decline, would be at the mercy of intervention by the Christian nations:

And to this maye bee added the greate number of Christians that are in all his cuntryes that haue bynne formerlye baptised, whyche doe farr exceede the Turkes in number, yea even in Constantinople it self; & these desire noethinge but armes & capiteynes, & they woulde ryse agaynest the Turkes for theyre libertye, & woulde furnishe men, money, & horses sufficiente. This I haue learned of diuers wyse & wealthye Greeks that doe wyshe for this helpe with tears.[6]

Such evidence at least affords proof that almost exactly two hundred years before Byron first set foot on Greek soil an Englishman had discussed with wise and wealthy Greek friends the feasibility, given certain conditions, of a Greek rising in the name of liberty.

Throughout the greater part of the sixteenth century the ratio between the strength of the forces of Europe and the Ottoman Empire remained finely balanced. The European Powers had no choice but to treat the Ottoman Empire as a military rival, and in the power struggle as a diplomatic equal. Suleiman the Magnificent had begun his long triumphant reign of conquest, which lasted forty-six years (1520–66), by taking Belgrade in 1521; and after more than six months siege, Rhodes in 1522, following a valiant defence by the Knights of St. John of Jerusalem. The Knights were allowed to capitulate on honourable terms and retired first to Crete and then in 1530 to Malta.

Though this is not the place to follow Suleiman's further conquests, nor to unravel the complicated political history of the period, mention may be made of his armies' decisive victory over the Hungarians at Mohacs in 1526—a key battle in European history—and the levelling of the score when the Turks were repulsed from Vienna in 1529. When Suleiman died in 1566, his voracious appetite for territory was not appeased, nor his ultimate ambitions for the conquest of Europe realized. For at the very close of his reign the Knights of St. John had defied his great siege of Malta, in spite of the fact that the Sultan's vast and powerful fleets had been deployed for four months against the little island. However, it was not until 1683 that Jan Sobieski, King of Poland, finally stemmed the Turkish tide of invasion in Europe by throwing the infidel back from the gates of Vienna. But the death of Suleiman the Magnificent is held by a majority of historians as marking the peak point, the apogee of the menace and power of the Ottoman Empire. After the Sultan's death corruption was soon to spread at home, although there was left some further glory to be won abroad.

The rise and rapid expansion of the Ottoman navy during Suleiman's reign, under the half-Greek corsair Barbarossa provides one of the most surprising developments in history; one, moreover, which is relevant to our theme in contrast to future events. Barbarossa—or Kheir-ed-Din, "Protector of Religion" to give him his true name—contrary to the traditional Christian view, was not just another murdering Barbary pirate, nor an "unlettered Turk", for he spoke at least six languages, but emerges clearly as a man of immense ability, a national hero who, after organizing the Ottoman navy and creating an efficient dockyard system at Constantinople, went on to found a new Kingdom of Algiers and make himself master of the whole North African coast. He settled the way of life and trade throughout the Mediterranean right up to the beginning of the nineteenth century. He and his brother Aruj were both men of creative violence; but what is strange is that it is probable that they had no Turkish blood in their veins, being almost certainly descended from a retired Janissary recruited from a Roumeliot or Greek family, who lived on the island of Lesbos which the Turks had captured in 1462. But both brothers were Christian-hating fanatical Moslems, notwithstanding the fact that their physical ancestry was in all likelihood Greek. By their exceptional prowess in navigation and fighting at sea, they succeeded in making Turkey the dominant maritime power which was to control the Mediterranean ports and the Barbary Coast for centuries. And if the years 1538–1566 may rightly be regarded as the most spectacular in the history of the Ottoman Empire, this was in no small measure due to Suleiman's Admiral, Kheir-ed-Din Barbarossa, who had indeed turned the whole Mediterranean into a Turkish lake.

After Suleiman's death and the glorious years of victory, the Turkish decline was not immediately apparent. Ottoman dominance of the inland sea continued, though Turkish sea-power had been shaken by the failure to capture besieged Malta in 1565, as also by the crushing defeat inflicted by the Christian fleet (raised by the Pope and commanded by Don John of Austria) at Lepanto in the Gulf of Corinth six years later. Selim II—nicknamed "the Sot"—succeeded his father Suleiman and during the eight years of his reign gained ground from Persia and Venice. He also achieved a conspicuous triumph in conquering Cyprus in 1571, the same year as the battle of Lepanto. Interestingly enough, the Christian fleet which had won at Lepanto had been intended to save Cyprus, but arrived too late. Cyprus of course publicized the Turks in England through Shakespeare's *Othello*. But Lepanto was not decisive; the Turks recovered from their defeat and were able to make peace on favourable terms in 1573. The main interest of Lepanto here is that a large number of the galley-slaves in both the Turkish and Christian fleets were Greeks, many of whom lost their lives. Yet the year 1571 does mark a shift in the balance of power between Turkey and Europe. It was a watershed. But it was not until much later in the second half of the seventeenth century that, pressed between Austria and Russia in the north and Persia in the east, the rather ramshackle frontiers of the Ottoman Empire began to retract and dwindle.

When in 1715 the Turks reconquered the Peloponnese, loosening the final hold of Venetian imperialism there, evidence relates that the Greeks welcomed the return of their former masters, as they had done also in Crete and Cyprus. There were reasons for this. In Cyprus the Venetians had treated the poor Greeks as worse than slaves, oppressing and torturing them; but when the Turks came back the tables were reversed. It was much the same story in Crete, although that island was the only part of Greece where there had been any considerable apostasy to Islam. In both islands there were naturally exceptions—as there were, too, in the Peloponnese and the Ionian islands—mostly among the better class Greeks who could more easily establish sympathetic cultural ties with the Venetian aristocracy than with the Turks, both being part of Christendom, though they regarded each other as heretics.

If a majority of Greeks did prefer the Turks to the Venetians as their overlords, it is obvious that it was only a choice of evils. In Crete, as elsewhere, the Turkish rule was exacting not so much from calculated harshness as from the indifference of the Sublime Porte to the economic plight of the people. For the Turks were nothing if not a warlike people always on the move; so that their social and administrative system remained totally unsuited to a Greek pastoral and settled conception of life. In the occupied lands the two main functions of Turkish officials were to collect taxes and raise more troops for fresh expansion. The slightest sign of a declining revenue led to cruelty or deliberate oppression, because the Turks cared nothing for the distress or poverty of the *rayah*. Only by waging war could the supply of slaves be maintained at a level sufficiently high to fill the administrative posts, man the armed forces, and fill the imperial coffers. Any reduction of the enslaved Christian population would rob the State of tax-revenue. There was a Greek rising in Epirus in 1611 and an Albanian revolt in the Peloponnese in 1647. Areas like the Mani which had never

45

paid the head-tax were now forced to do so, and the collection of it transferred to the army. But from the middle of the seventeenth century the Ottoman Empire had stopped expanding. The old feudal system was cracking at its outer borders. The rock of successful warfare and conquest had started to crumble.

A sensible dictum of the Florentine statesman Machiavelli is that in dealing with the conquered one must either crush or conciliate. Yet in their treatment of the Greeks the Turks had done neither, seemingly content by their exactions to gall the pride of the *rayah* to the limit. But they had not destroyed Greek social organization; nor had they wholly deprived the Greeks of weapons. The Byzantine Emperors had enrolled some of the wild shepherds and muleteers who lived in the mountains into an irregular militia, known as Armatoli, for the protection of roads and the defence of passes. This system was at first enlarged by the Sultans, so that the Greek mountaineers had for long been trained in the use of arms and were expert in all the ways of mountain warfare. The Christian armatoles were a purely Greek police force, no Turks or Albanians being admitted to their ranks; but as later Sultans began to reduce the numbers of this militia, curtailing the power of their captains, the Greeks felt an increased hostility towards the Turks whose order they were no longer paid to defend. From armatole to brigand was only a short step. In the course of time many peasants took to the hills in order to escape from oppression, live free as brigands, and defend themselves when necessary. The title of klepht (robber) was given to them and became one of respect. The armatoles were supposed to suppress the klephts, but with the years the status of each grew more confused until there was no clear line left between them.

For decades before the outbreak of the War of Independence to be a klepht was more of an honour than a disgrace. These brave men, living austere lives in their inaccessible mountain hideouts called *limeri*, were glamourized by the people (rather as once were the Scottish Highland chieftains or Robin Hood and his men) as defenders of freedom and religion against the Turk. But George Finlay, philhellene and classic historian of the Greek Revolt, who was eager for Greece to recreate herself as a new modern state, was anti-sentimental in approach and harsh even when writing of the Greek past. He regarded the klephts as mere brigands, who both before the revolution, during the war, and even under the rule of King Otto, "plundered the Greeks more than they were ever plundered by the Turks." All the same, though the klephts were often ruthless in raiding helpless villages, and cruel to Moslem and Christian alike, they also possessed formidable virtues of courage, sexual continence and asceticism, combined with a picturesque image and an almost miraculous prowess in arms. Moreover, the klephts were to provide the major military effort of the War of Independence, for the Greek masses gathered round them, accepting the klephtic ideals of the Christian duty to resist the infidel. There existed the kind of liberty which according to the Greek proverb, "lives in the mountains" side by side with contests of endurance, simple piety, homeric feastings, and a chivalry which added up to a spiritual force that enabled the Greeks to fight on at moments when the cause seemed lost.

A klephtic chief in his *limeri* seldom found himself at the head of more than two or three hundred pallikars (gallant young men); more usually the band numbered some hundred or fifty who, hardy and active, roamed freely over the mountains by day, choosing dark and stormy nights for their devious enterprises. They slept in the open air wrapped in cloaks of goat-hair, their weapons limited to a long gun, a sword, a knife or dagger. The klephts preferred to fight singly: each man, as occasion arose, would shield himself behind wall or rock, shrub or tree, from the protection of which with his long gun he took sure aim at his enemy. Klepht marksmanship was famed to be prodigious; an example of this was the ability to hit an egg suspended by a thread from the branch of a tree at a distance of two hundred paces. Often an enemy's gunflash in the dark was enough for a klepht's bullet to find its mark, "firing on fire" they called it. The klephts feared only one thing, to fall alive into the hands of the Turk. Like the Vikings before them they had a horror of dying slowly in bed from disease. Therefore they courted death on the battlefield— "a good ball! (καλὸν μολύβι)" was a customary toast at their banquets. Like the Norsemen, too, or like the American Indians, they prided themselves upon their stoicism in silently enduring torture, the least of which was to have their legs smashed by the slow blows of a smith's hammer until every bone was broken. Also the klephts were inured to every kind of physical hardship, fatigue, hunger, thirst; they could fight on for as long as three consecutive days and nights without sleep or nourishment. Among the more attractive characteristics of the klephts was their chivalrous "taboo" against raping any women they had carried off to their lonely caves. Even if they held powerless for several days the wives or daughters of Turkish beys or Greek primates, to await ransom money, no harm would come to these women, not even though their husbands or fathers had themselves raped the wives and daughters belonging to the klephts. Not the smallest insult was permitted to such prisoners, fair or ugly, young or old, Moslem or Christian. This respect for women is illustrated in the following klephtic ballad where a klepht, eating beside a Greek woman captive, has demanded that she pour out wine for him:

> Skyllodimos sat and feasted
> Beneath a spreading pine.
> By his side was fair Irene
> To pour him out his wine.
> "Let me quaff, my fair Irene,
> Pour me wine till break of day,
> Till the star of morning rises
> And the Pleiads fade away.
> To your home I will then safe send you
> With ten of my comrades true."

> "I am not your slave, O Dimos,
> And will pour no wine for you.
> Noble is my husband's father
> And a chieftain's daughter I."[7]

But here the klephts must be left, to return later.

By the end of the seventeenth century the Barbary pirates were a menace all around the shores of Greece. As the activities of these predatory sea-faring corsairs increased, the Greeks rebuilt some of their coastal villages several kilometres inland as a partial refuge from the murderous raids of the marauding pirates. Watchtowers were built at strategic points on the cliffs and sentinels posted. Sometimes a warning fire would be lit on a height; so that island could signal to island on a clear night the message that the pirates were approaching. Then to escape murder, rape and wholesale loot the islanders would barricade themselves inside their houses until the danger had passed.

Just as the klephts were to play a principal part in achieving Greek independence, the policy of the Sublime Porte during the eighteenth century allowed the Greeks to develop the maritime power of the Greek islands. Many of these islands had either gained, or were permitted, a large measure of freedom. Some of them were allowed to be almost self-governing, with the provision that they paid a small yearly tribute to the Sultan and were punctual in supplying a modicum of sailors to the Ottoman navy. Such islanders had been familiar from earliest childhood with every danger and hazard of the sea, and so made superb seamen; and, being practically autonomous, the islands were able to support and encourage on their own initiative a growing maritime trade. When in 1783 Catherine the Great seized the Crimea the Turks lost their hold on the Black Sea, which for two centuries had been regarded as a Turkish lake. At the same time Catherine obliged the Turks to sign a commercial convention that supplemented the Kütchük Kainardji treaty of 1774, and permitted the Greek merchantmen to trade under the Russian flag. So the Greek merchant navy was able to expand still more. Greek ships, which hitherto mostly had been small coasting brigs, now grew larger; and instead of just timidly plying between island and island, sailed as far as Gibraltar and beyond. The ubiquitous, deadly Algerian pirates caused these ships to be armed. So their crews learnt not only navigation but fighting. But the Ottoman navy could rely upon no such ready mercantile support, a profound disadvantage which, as the Greek naval power became stronger, was to affect the struggle for Hellenic liberation which lay in the future a generation later.

Another event which was to help the cause of Greece was the promotion and increasing influence of the Phanariotes, who would produce such leaders as Prince Alexander Mavrocordatos and the brothers Alexander and Dimitrios Ypsilantis. There had already been spasmodic outbreaks of rebellion on land, such as a revolt against the Turks in the Mani in the southern part of the Peloponnese in 1659; but these risings were still due to local causes and were not yet influenced by the foreign Powers in the way they would be during the eighteenth century. Now wars were to become more complicated, but no less bloody, "trade" wars, in contrast to the religious wars of the sixteenth and seventeenth centuries. The Turks veered from a transient fanaticism to a lethargic torpor in their treatment of the Greeks. But they were becoming uneasy, realizing that something more than compulsion was needed; so they decided to make use of the Greeks—"their favourite Christians"—both by supporting them against the Catholics in all religious disputes and by giving the most wealthy and intelligent of them high posts in the Ottoman administration.

The promotion of the Phanariotes widened still more the gulf which already existed between the Hellenic *élite* of Constantinople and the rest of the oppressed subjects of the Sultan. For the Greek peasants and artisans, guided by their virtually uneducated village priests, lived lives wholly set apart from the sophisticated aristocracy of the Phanar. Not only had the Phanariotes diplomatic contacts with various European governments, but also links with Greek merchants domiciled in countries like England, France, Italy, Germany and Russia. So the Phanariotes moved into a very strong position; so strong in fact, that it looked as if they might almost have taken over the Ottoman Empire. This, of course, marked the beginning of a still further decline for the Turks.

But the Turks were by no means finished. They waged a series of wars with Austria, Poland, Russia, and Venice, resulting in the reconquest of the Peloponnese from the Venetians in 1715. The Greeks actually had welcomed and assisted the Turks in this, a sure proof that they had no thought yet of national independence.

Three decades of peace followed, after which it was recognized that there had been a change in the European balance of forces. Venice had ceased to be a great power, and Austria was beginning to yield in importance to Russia, which was seen to be the now dominant Christian power in eastern Europe; and because she was Orthodox and not Catholic, she had a special religious affinity with the Greeks.

Catherine the Great's attempt a generation later to undermine the Ottoman Empire through the insidious emotional means of the Orthodox faith was doomed to failure. Voltaire's faulty prediction as an outsider that Constantinople would presently become the capital of the Russian Empire, was tactless because in sentiment it bore no relation to the wishes of the Greeks. It is true that the Greeks raised a half-hearted rebellion in favour of Catherine, when the fort and harbour of Navarino were captured in April 1770; but this was the single success of the campaign. Greek and Russian forces penetrated the interior of the Peloponnese. But at Tripolitza they were confronted and defeated by mostly Albanian forces mustered by the Turkish governor. The rebellion collapsed. The reprisals were appallingly severe. The Albanians ran riot over the Peloponnese for ten years where they pillaged and terrorized the Greek inhabitants. At last the Turks forcibly intervened and sent the Albanians back to Albania. The Russians had abandoned the Greeks to their fate. The war went on, but there was no hope of any further new Greek rising on behalf of Catherine.

Although by the end of the eighteenth century Catherine's fantastic "Oriental Project", involving a partition of the Ottoman Empire, was over, her war against the Turks of 1787–92, which ended in the treaty of Jassy, was of major importance for the Balkans because for the first time it alerted the British government to a potential conflict of interests between Britain and Russia in the Near East. The French Revolution had deeply affected the races of Southern Europe. In Greece Theodore Kolokotronis, one of the most influential klephts, commented later, "according to my judgment, the French Revolution and the doings of Napoleon opened the eyes of the world." The impact of France was reinforced by the fact that educated Greeks read Rousseau and Voltaire, and by the publication in 1788 of *Voyage du Jeune Anarcharsis en Grèce Vers le Milieu du Quatrième Siècle Avant l'Ere Vulgaire* by l'Abbé Barthélemy. In the eyes of Greek intellectuals Paris began to rival St. Petersburg as a focus of Greek aspirations. Adamantios Koraïs, an expatriate leading Greek scholar from Smyrna, had settled there in 1788 and was devoting his life to a revival and purification of the classical Greek tongue. Neither were ideals of a Greek renaissance one-sided; for they were reciprocated by the French. The French Foreign Office had even toyed with the idea of annexing the Peloponnese.

So France and Russia continued to be rivals in the southern Balkans, and in the final decade of the century Russian agents were once more busily engaged in the Peloponnese, acting from their consulate at Patras. In 1790 a Greek deputation attended Catherine's court, offering to recognize her grandson Constantine, then aged ten, as their Emperor. But by this time Catherine was bored by her "Greek dream" for Constantine. Nor had the boy himself, although he had been reared by Greek tutors, ever shown the slightest interest in ascending the throne of a resuscitated Byzantine Empire. Meanwhile the French had established a consulate at Yannina where Ali Pasha, a powerful and sinister figure, had made himself governor of Epirus in defiance of the Sultan. By an almost sublime mixture of ruthlessness and cunning he had created a state which was virtually independent of the Porte. So the rivalry for the control of the southern Balkans had now become a triangle through the rising power of Ali Pasha. In England Pitt, and in Prussia Frederick the Great, both viewed with considerable apprehension what was happening, neither of them relishing the unwelcome possible contingency of the Tsar of Russia supplanting the Sultan at Constantinople. But by this time certain momentous questions were being widely canvassed and asked: Should Greece be permitted to become a dependency of Russia or, more remotely, of Austria? Would she be acceptable to Europe as a colony of France or of Britain? Could she be tolerated if she became an addition, an annexe to the outlaw empire of Ali Pasha of Yannina? Or, after all, wouldn't it perhaps be most convenient if she remained, by mutual consent of the Great Powers, a province of a refurbished and shored up Ottoman Empire? Only one thing was certain, as rivalry grew between the Powers; Europe was faced with an entirely new historical situation, the "Eastern Question". And Greece was back in history.

"Philhellenism" was the generally accepted term in Europe for that enthusiasm for the welfare of Greece, combined with an active faith in her future as a nation which was shared by many hundreds of foreigners from different countries in the early years of the nineteenth century. Such devoted enthusiasm was partly the effect of a widespread, classical education (for instance in the English public schools, the birthright of a cultural *élite*, much fostered by the Grand Tour) which dated back to before the eighteenth century. Of course many philhellenes, scholarly men of the study, were no doubt little more than sentimentalists who regarded the modern Greeks as the direct descendants of the inhabitants of ancient Hellas, who had bequeathed to the world incomparable treasures of literature and art. So the notion had grown of a compelling moral obligation on Europe to do everything possible towards aiding the resurrection to fresh nationhood of a race whose past had given to Western civilization so much that was priceless. To restore liberty to Greece would be the just repayment of a debt.

In the successful eventual restoring of that liberty, one of the most curious and significant factors was the imponderable spiritual triumph of the poets. For the poets were finally proved right. Shelley had written that poets were "the trumpets that sing to battle", and before the war was over, poets of varying nationality had succeeded in transforming the poetry of national aspiration into effective outward action and could fairly be claimed as "the unacknowledged legislators" of Greece. Sir Harold Nicolson has recorded his belief that "Lord Byron accomplished nothing at Missolonghi except his own (virtual) suicide; but by that simple act of heroism he secured the liberation of Greece;" furthermore, that without Byron's idealistic support of the Hellenic cause there would have been no subsequent Battle of Navarino and that the whole history of the Balkans would have developed on different lines.[8]

Of the Greek poets whose trumpets blared to battle in their own tongue, the most important and moving voice in the early days was that of Rhigas Pheraios, a revolutionary national poet and propagandist who had grown up and been educated at Velestinon in the Pelion region of Thessaly, an area which was then almost independent. But he killed a Turkish official in a quarrel and took refuge as a klepht. He had learnt French and German, had travelled, and in 1796 he set up an illegal revolutionary press in Vienna. He had planned to visit Greece to distribute nationalist tracts in 1797 but was betrayed to the Austrian police, condemned and executed by order of the Pasha of Belgrade in 1798. One of the most celebrated of his songs, published in the last quarter of the eighteenth century, is his *War Hymn* which opens as follows:

> How long, my heroes, shall we live in bondage,
> alone like lions on ridges, on peaks?
> Living in caves, seeing our children
> turned from the land to bitter enslavement?
> Losing our land, brothers, and parents,
> our friends, our children and all our relations?
> Better an hour of life that is free
> than forty years in slavery!

Rhigas Pheraios touched the conscience of the Greek people and in so doing woke it to a new, glowing life. Also there was Adamantios Koraïs who, after the death of Rhigas, helped to spread the intellectual ferment already working among the Greeks. The son of a Smyrna merchant, he had lived in France, and in the capital itself after 1788, and did much to advance the cause of Greek independence by laying stress upon the classical past and by codifying the present language so as to make it intelligible to all classes of people. Koraïs played an important part in calling to birth the new nation.

When Byron was on his first visit to Greece, with his friend John Cam Hobhouse, he wrote home from Patras in November 1809 that he was going to Athens to study modern Greek, which he did with conscientious "zeal and industry". The real importance of this first journey was Byron's discovery of Greece, not as the cherished fable of scholarship and past poetry, but as "a real land, a living people, and a living tongue". He wished that more Grecian tourists "would turn their minds to the language of the country, so strikingly similar to the ancient Greek is the modern Romaic as a written language." Although he had no care for collecting dead things, for what he called "antiquarian twaddle", Byron catalogued for his own use a list of fifty-five modern Greek authors and was fully knowledgeable about the revival of Greek learning. The best Greek, he said, was spoken at the Phanar and at Yannina. The spread of education among the Greeks at this time proved to be one of the heralds of liberty.

Throughout Greece schools, literary clubs and secret societies were formed for the purpose of raising the Greeks from the degradation to which they had been reduced in the previous century. Of these societies two, the *Philomuse Society* founded at Athens in 1812, and the *Philike Hetairia* (Society of Friends) set up at Odessa, the new Russian port on the Black Sea, in 1814, although they were symptoms rather than the cause of the Revolution, may well have accelerated it. The *Philike Hetairia* was in origin a political society, but developed into a revolutionary conspiracy of Greeks (many of whom lived abroad) pledged to hasten and control plans for the liberation of Greece. The Society taught the Greeks scattered in the multiple provinces of the Ottoman Empire that, once arms had been taken up, immediate assistance could be relied upon from Russia and that the enterprise was therefore less desperate than it might seem. But the influence and power of these secret societies can be overrated; for many of the last, most prominent Hetairists were more under the influence of Russian orthodoxy than interested in Greek independence. Besides this, many of the most distinguished men of the Greek Revolution were not Hetairists.

A majority of these "best philhellenes", who were not Greeks, were British and will appear later in the narrative. The movement of course was much more than just Byron, helped by all manner of adventurers and eccentrics. It was a portion of a wide international radical movement in which protest was combined with a mingling of motives such as religion, nationalism, pure commercial avarice and genuine romantic heroism. The broad international range of philhellenism, after the French Revolution ("Bliss was it in that dawn to be alive . . .") and then Napoleon, became apparent when devoted zealots arrived to fight for the Greek cause, not only from Great Britain, but from a diversity of countries, such as France, Germany, Denmark, Switzerland, Italy and the United States of America. Yet it was from the British Isles—an impressive number from Scotland and Ireland—that most of these enthusiastic philhellenes came, some of whom have given their names to the streets of several Greek cities and towns, and are still honoured and remembered today. As C. M. Woodhouse insists:

> it would be false patriotism to deny the predominance, both in numbers and in decisive effect, of the British contingent. No other country can parade even one rival, let alone an equal number, to match the roles played by half a dozen of the British. The names of Lord Byron, Sir Richard Church, Sir Edward Codrington, Captain Frank Abney Hastings, George Finlay and George Canning, are immortal in Greece; and rightly so. Only their fellow-countrymen fail to appreciate their services to the first of the new nation-states to achieve independence in the nineteenth century.[9]

Europe for some time had been suffering from ultra-conservative governments. By the beginning of the new century the signs in Greece of a national renaissance and possible revolution by the oppressed people were unmistakable; but nobody knew how the change in their status would be brought about or what it might entail. The signs had been the formation of the *banditti* called klephts, the founding of the *Philike Hetairia* and the growing numbers of enthusiastic philhellenes. There were liberal upsurges in other countries such as Spain and Italy. After Napoleon's meteoric career was finally destroyed on the field of Waterloo in 1815, the Congress of Vienna had been convened to try and determine the future course of affairs in Europe. England had refused to join the "Holy Alliance" of Tsar Alexander I, and France had not been invited. But the member states, Russia, Austria and Prussia, clearly revealed their belief that the best solution lay in an authoritarian return to the *status quo ante* 1789. These three Powers, in terms of *realpolitik*, had combined in an alliance of European despots pledged to damp down all revolutionary, even liberal ideas.

PART II

THE HEROIC STRUGGLE

CHAPTER IV

The Lion of Yannina
(Ali Pasha 1741-1822)

To the Greeks, even to-day, Ali Pasha the dictator of Epirus, who had cruelly tyrannized over their ancestors from his capital Yannina beside the lake, has remained something of an enigma. So double-sided and contradictory was his character that one might almost suppose him to have been the monstrous invention of some romantic imagination on a Shakespearian scale. A dynamic man of his time, who had risen from being a common brigand, he counted himself as an Albanian, though his remote paternity may have stemmed from a dancing dervish from Asia Minor who had wandered into Albania. But without doubt there was a touch of mystery, a lurid streak of menace in Ali's character that made a strong appeal to the romantic imagination of his period. His wars and his diplomacy were both fantastic and unpredictable. At the height of his power this autocrat of the greater part of European Turkey was able to hoodwink, or beguile by his soft manners, some of the foremost men of his age, among whom were the young Byron, Napoleon, Potemkin, Nelson, Collingwood and Victor Hugo.

Byron, on his first visit to Greece with his friend John Cam Hobhouse in 1809, succumbed to Ali's Oriental glamour, seeing in this sadistic monster a paragon of valour. Byron also correctly noted that during the period of his *pashalik*, acting in his capacity of patron of the arts and letters, Ali Pasha had made Yannina in wealth, refinement and learning, the most civilized cultural capital of the Greeks, a fair rival of Athens. Victor Hugo called him "the only colossus and man of genius of the time worthy to be compared with Napoleon", and added that Ali "was to Napoleon as the tiger to the lion, or the vulture to the eagle".

The paradoxical self-contradictions in Ali Pasha, the diamond-hard, cold calculating opportunist, liar, swindler, mass murderer and sadistic torturer, vicious sensualist with a harem of six hundred women, and millionaire, were combined with virtues such as a remarkable physical bravery, notable personal charm, refined aesthetic taste and a sardonic wit. But it was his ruthless opportunism which predominated—"for mine own good all causes shall give way." He would often seem to be gentle, his expression open, gracious and alluring, but he was skilful in concealing his craftiest evil intentions in a twinkling blue eye. Truly, to invoke Shakespeare once more, there was "no art to find the mind's construction in the face". And it was Ali Pasha's inflexible hardness of will, together with blind ambition, plain perfidy and savagery, that won for this rebel Pro-Consul of the Porte so much power and independence. He became the master of Southern Albania, all of Western Greece, parts of Macedonia; and (through his son, Veli) he dominated Thessaly, and for a while found himself in a position to exercise control even over the Peloponnese. His genius lay in his ability to weld the fierce tribesmen of different districts into an effective model army. Then, either by taxation or extortion in the conquered regions, he acquired a colossal fortune which enabled him to win by bribery what he would have failed to win by force. He grew powerful enough to secure concessions for himself even in Constantinople.

Nothing shows up the weakness of an Empire in decline so clearly as a loss of grip on its colonies. Unwittingly, Ali Pasha helped to nationalize the Greeks—something which not the memory of Byzantine power nor the Orthodox Church could do —by fanning the smouldering incipient fires of revolution against the Turks. After the fighting had actually broken out, for purely selfish reasons he helped the war because his defiance of the Sultan had the effect of diverting some twenty thousand Turkish troops away from the Peloponnese. When early in the nineteenth century "Black" Ali made himself autocrat of Yannina and the *pashalik* of Southern Albania virtually became an autonomous state, he probably did more than any other single person to set in motion the collapse of the Turkish Empire in Greece.

Ali Pasha was born in 1741 in the south of Albania at Tebeleni, a village perched on a rocky peninsula high above a turbulent river. It was hemmed in on every side by barren mountain ranges, bleak ravines and desolate gorges, all on a gigantic scale. This, a place of sudden violent storms, was the natural habitat of a vigorous lawless people, capable of devastating passions, who sometimes knew too little of the qualities of mercy or of gentleness. Ali, whose father had died while he was an infant, had absorbed as a boy the colour of his surroundings, and, starting as a cattle stealer and robber chief, he had developed both his cunning and the more savage characteristics of his race. The Albanians were half shepherds, half warriors, possibly of Scythian origin, who spoke a mixed language and called themselves Skipetars. They were part and parcel of their native mountains and, having inherited heroic traditions from a long forgotten past, they thought of themselves as palikars, or gallant young men. It was the custom for such gallant Skipetars to form close personal attachments, to swear eternal vows to one another which were held sacred and invariably proved to be inviolable.

Ali's father, Veli, had married as his second wife a woman of quite extraordinary character called Khamco, who had about as much gentleness in her nature as Tamora, Queen of the Goths. As well as Ali, she had borne her husband a daughter named Shainitza. On the pretext of safeguarding the rights of her children, Khamco had thrown her veil aside to take up arms, and, leading a troop of ferocious soldiers, she had terrorized the countryside round Tebelini. However, her affairs did not always prosper. As the result of an alliance between the villages of Gardiki and Khormovo, an ambush was laid for Khamco who was taken prisoner. Her enemies decided to teach her a lesson, which she never forgot. "They treated her very badly, shut her up in a dungeon by day, and took her out each night and forced her to submit to the embraces as well as the insults of the men of each house in turn. A Greek merchant of Argyro Castro heard of her misfortunes and felt so sorry for her that he paid her ransom of 23,000 piastres."[1] Soon after she returned to Tebelini.

From that moment Khamco's main object was to inspire in her

son's breast a burning lust for vengeance, which had to bide its time. To avenge his mother's dishonour on those who had imprisoned and outraged her became a supreme purpose of Ali's life. Before he died the wrongs his family had endured had been fully expiated by a holocaust of thousands of innocent victims. The motive forces of hatred and ambition enabled Ali Pasha to pit his power until his death against the whole might of the Ottoman Empire. Yet his total triumph would, of course, have been fatal to the Greek cause, resulting in an Albanian rather than a Hellenic Kingdom. In 1761 at twenty Ali was a handsome young man who wore his fair hair long; with intelligent blue eyes that flashed with fire or melted to charm. He was of medium height, but gracefully built and in splended physical condition. He could be winningly talkative—an irresistible personality. At this time he had fallen foul of Kurd Pasha of Berat, head of the police in Southern Albania, Thessaly and the Peloponnese, on account of his by now almost legendary looting exploits, and was taken prisoner with his gang. While most of his comrades were hanged, the Wolf—as Kurd was called—took a fancy to Ali and spared his life which he may have judged too distinguished to be wasted. But the Wolf was related to Khamco and this may have caused him to decide to be lenient to her son. At any rate, Ali stayed on in the wealthy town of Berat, with its mosques, minarets and pleasant gardens, for some years, where he was so kindly treated that he eventually plucked up courage to ask for the Wolf's daughter's hand in marriage.

The Wolf refused and married his daughter instead to Ibrahim Pasha of Valona, a man of superior birth and station to Ali. Like his mother who always demanded her own way, Ali, riven by black anger, nursed a violent life-long hatred towards Ibrahim. Disguised as a beggar, he left Berat and took to mountain banditry once more. The Wolf had put a price of 5,000 piastres upon his head. While in hiding with his friends, Ali thought of a ruse: two of his friends were to drape a few of his clothes over the body of a ram, then fire at the animal, and forthwith return with the bullet-holed and bloodstained garments to Ibrahim, assuring him that they had killed Ali. This they did and successfully collected the

5,000 piastres reward, which they handed over to Ali. He straightway used the money to recruit and finance a larger, stronger gang whose misdeeds quickly drove the Wolf beyond endurance. Now the Wolf sent out a powerful force to suppress Ali, who had concealed himself in a Christian village before being received and welcomed by Caplan Pasha of Delvino, the Wolf's most implacable enemy. Ali, temporarily tired of the dangers of his restless life, for the moment was prepared to live peacefully, and Khamco judged this the right time to find him a wife. She approached Caplan Pasha, with the result that at the age of twenty-four Ali was married to Caplan's daughter Eminé, who also was called by the delectable name of Umm-Gulsum. The marriage, which was celebrated at Argyro Castro in grandiose style, added much to Ali's prestige. Khamco was delighted to have joined her son to such a rich, all powerful family. Two boys were later born of the union, Mouktar in 1769 and Veli in 1771.

How Ali Pasha, who only became the unchallenged despot of Epirus after fifteen years of intrigue and the pitiless murders of many of his rivals (sometimes with their families), managed to acquire the title of Pasha of Yannina is typical of his crafty methods of dissimulation. The year was 1788 and he was forty-seven years old. His mother Khamco had just died of cancer of the womb, screaming in paroxysms of fury for revenge on the people of Gardiki and Khormovo, and adding to her will a curse on her children if they should fail in this. She also left a list of individuals to be assassinated and villages to be burned. Though Ali arrived after Khamco had died, he and his sister Shainitza solemnly swore to carry out their mother's evil wishes.

But first Yannina. . . . Marching from Trikkala, Ali took up a defensive position before the town, for the moment contenting himself with looting neighbouring villages. The alarmed beys inside Yannina called upon him to return to Trikkala. On his refusal they attacked him; but the fight finished in a draw. Ali bided his time, while reinforcing his position by abducting by night in a boat across the lake a daughter of the most important family in the town and marrying her:

He then persuaded his supporters in the town to send a deputation to Constantinople to petition that he might be made Pasha of Yannina, but he got word that his enemies were working actively against him in the capital, and were making some headway. He felt that the time for delays and half measures was gone, so he took the simple step of forging a decree announcing his appointment to the pashalik, for he was statesman enough to know that a *fait accompli* cannot easily be explained away. He had the announcement made in the town; the beys came out to meet him, and with much ceremony the decree was produced and drawn out of its crimson case; each bey touched it with his forehead in token of obedience; and Ali entered the town and occupied the citadel. On the following morning a second faked document was drawn up, confirming his appointment. His boldness was rewarded, for he presently found himself recognised by the Porte as Pasha of Yannina.[2]

When Lord Byron, on his first visit to Greece at the age of twenty-one, had ridden with Cam Hobhouse through the dark gorges, fearsome ravines, and adamantine mountains of Epirus in the autumn of 1809, Ali Pasha, whom he was to visit, was nearing seventy but had lost none, or little, of his vigour. But the ageing autocrat of Epirus, the "obese adventurer", had already many terrible crimes behind him. The two friends had sailed from Malta in September and had visited Patras and Preveza. Hope was high in Byron's heart for he was young and healthy and he loved Greece with the finest part of his passionate nature. Not the Greece of Lord Elgin and of the aesthetes; rather it was the living Greece of the present, the Greece of the klephtic songs and ballads which would soon make history by rising against the domination of the Ottoman Empire.

As the friends approached Yannina and the lake on which it stands, from the south a burst of sunshine suddenly illuminated the houses, domes and minarets which gleamed through the cypresses and orange and lemon groves, the lake shining, the mountains rising abruptly from its shores at the back. However, to quote Hobhouse's Journal: "As we passed a large tree on our left opposite a butcher's shop, I saw something dangling from the boughs, which at a little distance seemed to be meat exposed for sale: but on coming nearer, I suddenly discovered it to be a man's arm with part of the side torn from the body, and hanging by a bit of string tied round one of the fingers."

It was the arm and hand of a famous klephtic hero, Evthymios Vlachavas, who, desiring the ultimate liberation of Greece from the Turks, had tried in his rebellion of 1808 to take a first step by the overthrow of Ali Pasha. With more than a thousand rebels, who included some Souliotes, this patriot Vlachavas had operated near Arta, been betrayed and caught, and sent to Ali alive, together with a grisly trophy of sixty-eight heads of his dead comrades. He had been condemned to death, roped to a stake in a courtyard of the palace at Yannina, and been fiendishly tortured. Francois Pouqueville, Napoleon's consul at Yannina, who had once been his guest and feasted with him in the mountains in klephtic style, watched him as he faced his torturers, and afterwards described a scene as horrible as can be imagined; one which revealed the sadistic strain in Ali Pasha's character when he grew abnormally excited by blood-lust:

The rays of a burning sun shone upon the bronze head of Evthymios Vlachavas and glittering drops of sweat ran off his thick beard. Faced with an appalling fate Evthymios was calmer than the tyrant who was gloating over him, and I detected in the serenity of his eyes a consciousness that this would not only be his most frightful but his greatest and most exalted moment. Without flinching or making one sound the Greek chieftain endured the slow cruelties of the torturers. In the end he was dismembered and the pieces were exposed in various parts of the city as an example to the seditiously inclined. Then it was the turn of Dimitrios, a monk, who had been Evthymios' friend and constant companion: sharp laths were driven under the monk's nails, a chaplet of knucklebones was drawn tight round his head and he was hung upside down over a slow fire. Then he was covered with a board which was jumped on in order to break his bones, and at last he was walled up in a cell with only his head free. He took ten days to die.

Nor did women escape the shameless cruelty of those times. The sombre lake that Byron saw should have been haunted by female ghosts. "Dark Mouktar"—Ali's elder son—like his father and his grandmother—could control neither the impatience nor the violence of his passions and had even raped women publicly in the daytime streets. He had grown to be infatuated by a dazzlingly beautiful woman of Yannina, the twenty-eight-year-old wife of a Greek merchant, named Kyra Frosyni, the mother of two children. While her husband was away on business in Venice, Mouktar succeeded in making the accomplished, flighty, and flattered Frosyni his mistress. Mouktar had never tried to hide his obsession, which became common knowledge; so that his own wife Pasho began to be jealous. Frosyni, knowing that Mouktar was madly in love with her, played him for every material advantage, including a valuable diamond ring that she persuaded him to give her, which had originally been the gift of his wife Pasho. Frosyni, needing money, sold the ring to a jeweller, who in turn offered it to Pasho. When Pasho discovered this perfidy, she went, half-crazed by jealousy, to Ali Pasha and demanded vengeance against Frosyni. During Mouktar's absence on active service, Ali swore by the Prophet that Pasho should be allowed her revenge.

Fearing that his officers might warn Mouktar of his intentions, Ali himself went in the middle of the night to Frosyni's house, woke her up and showed her the ring, asking if she recognized it. Frosyni's first alarm had turned to terror as she realized that all was lost. She flung herself weeping at his feet, and begging for mercy. She offered him the whole of her jewellery, if only he would spare her life. But Ali, with customary avarice, but no clemency, took the treasure and then handed over Frosyni and her maid to the guard waiting at the door of the house.

The next day Ali asked Pasho if there were any more loose women with whom her husband had trifled, and without scruple she made him a list of fifteen of the most beautiful women in Yannina who deserved punishment. They were at once arrested and shut up, with Frosyni and her maid, in the Buldrun, a vile dungeon beneath the Castro where they were abused, being forced to serve the pleasures of the men who guarded them. Meanwhile, they had all been condemned to death.

At midnight, a day or two later, the guards came and took the prisoners to an opening in an underground passage where boats waited at the bottom of some steps. A thunderstorm was in progress and the dark lake water lay livid under the lightning-flashes. As the wretched women were brutally hustled into the boats, their shrieks of terror mingled with the crashes of thunder. The boats were rowed out to the middle of the lake and the women, who had been tied up in sacks, were dumped overboard, which was the barbarous but usual Mohammedan penalty for a woman's adultery.

Legend has it that Frosyni, with her maid clasped in her arms, jumped overboard before they could be tied in sacks, and that her body was recovered and given a proper burial by some Christians. Although in life she had been unfaithful, vain and greedy, time was kind to her memory for she blossomed not only into a Christian martyr but was universally regarded as a romantic early heroine of the Greek struggle for independence. Her alleged lonely tomb was later pointed out beneath a wild olive tree, overgrown with white irises. She had become the stuff of dreams and folk song:

KYRA FROSYNI
(1801)

Have you heard what happened
  on the lake at Yannina,
How seventeen were drowned with
  Kyra Frosyni,
Ah, Frosyni, famous and ill-fated!
No other woman wore a sari from Lahore,
Frosyni wore it first when she
  went out walking.
Ah, Frosyni, famous and celebrated!
Did I not tell you, Frosyni, hide the ring,
If Ali-Pasha sees it he will send a snake
  to eat you.

"If you are Turks, release me,
   here's a thousand florins,
Take me to Mouktar-Pasha, in two
   words I'll tell him:
'Mouktar my Pasha, where are you,
   come and save me,
Calm the wrath of Ali-Pasha, give him
   what you will.' "

The golden coins, the tears, they never
   reached the vizier,
And he gave you, with the others, for the
   fishes to devour.
I will throw a ton of sugar in the lake,
   to make the water
      sweet for you to drink,
Ah, Frosyni, famous, floating!
Blow, north wind, blow, north-east
   wind from Thrace,
Make wild the lake, take the
   princesses, and Kyra Frosyni.[3]

It will now be obvious that Ali Pasha was not only a man of inordinate ambition, but of an insatiable sexual appetite which was seldom allowed denial. As well as the enjoyment he derived from his harem of five or six hundred women of the most delicate and varied accomplishments, Vaudoncourt wrote: "He is almost exclusively given up to Socratic pleasures, and for this purpose keeps up a seraglio of youths, from among whom he selects his confidants, and even his principal officers." Ali would go to the most inhuman lengths to stock his treasury, or to fill his harem with children of both sexes. He even caused a beautiful girl to be dragged from the altar during her marriage service, with the result that her bridegroom afterwards shot himself. The Skipetars were prepared to kidnap any child of renowned beauty to satisfy their master's lust. If parents or relatives objected, likely as not they would be slain and their houses set on fire. An English doctor,

who had at one time ministered to the old tyrant's health, remarked with something like relish that "in the gratification of his
depraved appetites, Ali Pasha, of all modern sensualists the most
sensual, exceeded whatever the most *impure imagination can con-
ceive*, whether it may have drawn its sullied stores from scenes of
high-varnished debauchery, or from the obscurely tinted perspec-
tive of the low haunts of infamy and vice." But to complete the
portrait of this most bizarre and ferocious Pro-Consul, it will be
pertinent to examine Byron's reaction, not forgetting the poet's
youth at the time of his visit. As an English Peer of the Realm on his
travels, Byron was everywhere received with the honours due to
his rank; and upon the available evidence it would appear that Ali
Pasha was far more impressed by his visitor's ancestry than with
his poetry. Byron saw Ali Pasha at the height of his glory, dis-
playing all the pomp and arrogance which, within thirteen years,
would provoke the Porte to fury and lead to his defeat and death
at the hands of the Sultan's armies. A fairly lengthy citation of
extracts from Byron's long letter to his mother from Preveza on
the 12th of November, 1809, will add to the picture:

My dear Mother,
   . . . I have traversed the interior of the province of Albania
on a visit to the Pacha . . . as far as Tepaleen, his Highness's
country palace, where I stayed three days. The name of the
Pacha is *Ali*, and he is considered a man of the first abilities: he
governs the whole of Albania (the ancient Illyricum), Epirus,
and part of Macedonia. His son, Vely Pacha, to whom he has
given me letters, governs the Morea, and has great influence in
Egypt; in short, he is one of the most powerful men in the
Ottoman empire. When I reached Yanina, the capital, after a
journey of three days over the mountains, through a country of
the most picturesque beauty, I found that Ali Pacha was with
his army in Illyricum, besieging Ibrahim Pacha in the castle of
Berat. He had heard that an Englishman of rank was in his
dominions, and had left orders at Yanina with the commandant
to provide a house, and supply me with every kind of necessary
gratis; and, though I have been allowed to make presents to the

slaves, etc., I have not been permitted to pay for a single article of household consumption.

I rode out on the vizier's horses, and saw the palaces of himself and his grandsons: they are splendid, but too much ornamented with silk and gold. I then went over the mountains through Zitza, a village with a Greek monastery (where I slept on my return), in the most beautiful situation . . . I ever beheld. In nine days I reached Tepaleen. Our journey was much prolonged by the torrents that had fallen from the mountains, and intersected the roads. I shall never forget the singular scene on entering Tepaleen at five in the afternoon, as the sun was going down. . . . The Albanians, in their dresses, (the most magnificent in the world, consisting of a long *white kilt*, gold-worked cloak, crimson velvet gold-laced jacket and waistcoat, silver-mounted pistols and daggers,) the Tartars with their high caps, the Turks in their vast pelisses and turbans, the soldiers and black slaves with the horses, the former in groups in an immense large open gallery in front of the palace, the latter placed in a kind of cloister below it, two hundred steeds ready caparisoned to move in a moment, couriers entering or passing out with the despatches, the kettle-drums beating, boys calling the hour from the minaret of the mosque, altogether, with the singular appearance of the building itself, formed a new and delightful spectacle to a stranger. I was conducted to a very handsome apartment, and my health inquired after by the vizier's secretary, *à-la-mode Turque*!

The next day I was introduced to Ali Pacha. I was dressed in a full suit of staff uniform, with a very magnificent sabre, etc. The vizier received me in a large room paved with marble; a fountain was playing in the centre; the apartment was surrounded by scarlet ottomans. He received me standing, a wonderful compliment from a Mussulman, and made me sit down on his right hand. I have a Greek interpreter for general use, but a physician of Ali's named Femlario, who understands Latin, acted for me on this occasion. His first question was, why, at so early an age, I left my country?—(the Turks have no idea of travelling for amusement). He then said, the English minister,

Captain Leake, had told him I was of a great family, and desired his respects to my mother; which I now, in the name of Ali Pacha, present to you. He said he was certain I was a man of birth, because I had small ears, curling hair, and little white hands, and expressed himself pleased with my appearance and garb. He told me to consider him as a father whilst I was in Turkey, and said he looked on me as his son. Indeed, he treated me like a child, sending me almonds and sugared sherbet, fruit and sweetmeats, twenty times a day. He begged me to visit him often, and at night, when he was at leisure. I then, after coffee and pipes, retired for the first time. I saw him thrice afterwards. It is singular that the Turks, who have no hereditary dignities, and few great families, except the Sultans, pay so much respect to birth; for I found my pedigree more regarded than my title. . . .

His highness is sixty years old, very fat, and not tall, but with a fine face, light blue eyes, and a white beard; his manner is very kind, and at the same time he possesses that dignity which I find universal amongst Turks. He has the appearance of anything but his real character, for he is a remorseless tyrant, guilty of the most horrible cruelties, very brave, and so good a general that they call him the Mahometan Buonaparte. Napoleon has twice offered to make him King of Epirus, but he prefers the English interest, and abhors the French, as he himself told me. He is of so much consequence, that he is much courted by both, the Albanians being the most warlike subjects of the Sultan, though Ali is only nominally dependent on the Porte; he has been a mighty warrior, but is as barbarous as he is successful, roasting rebels, etc., etc. Buonaparte sent him a snuff-box with his picture. He said the snuff-box was very well, but the picture he could excuse, as he neither liked it nor the original. His ideas of judging of a man's birth from ears, hands, etc., were curious enough. To me he was, indeed, a father, giving me letters, guards, and every possible accommodation. Our next conversations were of war and travelling, politics and England. . . .

Your affectionate son,
Byron.[4]

Despite the strong moral influence of the French Revolution, with its stirring cries of Liberty and Freedom, the aftermath of the Napoleonic wars hardly touched Greece at all. In 1797 the centuries-long protection of the powerful Venetian Republic over the Ionian islands came to an end, when these islands were occupied by the French. And Ali Pasha's ambitions clashed directly with French interests. First he wanted to crush the free Greek community of Souli, against which at the end of the eighteenth century he waged a number of lurid wars; then he wished to gain control over the Ionian islands, with some of their mainland dependencies such as the towns of Butrinto, Preveza, and Parga, above all of Parga. In 1798 Napoleon's invasion of Egypt involved Ali Pasha not only in war with England but also with an unnatural temporary alliance between the Tsar and the Sultan; for both Russia and Turkey shared their fear of French interference in Greece.

After Napoleon's fall in 1815 the Greeks were proved to have been over-optimistic in considering that they could rely upon the support of the major European Powers, for they became much more the playthings of these powers, who now wanted only peace and quiet. Tsar Alexander I had planned the somewhat fantastic Holy Alliance, consisting of Russia, Austria and Prussia, as a league of despots to discourage liberalism and all revolutionary movements. Although the Holy Alliance was not taken too seriously by other governments (England refused to join and France was not invited), its stubborn reactionary spirit would dominate European politics for the next decade. In the eastern Mediterranean British official policy was scarcely more sympathetic to Greek aspirations than was the reactionary Austrian chancellor Prince Metternich, who had remarked with customary sardonic contempt that it was not possible even to define what was meant by the word "Greek", since it was used "indiscriminately to signify a territory, a race, a language or even a religion."

England had a twofold policy: she was anxious to block Russian aims in the Mediterranean, and to safeguard the security of the Ionian Islands over which, on evicting the French in 1814, she had assumed a protectorate. Though the Greeks at first welcomed the British to Corfu, they came later to regret the "English presence";

for Sir Thomas Maitland, the stern autocratic High Commissioner, by insisting on preserving strict neutrality when the struggle came, proved anything but helpful.

The seven Ionian Islands, running from north to south, are Corfu, Paxos, Levkas, Ithaka, Cephallonia, Zakynthos and Kythera, and in remote antiquity had been independent of one another. They were ruled collectively at first by Rome and then by Constantine from Byzantium. Subsequently, they were split up between Norman, Genoese and Venetian adventurers. Unlike other Greek islands, apart from Levkas, they hardly felt the Turkish yoke at all. But from 1387 onwards they fell in turn under the direct control of the rich Republic of Venice. When in 1797 the Republic of Venice collapsed, they were occupied by France. But in 1799 the islands were captured by a Russo-Turkish fleet, jointly occupied, and an unusual condominium was set up which changed to a Russian protectorate in 1801. This short-lived joint dominion became an autonomous state, the "Septinsular Republic", with its own flag and the right of making diplomatic contacts with other countries, although remaining subject to Turkish suzerainty. Russian troops stayed in occupation to safeguard the islands, which might otherwise have been seized by Ali Pasha. However, this somewhat thin autonomy disappeared in 1807, when the Russians surrendered their rights of sovereignty to the French by the Treaty of Tilsit. Along with the territory of the Ionian Islands went four towns on the mainland, the ports of Butrinto, Parga, Preveza and Vonitza, of which today Butrinto alone is not on Greek soil.

The short-lived Septinsular Republic was more than symbolically important because the Greeks on the islands were the first for three centuries and a half to enjoy the semblance of governing themselves. And the Great Powers, by creating the Septinsular Republic, had released forces whose future effect would pass out of their control. Napoleon himself highly appreciated his tenure of Corfu and wrote to Talleyrand, "I think that henceforth the chief maxim of the French Republic should be never to give up Corfu . . .". Nevertheless, in 1814 Corfu was occupied by the British after Napoleon's defeat at the Battle of Leipzig, and shortly became the capital of the "Ionian Republic" under British suzerainty. The islands were to remain as a British protectorate until the year 1864 when the "United States of the Ionian Islands" were generously and unconditionally ceded to the Kingdom of the Hellenes. The fact that all the Ionian people were proud to be Greek, convinced England that union with Greece would be both justified and desirable.

Coming events cast their shadows before, and an event happened in 1807 which was to have great significance for the future. Ali Pasha, who already held Preveza, decided to attack Levkas which was divided from the mainland only by a narrow strait. The Septinsular Republic entrusted the island's defence to a young Ionian aristocrat, Count John Capo d'Istria (he later adopted the Greek form of his name, Capodistrias) who at the age of thirty had already been appointed Secretary of State. His family had come to Corfu from Istria as long ago as the fourteenth century, and he himself had been born on the island in 1776. Capodistrias had grown up while the intellectual Enlightenment in France was spreading; but he was a staunch son of the Greek Orthodox Church, whose mother was a member of a solid family from Epirus. Like other Ionian nobles, Capodistrias had studied in Italy, at Padua University where he read medicine. But now he had become passionately interested in the national aspirations of Greece, though he believed that so small a country must rely upon the protection of a great power. This influenced him when he joined the service of Russia whose autocratic and religious traditions matched his own. He rose rapidly in the Russian service, concerned especially with Russia's desire to protect the Orthodox subjects of the Sultan.

Before he left for Russia, Capodistrias had gained valuable experience of war during his military defence of Levkas against Ali Pasha. He had shown a natural gift for leadership, and had conducted the defence with success. He had obtained help not only from the other Ionian islands but also from the mainland klephts who had flocked to Corfu for refuge. These armed bands of refugees included such heroes as Theodore Kolokotronis and Marco Botzaris, both of whom were to win great fame in the future War of Independence. These two rough chieftains and the cultured nobleman had discovered a mutual commitment to the ideal of Greek freedom, which all three were sworn to promote with their utmost powers. But after the Treaty of Tilsit, when the French took over, Capodistrias's destiny pointed to Russia, where he pursued a distinguished diplomatic career until he had risen to become the Tsar's joint Secretary of State at the Congress of Vienna. However, he never forgot his ambitions for Greece; nor the brotherhood he had sworn with the two klephts.

CHAPTER V

Today the Struggle

At the outset of the war it is essential to grasp the heroic magnitude of the task undertaken in the Greek struggle for independence. It was David against Goliath in national terms. For, although the might of the Ottoman Empire had long since passed its prime, with a declining administration and a body politic bleeding from a growing corruption, inefficiency and lethargy within, nonetheless Turkey was still a Great Power, and her image as the "sick man of Europe" still lay in the future.

For a very long time the Greeks could count on no support from any of the Great Powers, unless it was Russia. After the cataclysmic threat of the Napoleonic Wars, the reactionary rulers of Europe were wholly disinclined to encourage any sort of popular subversion. Besides, the Powers, except Russia, were all on reasonably friendly terms with the Turkish Empire and England and France were preoccupied with the safetly of their trade in the Near and Middle East. So England, unsure also of social stability at home, disappointed the liberal hopes of the Greeks. It was not until six years after the outbreak of the Greek war, in April 1827, that George Canning became Prime Minister and reactionary Toryism ended. His philhellene cousin, Stratford Canning, replaced a pro-Turkish ambassador at Constantinople and at last England could show open sympathy for the oppressed Christian subjects of the Porte.

At the moment of the Greek risings a contradiction in aims was clearly apparent. On the one hand, most Phanariotes, together with other wealthy Greek families of good standing, thought it in their best interest to preserve the *status quo* of the Ottoman Empire, so that, provided they exercised patience, they might perhaps inherit the Empire's advantages as more and more plum administrative posts were offered to them. On the other hand, conflicting with such hopes, was the fact of the Greeks' fervent re-awakening to a sense of their national identity. For Greece to be reborn as a nation it was necessary they should break completely with the Ottoman giant. Geographically estimated, the amount of Greek soil inhabited by Greeks within the Turkish Empire was not large; but to liberate this comparatively small area of land the Ottoman Empire would have to be disrupted. And neither of these two wholly opposite Greek points of view had been resolved—nor indeed even properly understood—when in March 1821 the War of Independence broke out in two separate uprisings.

Simultaneously, but with no effective co-ordination, the war started in far apart regions of the Turkish-dominated Balkans: in the Danubian principalities of Moldavia and Wallachia and in the Peloponnese. If the abortive invasion of Roumania by Prince Alexander Ypsilantis, which collapsed ignominiously, be excluded, the theatre of war of the entire struggle was confined to continental Greece, the Peloponnese, and the adjacent islands in their narrow seas. The fact that the Turkish Commander in Chief, Kurshid Pasha, was occupied in the long business of reducing the troublesome Ali Pasha provided both an opportunity and incentive to revolt. So on the 6th of March the Phanariote Alexander Ypsilantis, who was in the Russian service, accompanied by some Russian and Greek officers crossed the River Pruth and raised the flag of Greek Independence at Jassy in Moldavia. Though the Russian Court may have connived at this rising, officially the Tsar disowned it, and from the first this ill-fated invasion was doomed to failure. It was hampered partly by the defects of Ypsilantis's character, such as his visionary vanity, military over-confidence and incapacity to judge the conditions of the country, and also by the Russian disavowal of the strange fact of an alien nobility's attempt to arouse the enthusiasm of a peasantry for a cause other than their own. All that is relevant here is that the rebellion in the Roumanian provinces failed from the start, while the one in the Peloponnese surprisingly succeeded. In the Peloponnese the determined single object of the rising was simple—Greece for the Greeks.

Although the Greek historian Trikoupis, with other writers, had dismissed the founder members of the *Philike Hetairia* as men of straw, many of them expatriate Greek merchants imperfectly acquainted with the true position in Greece, the secret Society founded on Russian soil at Odessa in 1814 had, through the conspiracy of its agents in the Balkans, provided an impetus for future revolutionary activity. The *Philike Hetairia* let it be believed they had Russian support. But the Tsar's Foreign Minister, the Greek Count John Capodistrias, had refused to lead the rebellion and returned to Russia. On his refusal, the *Philike Hetairia* had invited the Phanariotes, Prince Alexander Ypsilantis and his brother Demetrios to become the titular heads of the two uprisings.

In the Peloponnese, as the time for decision came, many of the thriving notables were reluctant to commit themselves to the dangerous hazards of revolution without firm confirmation of the expected Russian aid. The Greek population's volatile enthusiasm had been roused by news of the uprising in Roumania; but fortunately for the Hetairist patriot priest and political and military leader, Dikaios Papaphlessas, rumours of the defeat of Alexander Ypsilantis came only after the rebellion in the Peloponnese had begun. The Peloponnese had a more or less homogeneous Greek population, and the rising was unleashed by limited local actions, and by outbreaks of violence and looting, encouraged by such patriotic leaders as Papaphlessas and the Overlord of Mani, Petrobey Mavromichalis. At first small bands of autonomous Greek irregulars operated locally against Turkish forces which were dispersed and confined to garrison towns and forts.

From the beginning the war was a savage people's war, a revolt of the peasantry and the klephtic chieftains against their detested masters who had subjugated them for so long and treated them as cattle. It was to be a war of mutual extermination, with brave deeds, but also hideous atrocities committed by both sides. Many of the first acts of violence were little more than massacre by bandits:

A Turkish tax-gatherer and his retinue were fallen upon and murdered. A band of sixty Albanian mercenaries were surprised and butchered by three hundred Greek klephts. This was in March, 1821; and in April the insurrection was general. Everywhere, as though at a preconcerted signal, the peasantry rose, and massacred all the Turks—men, women, and children—on whom they could lay hands.

> *In the Morea shall no Turk be left,*
> *Nor in the whole wide world.*

Thus rang the song which, from mouth to mouth, announced the beginning of a war of extermination. The Mussulman population of the Morea had been reckoned at twenty-five thousand souls. Within three weeks of the outbreak of the revolt, not a Moslem was left, save those who had succeeded in escaping into the towns.[1]

Meanwhile the national uprising had found another leader in Bishop Germanos, the distinguished Metropolitan of Patras who, according to the accepted popular account of the war, with other clerics and notable laymen, on the 25th of March, 1821, raised the flag of national rebellion at the monastery of Aghia Lavra at Kalavryta in the north of the Peloponnese. Probably this was not their intention. They would have preferred to delay their commitment until they were more certain of Russian support. They had stopped at the monastery in a despairing attempt to stave off, or at least delay, a summons by the Turkish authorities for consultation at Tripolitza, where they suspected they would be held as hostages. Yet it was customary for the bishops and primates to meet twice a year at Tripolitza to receive through the Pasha the Ottoman government's orders concerning taxation and police measures. This year the pretext was that the Turks wanted a consultation to devise a policy to counteract the intrigues which Ali Pasha was carrying on among the Greek population. while he was being blockaded in Yannina by the Turkish *seraskier* Kurshid Pasha.

Today the monastery of Aghia Lavra stands in its shady garden, with its historic plane-tree, a few kilometres up a mountain road above the small town of Kalavryta, and there the standard of the revolution may be seen with its stirring inscription: "Here is the historic holy standard Banner, that the Archbishop 'Germanos' of ancient Patras hoist(ed) here the day of Greek Revolution out under the historic plane-tree." It presents the Assumption embroidered by a Greek woman (Chissos) from Smyrna. There is a bullet hole through the crown of one of the angels made during the battle of Kalavryta.

From the monastery on the 6th of April, 1821, Archbishop Germanos, with a force of several thousand armed men, descended into the plain against Patras. Only a portion of his army, composed of undisciplined peasants, carried guns, the rest merely slings, clubs and daggers fastened to the ends of long poles. The Archbishop was accompanied by the Greek primates Papadiamanto-pulos, Londos, Zaimis and Sotiri, primates of Vostizza and Kala-vryta. The Greek population had already risen and proclaimed with fierce shouting the liberty of their country. The Greeks had set fire to the Turkish quarter of Patras and the Turks were launching shot and shell from the safety of the citadel. Greek and Turk indulged in a merciless massacre amid the burning ruins of the city:

the only prisoners that were spared, owed their lives to fanati-cism, some Christian youths being circumcised by the mollahs, and some Turkish boys baptized by the priests. . . . Germanos bivouacked during the night of the 6th, and on the following morning, conducting his army to the yet burning town, shut up the Turks within the walls of the citadel. The Christian in-habitants welcomed him with great demonstrations of joy; a crucifix was elevated in the square of St. George, the Grecian banners floated from the mosques, and the conflagration that had raged for near three days was at length got under. The arch-bishop and the other Greek generals . . . set forth a proclama-tion containing merely these emphatic words,—Peace to the Christians! Respect to the Consuls! Death to the Turks![2]

Unfortunately, the only immediate result of the rising at Patras was that the once flourishing port and capital of Achaia was destroyed; but every Turk who failed to reach the sanctuary of the citadel was slain. The undisciplined Greeks, however, led by commanders of little experience, were unable to reduce the citadel; and, as soon as it was relieved on April 15th by Yussuf Pasha, Germanos and his men were forced to retire to the mountains. Other unsuccessful attempts were made to reduce Patras; but the citadel remained in Turkish hands until Ibrahim Pasha evacuated the Peloponnese in 1828.

The long progress of the war, atrociously brutal, but heroically borne and inspired by the peasant population, was uplifted by the supreme heroism of such Greeks, for example, as Makriyannis. But the pattern of events was complex, often obscure in motive, and fragmented because of rivalries and sudden shifts of purpose among the various factions. From such a tangled skein of events it is impossible to draw out a simple thread of narrative; but the three main periods of the war can be clearly indicated. The first period lasted until 1824 and during this time the Greeks had to "go it alone", except for the help they received from bands of philhellenes from the different countries of Europe. During the second period from 1824 the tide turned against the Greeks when the disciplined army of Mehemet Ali, Pasha of Egypt, came to the aid of the Sultan. The third period began with the *deus ex machina* intervention of the European Powers in the autumn of 1827, and lasted until the end. Although it seems that the war could not have been won without the armed intervention of England, France and Russia, it remains doubtful whether the intrepid spirit which animated the movement for Greek freedom could ever have been permanently suppressed even if the Powers had persisted in their neutrality.

In the Peloponnese the Turks in spite of copious warnings were caught wholly unprepared, with the larger part of the Ottoman army under Kurshid Pasha, out of reach, engaged against Ali Pasha. The war began without any concerted plan or generally acknowledged leadership. But in the deep rocky south of the still almost unconquered Mani, Petrobey Mavromichalis, eighth and last and greatest of the sovereign overlords of the Mani (who became a paramount figure in Greek nineteenth-century history), led his clan against Kalamata and put all the inhabitants of the Turkish garrison to the sword:

> It was from the Mani that the first blow was struck. Petrobey and three thousand Maniots with Kolokotronis and a number of the great Morean klephts advanced on the Turkish garrison of Kalamata. After its surrender he issued a declaration of the Greek aspirations to the courts of Europe signed "Petrobey Mavromichalis, Prince and Commander in Chief". The banners of freedom were going up all over Greece, and the whole peninsula burst into those flames which, after four centuries of slavery, demolished the Turkish power in the country for ever and gave rebirth to the shining phoenix of modern Greece. Petrobey, at the head of his Maniots, fought battle after battle in these ferocious years; he takes his place as one of the giants in the struggle. . . . No less than forty-nine of his family were killed during this contest and his capital of Tsimova was re-named Areopolis in his honour: the town of the war-god Ares.[3]

Theodore Kolokotronis, the klepht chieftain who had once served in the British Ionian levies, had now returned to the Peloponnese where, fortified by a vision of the Virgin, he captured Karytaena in Arcadia and massacred the Moslem population.

The revolt spread rapidly, fanned to a jubilant flame by these initial successes. In a matter of weeks every Turk had been cleared from the open country, the survivors of the Ottoman ruling class finding themselves miserably besieged in the fortified towns. In April the flames of Christian liberty had leaped the Isthmus of Corinth and engulfed the whole of Boeotia and Attica, and in early May the Turks were blockaded in the Acropolis of Athens. In the Peloponnese several Ottoman fortresses still held out, such as Coron, Modon, Navarino, Monemvasia and Tripolitza; but one by one these were captured, with a repetition of merciless scenes of slaughter. In October 1821 Tripolitza, the capital of the vilayet (a province of the Ottoman Empire) was taken by storm and the

Greeks' cruelty reached a climax. Kolokotronis rode in triumph to the citadel over streets carpeted with dead bodies, and "the crowning triumph of the Cross" was celebrated by the cold-blooded murder of about two thousand prisoners of all ages and both sexes, but mostly women and children, some of whom were tortured before they were killed. These acts crowned and completed the success of the insurrection in the Peloponnese—a sorry climax —and now only Nauplia and Patras, with a few minor fortresses, were left in the possession of the Turks.

In seeking to balance the relative barbarism of each side in this desperate contest between two great racial antagonists, several factors must be kept in mind. Turks and Greeks were peoples of opposed traditions and cultures, and the Turks were Orientals. Certainly, their heroic virtues helped, but their vices hindered the Greeks in their long struggle for nationhood. Probably the Turks were the more cruel of the two. For instance, if a klepht lay dying on a lost battlefield, he would very likely ask his companions to cut off his head and carry it away with them, rather than let it fall into the hands of the Turks. It is true that a Greek pallikar seldom spared a Turk who fell into his hands; but unlike the pasha's executioners, he had neither the leisure nor the taste to refine upon the torment of his victim, or make it last through several days.

North of the Gulf of Corinth the fortunes of battle had been ambiguous. In Eastern Roumeli, which was of more strategic value than the country west of the Pindus mountains because it provided the overland route from the north into the Peloponnese, the Greeks had struck with vigour, under brave but inexperienced leaders. In the past many Greeks had chosen to serve under Ali Pasha, accepting both his favours and the peril of his whims. Among these were three of the most colourful revolutionary leaders of the rebellion, Odysseus Androutsos, Makriyannis, and Athanasios Diakos "the Deacon", so nicknamed because he had once studied for the priesthood in a monastery. The last two men proved to be dedicated, passionate patriots and were destined to win for themselves golden opinions in the annals of the war. The career of Androutsos, however, was to say the least equivocal, and ended dishonourably. A famous klepht at sixteen and in Ali Pasha's bodyguard, he rose to be a captain of gendarmes, and was later made Commander-in-Chief in Western Greece. He was linked with the English philhellenes through his half-sister's marriage to Trelawney, the swashbuckling friend of Shelley and Byron. But his character was devious and jealous. He came to terms with the Turks through suspicion of John Kolettis (the Vlach physician to Ali Pasha, and Plenipotentiary for Epirus in the First National Assembly of 1821) then surrendered to Gouras, the garrison commander of Athens, and was imprisoned on the Acropolis. He was found dead at the foot of the "Venetian" tower in the southern wing of the Propylaea, and was supposed to have died by a fall in attempting to escape. Finlay is harsh in his judgement of Androutsos, branding him as a traitor guilty of charges of collaboration with the enemy, "at whose name the finger of scorn is pointed by every Greek".

Athanasios Diakos had served as a klepht under Androutsos and, likewise, had been a member of Ali Pasha's bodyguard. He was also a member of the *Philiki Hetairia*. On the outbreak of the revolution he had collected a troop of his compatriots to fight the Turkish forces which were moving southwards from Thessaly against the insurgents. In April the Greeks captured Amfissa and Levadia and very soon Athens (in those days no more than a large village, although strategically important) was blockaded. Kurshid Pasha's efficient commander Omer Vrioni, a Moslem Greek who was descended from the august family of the Palaeologi, inflicted a number of defeats on the Greeks. But now, moving south from Larissa, Vrioni's army was opposed in the plain of Lamia by the troops of Diakos at the bridge of Alamana, across a tributary of the River Sperchios, not far from the pass of Thermopylae where in 480 B.C. King Leonidas and his three hundred Spartans had resisted the Persians.

The bridge was heroically defended on May 5th by Diakos and the Bishop of Salona, with only seven hundred Greeks, against a far superior Turkish force. Unfortunately, after the most gallant fighting, both Diakos and the Bishop were captured and executed. Diakos was taken to Lala, impaled on a spit, and roasted alive by the Turks. The record of his defiant spirit during his martyrdom has been preserved in a popular folk-poem, one of the few ex-

amples of a klephtic ballad which throws a definite light on Greek
history:

DIAKOS

A great darkness is rushing down upon us, black as a raven.
Is it Kalyvas who comes, is it Leventoyanni?
"Tis not Kalyvas who comes, nor Leventoyanni;
Omer Vrioni is rushing upon us with eighteen thousand men."
Diakos, as soon as he heard of it, was sorely troubled;
He cried out shrilly, and spoke to his lieutenant.
"Gather my company together, collect the pallikars,
Give them powder in plenty and bullets in handfuls
And let them go down quickly to Alamana,
Where there are strong bastions, and goodly entrenchments."
They take light swords, and heavy guns,
They come to Alamana, and occupy the bastions.
"Take heart, my lads," he says, "fear not,
Stand up boldy like Hellenes and like Greeks."
But they were afraid, and scattered into the woods.
Diakos remained under fire with eighteen warriors,
For three hours he fought against eighteen thousand;
His gun was shattered, and broke into pieces.
And Diakos drew his sword and charged into the enemy's fire;
He destroyed numberless Turks and seven buluk-bashis.
Then his sword broke off at the handle
And Diakos fell into the hands of his enemies alive.
A thousand men went in front of him and a thousand behind.
And Omer Vrioni asked him secretly on the way,
"Will you turn Turk, Diako mine, change your faith,
Make obeisance in the mosque and leave the Church?"
But Diakos answered him, and spoke angrily;
"Go, you and your faith, you infidels, to destruction!
I was born a Greek, and a Greek I will die!
If you wish a thousand florins and a thousand *mahmoutis*
I would that you might grant me but five or six days of life,
Until Odysseus and Thanasi Vaya come!"

Soon as he heard this, Halil Bey wept, and said:
"A thousand purses will I give you, and five hundred besides,
If you will destroy Diakos, the fearsome klepht,
For he will bring low Turkey and all its government."
They took Diakos, and impaled him,
They stood him upright, and he mocked them,
Insulted their faith, and called them infidels.
"Dogs, though you impale me, it is but one Greek lost.
Odysseus is still well, and Captain Niketas,
And they will bring low Turkey and all your government."4

Apart from the atrocious cruelty and stoical heroism of this ballad's story, it reveals a point of great interest. In the line "stand up boldy like Hellenes and like Greeks" the words Hellenes and Greeks imply an unusual sentiment in a klephtic ballad. Although for many years the Hellenic idea had been canvassed, and to a certain extent successfully popularized, the national bond which drew the Greeks together at this time was less Hellenism than Orthodox Christianity; not the classical body of the country but its Byzantine soul. The long static tradition of ikon-painting, with its glowing inner spiritual luminosity, may be regarded as the symbol and epitome of Greek continuity. It was the devotion of the Greeks to their Byzantine Christianity that enabled them to maintain, unchanged, an undying hostility to the infidel.

And in a sense it is the same today. The ordinary Greek villager would be much less interested in such fabulous forbears as Homer, Plato, Pericles, Miltiades at Marathon or Leonidas at Thermopylae, than he would, were the subject broached, by a reminder of the deeds of the klephtic chieftains like Androutsos, Botzaris, Mavro-michalis, Karaiskakis, and Kolokotronis wearing his fireman's helmet, in all the kilted and moustached pallikars, and of course in Diakos and his men waving their scimitars, fighting like lions by the bridge of Alamana against the blaspheming Turk.

Other men who have never lost their romantic gloss were the heroes of the Greek war at sea, led by such Admirals as Miaoulis of Hydra and Kanaris of Psara. The expertise of the thousands of

anonymous sea captains and ordinary seamen was a second deter-
mining factor in the fortunes and progress of the war. Most Greeks
had learnt to handle a boat from infancy, and grew up to be brave
and adroit sailors; indeed, the long seafaring tradition of islands
like Hydra and Chios persists to the present day in some of the
wealthiest shipping dynasties. In a war fought for the most part on
or near the large peninsula of the Peloponnese, whose principal
fortifications lay along the coast, control of the routes of communications, entrances to the Gulf of Corinth and the Isthmus of
Corinth, with the mainland were all-important.

While the Greeks were by nature and tradition the finest
sailors in the Mediterranean, the Turks, from their origins, were
by no means a maritime race. The Greeks were always prepared
to dismiss them with contempt as "landlubbers". Certainly, late
in Turkish history, in the early sixteenth century, a formidable
navy had been forced upon the Turks by the genius and will-
power of Kheir-ed-Din Barbarossa, Sultan Suleiman the Magnificent's High Admiral, who, acting from the Barbary Coast, had
successfully fought Spain, Genoa and Venice, and made the
Ottoman Fleet a terror and a byword for piracy. But those days
were over. Now in April 1821 it was a different matter. When the
islands revolted, Spetsai on the 7th, Psara on the 23rd, Hydra on
the 28th and Samos on the 30th, the Ottoman Government found
themselves in a predicament about equipping a fleet to fight the
very people from whom they had formerly drawn their recruits.
They were obliged to man their ships with impressed crews of
untrained dock-labourers, peasants, fishermen and boatmen, supplemented by a motley collection of Algerian pirates and Genoese
and Maltese mercenaries who were mostly ignorant of the sea.
Although the Turks had once been invincible on land, they were
more helpless at sea, and there was some derisive talk among
British seamen, describing the Turkish fleet as being "adrift in the
Archipelago". Although in bulk and tonnage the Turks were
vastly superior, on many occasions they proved no match for the
Greek brigs and fully armed frigates whose crews were well
trained, if not always well disciplined. Under such circumstances,
though the need for action was imperative, it was small wonder

that the Ottoman navy was laggard in leaving the Dardanelles. When at last it did so, it had only eight warships and these were under-navigated by crews who had little more than a rudimentary knowledge of seamanship.

The Greek fleets were split into two squadrons, the larger one of thirty-seven sail under Admiral Iacobos Tombazis cruised the archipelago on the lookout for the appearance of the Turks. The other squadron, commanded by Andreas Miaoulis, sailed to blockade Patras and keep watch on the coasts of Epirus. It must, however, be here admitted that the Greeks opened the war at sea with some hideous atrocities, a counterpart to the cruelty of the war on land. Finlay records how eight brigs from Spetsai captured by surprise an Ottoman corvette of twenty-six guns and a brig of sixteen guns at Melos, and that the Turks on board were taken to Spetsai and tortured before being executed. Another such incident he describes thus:

Two Hydriot brigs, commanded by Sachturi and Pinotzi, captured a Turkish vessel with a valuable cargo, among which were some rich presents from Sultan Mahmud to Mehemet Ali, pasha of Egypt. A recently deposed Sheik-êl-Islam, or patriarch of the orthodox Mussulmans, was a passenger on board, accompanied by all his family. It was said that he was on the pilgrimage to Mecca. He was known to have belonged to the tolerant party of the Ottoman government. There were other Turkish families in the ship. The Hydriots murdered all on board in cold blood; helpless old men, ladies of rank, beautiful slaves, and infant children, were butchered on the deck like cattle. An attempt was afterwards made to extenuate this unmerciful conduct, by asserting that it was an act of revenge. This assertion is false. Those who perpetrated these cruelties did not hear of the execution of their own orthodox patriarch until after they had murdered the orthodox patriarch of their enemies. The truth is, that both by land and sea the war commenced as a war of extermination. Fanatical pedants talked of reviving the glories and the cruelties of classic times as inseparable consequences of Greek liberty. They told how the Athenians had exterminated the inhabitants of Melos, and how the Spartans had put all their Athenian prisoners to death after their victory at Aegospotamos.[5]

When starvation caused the surrender of the fortress of Navarino on August 19th, another massacre followed, but against the will of the Greek leaders who had intended to transport their Turkish prisoners to Egypt. One of the blockading Greek ships lay ready anchored in the harbour; but while valuable Turkish property was being loaded on board, a dispute flared among the Greeks about the manner in which the ladies' bodies were to be searched for gold and jewelry. This led to a general massacre and only those Turks who were already on board escaped death. A Greek ecclesiastic, Phrantzes, was present and has described with shame and indignation the scenes he witnessed:

> Women wounded with musket-balls and sabre-cuts, rushed to the sea, seeking to escape, and were deliberately shot. Mothers robbed of their clothes, with infants in their arms, plunged into the water to conceal themselves from shame, and they were made a mark for inhuman riflemen. Greeks seized infants from their mothers' breasts and dashed them against the rocks. Children, three and four years old, were hurled living into the sea and left to drown.

However, one must be fair and prepared to admit that the atrocities were pretty well equal on both sides. In such a war between an enslaved people and their fanatical oppressor, particularly when religions clash, it is not possible to eradicate sadism. Tragically, until war itself is exorcized, it seems certain that man's inhumanity to man will continue to make countless thousands mourn.

With the exception of Admiral Miaoulis, the Greek heroes of the war at sea, such as Constantine Kanaris, were less admirals in the manner in which they fought their engagements than "marine commandos". They would concentrate upon a single dashing exploit, with little or no reference to combined naval strategy or regard for the follow-up of success. The Hydriot Admiral Tombazis, who came from one of the most aristocratic and richest families on the island, was an honourable and well-intentioned man, but was given to consulting his inferiors over vital decisions rather than trusting in his own better judgement. The Greek squadrons were very democratic. Perhaps not even Nelson himself could have maintained strict discipline in a fleet where every ship held a close-knit clan and every common sailor found a voice.

Towards the end of May a Greek squadron under Admiral Tombazis contacted the Ottoman fleet. Although the Greek ships outnumbered the Turks, they were inferior in size and weight of ordnance; so they cautiously stayed beyond range of the Ottoman guns, while awaiting an opportunity to attack. This came on the morning of the 24th of May when a Turkish line-of-battle ship, separated from its companions during the night, was sighted north of Chios. The light Greek vessels gave chase and were soon over-hauling the slow-moving Ottoman. The Turkish captain altered course, steering for Mytilene under full press of sail; but unable to throw off the Greek squadron he again changed course and anchored in the bay of Eressos on the north-west coast of Lesbos and cleared for action. Sailing under the stern of the Turkish frigate a Greek ship fired a hail of shot which proved harmless against the solid timbers of the Turk. Admiral Tombazis then ordered a cease fire and called a council of war to meet on his flagship. It was resolved to make use of fire-ships, which had been fitted out at Psara. One of these fire-ships was commanded by a man named Pappanikolis, "the burner", who was successful in firmly fixing the bowsprit of his *brûlot* under the prow of the Turkish frigate *Ferman dïynemez*, the "Moving Mountain". Now he applied the fire, knowing that he himself would almost certainly be destroyed with the enemy vessel. What happened on the 27th of May in the bay of Eressos is described by Finlay:

> The flames mounted into the sails of the fire-ship in an instant, for both the canvas and the rigging were saturated with turpentine, and they were driven by the wind over the bows of

the line-of-battle ship, whose hull they soon enveloped in a sheet of fire. The flames and the dense clouds of smoke which rushed along the deck and poured in at the ports, rendered it impossible to make any effort to save the ship, even had the crew been in a much better state of discipline than it was. The cable was cut, and two launches full of men left the ship. Many of the sailors jumped overboard and swam ashore; but it is supposed that between three and four hundred persons perished. About 11 a.m. the magazine exploded, and left her a complete wreck. This conflagration was the naval beacon of Greek liberty.[6]

So Pappanikolis, whose marble bust may be seen today on the waterfront, became the hero of Eressos. After a few days, as a reprisal, the Turks massacred the Greek community at Aivali on the mainland.

Admiral Constantine Kanaris of Psara, who was to destroy the Turkish fleet off Chios a year later, was a man of incomparable skill and courage whose dashing naval exploits earned him an enduring fame beyond the limits of Greece. He was one of the heroes of the revolution.

But perhaps the best known and best loved of the Greek admirals was Andreas Miaoulis. From early childhood he had worked on his father's vessel where he acquired a mastery of seamanship. During the Napoleonic wars he had amassed a fortune by successfully running his cargoes through the French blockade of the Mediterranean. His personal character was exemplary, raising him high above some of the cruder self-seekers by whom he was surrounded. Miaoulis proved himself to be a natural sailor and a naval genius; yet he was so little literate that he could only laboriously add his signature to his letters and despatches. A photoprint copy of one of his letters in my possession, dated 12th of January, 1828, is addressed "To the Honourable Committee of the Chiots!" who had escaped the terrible massacre of February 1822 on Chios and were then living on the island of Syra. A translation of part of it may be of authentic interest. The handwriting is that of Papadopoulos, one of Miaoulis's secretaries. Only the last four words were written by the Admiral:

Gentlemen!

The clear danger of Chios, and the urgency of the occasion forced us to set sail aboard the Two-Decker without the least supply of provisions.

We therefore apply to your honour according to the order of the provisional Secretary of State for the Navy under No. 1231 and 1250—and enclosing for you a note of what they need for a campaign for one month, we ask you to show here and now your most active character, and to arrange that small boats be provided for the purpose and sent to the Two-Decker, if possible, within two hours, so that the enemy of the freedom of the Chiots might not also take the opportunity and carry out his destructive plans, and then, you're finished! We shall arrive too late.

We think it unnecessary indeed for us to bewail the miserable condition and the total lack of supplies, in which the national fleet is found, when we heard with the beating of our heart, that much-suffering Chios was even again being threatened by her blood-thirsty and inhuman enemies. But the reputation of your energy with regard to the present campaign, and the untiring and sincere devotion of yours to the emancipation of your wretched fatherland and the immediate presence of your envoy Mr. Glupippes, compelled us, as each and every one has feeling, to send out the national fleet instantly, and to sail out also ourselves with the Two-Decker immediately afterwards, as we were able, having provided food only as far as here. . . .

Therefore trusting to your true patriotism, we beg you to send us speedily all the money you have in hand from the taxes, and as much food as you can from the note, realising in consequence that you are sending us out afterwards to Chios in good time. . . .

I remain in proper esteem of your honour,

The Patriot
Andreas Miaoulis.

From the Two-Decker, the "Hellas"
12 January 1828.

James Emerson, who visited Admiral Miaoulis on the 23rd of May 1825, wrote his personal tribute: "My reception from Miaoulis was in the highest degree kind and hospitable and, on learning that my intention was to stop for a short time with the fleet, he requested me to remain on board his own vessel, and immediately assigned me a state room off his own cabin. Miaoulis is a man of from 50 to 60 years old, his figure somewhat clumsy, but with a countenance peculiarly expressive of intelligence, humanity, and good nature. His family have been long established at Hydra, and he has himself been accustomed to the sea from a child." Emerson tells the traditional Greek story of the young Miaoulis, during the Napoleonic wars, being captured by Nelson, and regaining his liberty both because of his frankness in admitting the justice of his capture, although his ship was not French, and by the natural sympathy of one great seaman for another. Emerson goes on: "I never met any man of more unaffected and friendly manners. He seems totally above any vaunting or affectation, and only anxious to achieve his own grand object—the liberation of his country, alike unmoved by the malice and envy of his enemies, or the lavish praises of his countrymen. The bravery of his associates is mingled with a considerable portion of ambition; but with him there seems but one unbiassed spring, of steady sterling patriotism."[7]

The barbarous intricate campaigns of the first year of the war finished with the Turks retiring into Thessaly. Gains and losses in those confused initial actions may have been fairly equally divided; but the Greeks were the virtual victors by the simple fact that they had succeeded in surviving and were still under arms. If the abortive rebellion led by Alexander Ypsilantis had failed in Roumania, his brother Demetrios had been much more successful in the Peloponnese and had cleared southern and eastern Greece of the Turks.

In the west and north, however, the Turks had won their victories: in Thessaly, Macedonia and Thrace, at Agrapha, in the valleys of the rivers Aspropotamos and the Arakhtos at Arta, and in the mountainous regions of Pelion, Ossa and Olympus, as in the three-pronged Thracian peninsula of Chalcidice where Mount Athos stands. In these districts the Christians had been worsted, forced to lay down their weapons and return to their daily occupations. But the contrast in the Peloponnese remained impressive; for, with the exception of a few garrison-towns and the island of Euboea, the Greeks now held all of the country south of a line drawn from Thermopylae in the east to the cape of Actium in the west. And, more important still for the future, they felt confident enough to convene a National Assembly before the close of 1821, and to proclaim in January 1822 a Constitution at Epidaurus. Shelley, writing from Pisa in Italy on December the 11th, 1821, expressed his hopeful idealism: "The news of the Greeks continues to be more and more glorious . . . it may be said that the Peloponnesus is entirely free, and that Mavrocordato has been acting a distinguished part, and will probably fill a high rank in the magistracy of the infant republic."

CHAPTER VI

Makriyannis

Contrary to some of the bitter and sordid brutalities of much of the first year's fighting, there is everything to lift the heart in the character of Makriyannis, one of the war's noblest heroes. Makriyannis (whose name by derivation means tall or long John) was as brave a champion as any of the uprising of his people against the tyranny of the Turk, and his life (1797–1864) for more than half a century was entirely bound up with the story of revived Hellenism. His *Memoirs* are invaluable for elucidating how the people felt while fighting during those long troubled years when modern Greece was being born. His work remains a record of supreme importance because it enshrines the conscience of a resurgent nation.

The facts of Makriyannis's life may be briefly tabulated. He was of humble origin, the youngest son of a poor shepherd from a tiny village near Lidoriki in the mountains of central Greece. He married in 1825 and had twelve children, but the first four died in infancy. He began as an illiterate; yet in early manhood he became a prosperous merchant. During his youth he had been sworn in as a member of the *Philike Hetairia*, and fought from the beginning of the rebellion and was eight times wounded. At the age of thirty-two he taught himself to write in order to record his memories, and eventually produced a work of historical value whose main ingredients are patriotism, religious fervour, and an uncompromising toughness in defending the Greeks' pride of achievement. Makriyannis's *Memoirs* are also a work of art; for he was a born writer, possessing a fiery imagination fed from the deep sources of both experience and traditional folk-song. Makriyannis rose

97

from a shining commander of irregulars to become a general and he survived the war.

In weighing the literary importance of the *Memoirs*, it is impossible not to be impressed by the opinion of George Seferis, Greece's Nobel Prize winner for literature, who sent a gift-copy of the 1947 edition to C. M. Woodhouse with the inscription: "For my learned friend Monty, this illiterate my master in Greek"; and also by Woodhouse's own tribute to "the first great artist in written demotic". While reading Makriyannis, Woodhouse seemed, he says, to be listening "to the language of the Homeric *pallikária*, spoken centuries before Homer" and points out that the General was a poet—"he could not have been Seferis's master otherwise". Makriyannis was, on more certain evidence than was Shakespeare, "self-school'd, self-scann'd, self-honour'd, self-secure".

But at the same time Makriyannis's honourable soul was enshrined in the body of a tall strong peasant. He was of course a tough man of his age who could, as occasion demanded, write a bawdy jest, be unrelentingly severe in taking what he considered just retribution, but also blame his own side when he believed it to be at fault. Above all, he repeatedly showed compassion for the wronged and suffering, whether they happened to be his friends or his enemies. An arbitrary quotation or two concerning the first year's fighting will illustrate the honesty and simplicity of his style:

In March 1821 I took some money and crossed to Patras. The Turks were suspicious when they saw a man of Roumeli; I was in danger. When I was in the Russian consulate . . . the Greeks began to ask me stupid questions. I was lodging in what was called Tatarakis's Inn. There were people from Yannina and Arta staying there. I went to the consulate, told them of the happenings in Roumeli and of the ill fate of Ali Pasha. He had made a sally from the fort opposite the palace in the city of Yannina and a multitude of his men were killed. He had lost the flower of his army.

These people did not believe a word of what I said—they

wanted Ali Pasha to win and deliver them—him! Ali Pasha the tyrant, to aid the cause of Greece and bring freedom to our country, this man who, had he gained the day, would not have left us our nostrils to breathe with![1]

In writing his account of an action, similar to many others, which took place in June when some eighty Greeks were attacked in a mountain pass dominated by six thousand of Kurshid Pasha's troops, Makriyannis reveals his qualities of fair-minded realism, his faith in God and his patriotic fervour. The Greek position was defended by Bakolas Gogos, an armatole under Ali Pasha and an uncle of Karaiskakis:

After the Turks and the Greeks had fought like lions for more than eight hours, over a thousand Turks were killed, and their skeletons remained unbroken for a whole year; the bones had dried hard. So many of them fell dead and were wounded that Arta was full of fugitives. The Greeks drove them before them with their daggers and hunted after them as far as Komboti, causing great slaughter and seizing much booty. Neither the Greeks nor the Turks could be accused in the matter of their bravery; both sides fought like lions. However, injustice was vanquished, for all bravery could do, because the Turks had gone far from the ways of God. On that day all the leaders and the soldiers did their duty. Gogos of beloved memory outshone all others in his glory. Our country owes him thanks. He fought like a lion and commanded like a philosopher. And, on that day, our country raised its head again.[2]

Makriyannis always did his best to instil into his men a sense of honourable behaviour. He was against all forms of atrocity, pillage and looting, becoming furiously incensed if he found out that in these matters his soldiers had disobeyed him. During the year 1824, when he was fighting in Arcadia, he discovered that some of his troops had plundered a village near Tripotamon in defiance of his commands. When the abused inhabitants came to him weeping, he could not help them and felt a deathly shame. So he went off

secretly with his ensign and a few picked followers and reached a
river which was in spate, since it was near Christmas. Makriyannis,
with his sworn band, made the dangerous crossing on their sturdy
horses, and had soon lit a fire and were having a meal. But the
guilty soldiers had followed close behind and on their way had
taken prisoner four Peloponnesians whom they had grossly ill-
treated; they had half killed them by making them carry half the
troop across the river upon their shoulders until they were "as
black as niggers from the cold". Makriyannis, in his graphic
manner, tells the full story:

They were left naked and they were crying like little children;
and they were trembling from the cold. I pitied them deeply
and declared that a wild beast was a wild beast but a man was
even worse. When these men had caught sight of me they had
shouted out in anger against me, and said, "When we learned
that it was you, Makriyannis, who was passing, you who keep
the strictest order among your men, we felt confident and left
our goods without hiding them; and you have robbed us. At the
river we risked our lives to get them across: and they have taken
our weapons and our clothes and we are shivering and we shall
die of cold." I gave the men good treatment and told them to
point me out those who had robbed them. I was resolved to
shoot it out with these. I rode hard and caught them with the
men's goods. I took with me those who had been robbed and
those to blame and came in the evening to the village where I
was to quarter. I sent a man out to cut some good stout
saplings and summoned all my officers. I told them, "We had
most of you for so many years, have I ever left you without pay
or hungry? When we did our duty like patriots the people of
the country respected us and gave us food with pleasure, and
gave votes of thanks for us to our Government, and would give
us our pay. While you behaved honourably I was your commander. Now that you have taken to acting on your own you
have plundered a village where they were waiting for us, as
men for their brothers and as Christians for their fellow Christians and you rob them of their goods and their cattle so you

have whole flocks with you. Don't expect me to be your herds-
man: be off and find another leader or let the villagers come
and you give them back the goods and the cattle of the village
with nothing held back: when the villagers have given me a
full receipt you can stay on my side once more. Or else find
some other leader. And I'll tell the Government what's
missing in the village so they can hold it back from your pay
and the people will be paid back." So we sent for the villagers
who took their property and I had a receipt from these
same people.

When I had brought before me those who had robbed the
man at the river, I set five of my officers to lay hold on each of
them. I was to give the thrashings. I got out my pistols and said,
"If any one of those who are holding these men leaves go or
tries to protect them let him have his arms ready and we'll
shoot it out. I'm not having men turned into beasts to ferry
people across the river on their shoulders and then be robbed in
kind thanks!" I had the four of them thrown on the ground and
held asprawl, I thrashed all of them in turn till the blood flowed
from their buttocks. I was worse off than they; my hands were
bleeding and I was sick for many days after. Then I had them
wrapped in raw sheepskins, gave them a month's pay and gave
them free passes. I left them in the village to be tended to till
their recovery. I tell you, brother readers, from that time on I
never came across a dishonourable or a thievish man in my
troop and wherever any of my men went they were welcomed
by the country folk like their brothers.[3]

So much for the moral quality of the man.

During the early months of the war the Turks committed a
crime that shocked the conscience of all Christian Europe. They
executed the Patriarch of Constantinople. The massacre at Tripolitza because of so many unburied Turkish corpses, had been
followed by disease which accounted for the lives of thousands of
Greeks; but such losses were little when compared with the result
of the Sultan's vengeance. News of the Greek atrocities in the

Peloponnese could do none other than stoke the fires of Moham-medan fanaticism, whose flames raged uncontrollably. Among the scattered Greeks of the Empire there was no discrimination, guilty and innocent suffered alike. The Sultan ordered the arrest of every available member of the *Philike Hetairia* several of whom were executed to expiate the blood of the Mohammedans.

But Sultan Mahmud, in the fierce intensity of his wrath, was bent on one white-hot act of vengeance which would strike terror into his subjects and teach the whole Greek world a lesson. Under Ottoman rule the higher State officials were held to be responsible for the conduct of the people they ruled; and in April the Drago-man of the Porte, Murusi, wearing his official dress had been publicly beheaded. But worse was to follow. On Easter Sunday, the 22nd of April, the Patriarch Gregorios, who was both the civil and religious head of the Greeks, was executed by order of Mahmud as an accessory to the rebellious activities of the *Philike Hetairia*. At midnight Gregorios had celebrated solemn mass as usual, surrounded by his prelates. At earliest dawn the new Drago-man invited the Patriarch to attend a meeting in the hall of the synod. When he appeared a *firman* of the Sultan was read deposing Gregorios and ordering the assembled clergy to elect another Patriarch. While the new Head of the Orthodox Church was being ceremoniously invested, the venerable deposed Patriarch was led away to his execution. Still wearing his sacred robes, he was hung from the lintel of the gate of the patriarchal palace, with a sentence of condemnation pinned on his breast. The old man met death with courage, dignity, and a pious resignation. The body remained suspended for three days, after which it was cut down and delivered to the Jews to be dragged through the streets and thrown into the sea. Subsequently, it was picked up by an Ionian ship, recognized, and taken to Odessa where it was welcomed by the Russian authorities as a holy relic and buried with military pomp and the ecclesiastical honours of a martyr.

Though Gregorios was certainly a man of superior talent and clear virtue, whose private character had commanded great respect, he had always been perfectly well aware of the intrigues of the Phanariotes, and had no doubt supposed that Russia would act as a shield of safety for the rebels. Apparently, his conscience was at ease when he died, believing it to be his duty as a Christian priest to conceal the existence of an Orthodox conspiracy from the Infidel; but it is to be questioned whether in his position as Patriarch his moral feelings should not have been more strained and divided. According to the laws of the Ottoman Empire, Sultan Mahmud in ordering his execution was strictly within his rights. So the Turks believed Gregorios to be a perjured traitor. The Greeks to this day cherish him in their hearts as a holy martyr.

However, the Sultan's deed of vengeance had sent a thrill of indignant horror through Christendom, from Constantinople itself, through the mountains of Greece, to the palaces of St. Petersburg. For a time it appeared possible that the execution of Gregorios might even unite the Powers in an anti-Turkish war. To Francis I, the Emperor of Austria, it was almost as bad as if the Pope had been murdered. In Russia, given the sign, the entire population would gladly have risen to avenge the Orthodox Patriarch; but the Tsar, Alexander I, happened to be out of the country, and was anyway too closely committed to the *realpolitik* of Metternich to be in the mood to sanction a war; so he contented himself with a vigorous protest and withdrawing the Russian ambassador, Stronganoff from Constantinople. In England, Castlereagh believed that a period of rest in Europe was essential after the dangers and exhaustion of the Napoleonic wars. Therefore, a proposal for a demonstration by the Great Powers to protect the Christians came to nothing, and so for the time being, Turkey was freed from any threat of European intervention on behalf of the rebels.

The war continued, with no half measures, no holds barred. The first year's fighting had seen the success of the Greek guerilla forces. By the end of 1821 the Greeks were masters of the Peloponnese, except for Nauplia, the fortresses of Coron and Modon in the west, Patras, and Rhion (with Antirrhion) at the mouth of the Gulf of Corinth. Nauplia surrendered in the following year; and the Acropolis of Athens also succumbed to Greek pressure in June 1822. But, on the other hand, by the beginning of 1822 several isolated Greek risings had been suppressed by the Sultan's armies, and the countryside north of Yannina and Mount Pelion restored to Ottoman rule. The Turkish counter-stroke to the west of the Pindus mountains in central Greece had thrust successfully southwards as far as the Gulf of Arta and the pass of Thermopylae, again putting the Greeks on the defensive. But to succeed strategically the Turks would have needed to capture Missolonghi on the Corinthian Gulf and here at present they failed.

The main problem for the Greeks now was to produce order out of chaos, to evolve from conditions close to anarchy some system of effective national government. Unfortunately, they showed themselves less capable of doing this than of prosecuting a successful guerilla war. Sectional patriotism, local feuds and jealousies, such as had undermined the civilization of ancient Hellas, proved just as intransigent and as characteristic of the modern Greeks. The political history of this time provides a contrast of sordid intrigues, contemptible peculations and a general incompetence, with the fortitude and heroic patience of the people. Nobody appears to have known the right way to construct a constitution. Yet such was the demand of the people for some form of a central executive that on June 7th, 1821, an oligarchic committee, or Senate of the Peloponnese, was set up which derived special strength from the prestige and patronage of Germanos, Archbishop of Patras. But its authority only survived until the crime of Tripolitza. The prelate's power of eloquence, high dignity in the church, side by side with the memory of his energy at the beginning of the revolution at first made him looked up to by the people; but, alas, their admiration slackened when it became only too obvious that an inordinate pride, wordly ambition and a love of luxurious pleasure lay hidden under the mask of religious fervour. Germanos quickly threw aside his hitherto respected sanctity, and revealed himself in Council and on the field clothed in gaudy apparel, with the assumed airs of a sovereign.

In June Prince Demetrios Ypsilantis had returned to the scene and had claimed that, because his brother Alexander was chief of the *Philike Hetairia* and therefore *ipso facto* Prince of Greece, he himself was entitled to act as his brother's viceroy and become lieutenant-governor of the country. Although—in view of Prince

Alexander's past failure—this was an extravagant and foolish pre-
tension, Demetrios, who was believed to be supported by Russia,
was welcomed by the soldiers and peasants. But the oligarchy
centering round Germanos used the Archbishop's influence, while
it was still at its zenith, to oppose and cry down Ypsilantis. Where-
upon Demetrios resorted to a bold stratagem. Suddenly he left
the camp before Tripolitza and let it be known that all his efforts
for Greece were being nullified by the selfish hostility of the primates and senators. The soldiers rose up in arms to support him;
and for a time the lives of some of the oligarchs were in danger.
The upshot was that they promised to accept the authority of
Prince Demetrios, who was brought back in triumph and confirmed in power. But regrettably Demetrios lacked the compe-
tence to hold the authority he had won and gradually, as his
power was corroded by his associates, his popularity also declined.

In the midst of these quarrels and confusions on the 3rd of
August another more important figure had arrived in the Peloponnese. This was Alexander Mavrocordatos, a Greek Phanariote
born of an old Constantinopolitan family, and much respected
as a man of honour and a sincere patriot. But not even Mavrocordatos could compose the chaos which he found, and he soon
left for Missolonghi, where later he was to organize the defence
of the first seige. Originally, he had arrived in Greece from Pisa
in Italy, where he had given Mary Shelley some "delightful and
improving lessons in the classics, from 'a real Greek Prince',"
although in fact Mavrocordatos was not a prince. In her diary for
Sunday, April 1st, 1821, Mary Shelley wrote: "Read Greek.
Alexander Mavrocordatos calls with news about Greece. He is as
gay as a caged eagle just free." A further entry for the 24th of that
month records: "Alex calls in the evening with good news from
Greece. The Morea is free."

Obviously at first the Greeks were jubilant at achieving a degree
of success they had hardly expected, and turned with an efferve-
scent optimism and elation to the task of forming a central Government. But at the very moment of triumph the unity of the nation
collapsed. Discord showed itself in the natural rivalry between the
military and civilian figure-heads. Demetrios Ypsilantis, from

Russia, represented the old Phanariote dream-conception of a revived Byzantine Greece, while from the west, "in fact from Mrs. Shelley's boudoir, there arrived the plump little figure of Alexander Mavrocordatos, with his gold spectacles and his European clothes, who was opposed to any dependence upon Russia, and who aimed at creating a new Hellas, national and self-sufficing, which should look only to the Western Powers, and particularly to England, for support."[4]

The result of the country's disintegration into these fissile factions was that before the end of the year 1821, Greece was divided into three main regions, each nominally under an almost powerless central Government. There was western Hellas administered by Mavrocordatos from Missolonghi; there was eastern Hellas controlled by Theodore Negris who convoked a meeting at Salona of deputies from Attica, Boeotia, Megaris, Phocis, and Eastern Locris, called somewhat portentously the Areopagus; and lastly there was the strife-torn Peloponnese. Nor must the islands be forgotten, most of which—though not of course the Ionian Islands which were under British rule—had rallied to the Greek cause. But it was only after interminable negotiations between these various factions, largely due to the statesmanlike moderation and persuasion of Mavrocordatos, that conciliation was finally achieved, and a constituent assembly held at Epidaurus in January 1822. The Constitution of Epidauras, drafted mainly by Mavrocordatos and Negris, while it undoubtedly represents "a landmark in Greek history", achieved its professed objects only on paper. Although the proclaimed ideal of the Constitution was stated with both brevity and dignity, it spelled out an aspiration rather than a fact:

> The Greek nation, under the fearful domination of the Ottomans, unable to bear the heavy and unexampled yoke of tyranny and having with great sacrifices thrown it off, declares today, through its lawful representatives gathered in National Assembly, before God and man, its political existence and independence.[5]

The past participle "having thrown off" unfortunately proved to

be nothing if not premature. All the same, Alexander Mavrocordatos was elected the first President of Greece and the blue and
white flag of modern Greece replaced the old black flag of the
Hetairists.

For a time the Greeks at Epidaurus may have misled Europe;
but they did little to organize Greece. Mavrocordatos, a man of
cultural experience and unquestioned probity, far superior to most
of the leaders of the revolt, yet lacked those essential qualities of
firmness and breadth of vision necessary if a statesman is to understand the wider issues involved in governing men. Moreover, he
was no soldier. In fairness, however, to Mavrocordatos, it is
reasonable to doubt whether at this point in history even the
wisest paragon of rulers could have produced order out of the
chaos in Greece. What was needed was some awful catastrophe
to make the Greeks forget their selfish rivalries and ambitions,
some event that would unite them in a common fear and rage for
revenge. And that bitter lesson was not long in coming.

CHAPTER VII

The Lapse into Civil War

After Epidaurus, in spite of the confusing operations of both civil and military factions, the existence of Greece could no longer be doubted. Then a totally unexpected catastrophe occurred which, for the time being at least, had the effect of binding the Greeks more closely together. This "uncouth event" of the Turkish massacre in February of the people on the island of Chios, also shocked the conscience of Europe and radically altered the attitude of the dominant Powers.

When, not long after the proclamation of the Constitution of Epidaurus, the ministers of the Holy Alliance, with other Powers, had reassembled at Verona, Europe was still much influenced by those reactionary bigots who were afraid of the spread of the contagion of liberalism. There was in progress, and as yet unrepressed, a republican rising in Spain, and the Latin colonies of South America were about to achieve their independence. The ministers of the Holy Alliance refused even to admit delegates from the new State of Greece, regarding its lately self-appointed Constitution as being beneath discussion. Foremost among others, Metternich did not want the Greek revolution to succeed.

The Conference thought of the Greeks as rebellious subjects of the Sultan and advised him to try and pacify them, perhaps by showing more respect for their religion. Nor was there any justification in 1822 for suspecting Britain and Russia of being more pro-Greek than the other Powers. Russia, for instance, had no intention of giving freedom to the Poles, nor Britain to the Irish. But Great Britain, because of her occupation of the Ionian Islands, was obliged to be concerned with the interests of the islands' shipping, as well as that of her own ships in Greek ports. For these reasons the Ionian administration recognized the Greek naval blockade of the mainland, while still preserving a policy of strict neutrality. In fact, both British policy, and Metternich's policy within the Holy Alliance, sought mainly to prevent a war between Russia and Turkey developing out of the Greek revolution.

This latent threat of a wider war was increased by the calamity that overtook the wretched inhabitants of Chios. Until now the prosperous island of Chios had been in a somewhat privileged position. Since the Turks had first captured it in 1566, despite several abortive risings, the islanders had enjoyed a certain measure of independence. Chios was close to Turkey, only five miles of strait separating it from the peninsula of Karaburnu in Asia Minor. It was one of the seven alleged birthplaces of Homer, as suggested in a Homeric Hymn:

> A man that is blind, in scarry Chios living,
> supreme in song both now and in times to come.[1]

But at the time of the revolution Chios was more renowned as the chief source of mastic, a resin obtained from the lentisk tree and used for flavouring a popular Levantine liqueur and later in the manufacture of chewing-gum. The Greeks called the quiet villages where they "milked" the trees Mastikhokhoria.

Soon after the outbreak of the War of Independence Chios had been attacked and occupied, rather against the wishes of its industrious and peace-loving inhabitants, by a force of free-lance patriotic adventurers from Samos, acting independently of any trustworthy higher authority. So valiant a part was Samos to play in the war, that "to go to Samos", became a phrase used by the Turks as an equivalent for certain death. However, notwithstanding the victories she won, Samos was restored to Turkey when the war ended and, like Chios, did not become re-united with Greece until 1912.

The news of this attack on Chios had aroused the wrath of the Sultan, who considered it a personal insult he was bound to avenge. Historians also record that the ladies of the Imperial

Harem indignantly called for the extermination of the insurgents who were devastating their highly prized mastic gardens. Be that as it may, the revenge carried out on Chios was one of the most brutal episodes in a chronicle of violence. Though the Turkish commander seems to have tried to curb some of the worst excesses of the "blood bath", less perhaps in the interests of humanity than of avarice, the Ottoman troops, who had been reinforced by crowds of fanatics from the mainland eager to join in the "holy war", proved impossible to control. The vengeance of the Turks was heavy. The unfortunate, mostly unarmed, poor inhabitants were all treated as rebels. Some of the more wealthy families managed to buy Turkish protection with large sums of money, while others escaped to the ports where they were taken off in ships from Psara which had hurried to Chios to try and help the islanders.

In the town the bloodshed ceased as soon as the fanatical volunteers realized that they might add profit to vengeance. They rounded up all those Chiots whom they thought they could sell in the slave-markets of Asia Minor and decamped with their booty. Three thousand Chiots had taken refuge in the monastery of Aghias Mynas and were called upon to surrender. They refused. The building was stormed, and the men were put to the sword and suitable women and children reserved for the slave-markets. Two thousand others had sought asylum in the monastery of Nea Moni. The Turks treated this monastery in a similar fashion. Some of the occupants had taken refuge in the church. The doors were burst open. The Turks, after murdering even the women who were on their knees praying, set fire to the screen of paintings in the church, as well as to the wood-work and roofs of the other buildings in the monastery, and abandoned the Christians who were not already slaughtered to be burnt in the general conflagration. By the end of May—the figures differ slightly in various historical accounts—it was calculated that 25,000 Chiots had been massacred and some 45,000 enslaved, and that a flourishing community of 100,000 souls had been reduced to a remnant of barely 2,000. The beautiful island of Chios was left a sad and depopulated ruin.

And yet for the Greeks the disaster at Chios turned out to have certain long-term advantages; for this horror perhaps did more than anything to recommend the Greek cause to Europe. To the Turks it was no more than a reprisal for what had happened in the Peloponnese; but few Europeans had heard of the Greek atrocities at Tripolitza. Moreover, suddenly in 1824 Chios was immortalized by the French painter Eugène Delacroix. In his "Scenes of the Massacres of Scio" Delacroix, with his gift for romantic bravura had found a subject perfectly suited to his sometimes slightly sinister genius. For it was just such dramatic details of frenzy and bloodshed, of forlorn suffering that he loved to depict, a drama round which the controlled violence of his imagination could expand, and which, besides, was now in fashion. Similarly, in prose and verse, the words of Byron and Shelley were swift to inspire Europe, transcending all meaner, sordid considerations of power politics. Such spiritual inspirations helped to encourage the philhellenic movements in London, Germany and Switzerland, and there was even talk of a foreign loan for Greece from as far afield as America. By now a small contingent of foreign philhellenes was already fighting in Greece. When in 1822 Mavrocordatos returned to his western command from Corinth, he marched at the head of a corps of about a hundred foreign officers, French, German, Polish, Italian and Swiss. British philhellenes were also in the field but independently, most notably the brave sailor, Frank Abney Hastings, of whom more will be heard. There were no Russians, unless they were Greeks who had acquired Russian nationality.

About the middle of 1822 the unhappy Chiots were partly, if equivocally, avenged. On April the 10th the Greek fleet of fifty-six sail had put to sea under Admirals Miaoulis and Kanaris. After an indecisive naval engagement off Chios at the end of the month, Admiral Kanaris had determined on a daring raid with fire-ships from Psara, the final result of which would be to force the Turkish fleet to abandon the open sea and to seek safety and shelter behind the guns of the Dardanelles.

On the night of June the 18th all the principal Turkish officers had gathered together on board the flagship to celebrate the

Mohammedan feast of Bairam with the Capitan Pasha. The sky was pitch black; but the flagship, profusely decorated with coloured lanterns, made a brilliant target. Music and the shouts of revelry of some three thousand carefree and careless men reached the ears of the Greeks. A feeble watch was being kept. Suddenly two Greek fire-ships slid like avenging ghosts between the lines of illuminated Turkish vessels. One of these, directed with cool-headed precision by Kanaris himself, made straight for the flagship of the Capitan Pasha. Kanaris ran his bowsprit into an open port of the enemy vessel, attached his grappling irons and lighted the train with his own hand. He then slipped with his men into a boat and rowed off as the fire-ship, its sails and rigging soaked in turpentine burst into flame. The wind soon carried the fire to the Ottoman ship, which enveloped it in a mighty conflagration. The Turks, completely surprised, had no time to save themselves and very few survived of the three thousand men on board. And among them were several hundred wretched Chiot prisoners. The shrieks of the dying struck all who heard them with cold horror. Kara Ali himself leapt into a boat brought alongside; but he was struck by a falling spar and carried dying to the shore.

While this episode earned for Constantine Kanaris widespread and undying fame as a naval hero of the revolution, it is doubtful whether the frantic acclaim which followed found an echo in the hearts of the surviving Chiots. For the unfortunate island was now subjected to a second devastation, as a reprisal, to complete what had been left undone before. This time not even the mastic villages were spared.

On mainland Greece the campaigning season of 1822 amounted to a series of serious setbacks that combined to reduce the acres of territory already freed by the infant state. Before even the massacre of Chios, the Turks, who were commanded by Omer Vrioni, had successfully quelled the rising in Euboea, the largest island next to Crete, which runs for nearly a hundred miles almost parallel to the mainland route from the north and is necessary to its defence. The first misfortune which befell the Greeks in 1822 was the death on January 24th of Elias Mavromichalis, the eldest son of Petrobey, who had been asked by the provincial government of Eastern Greece to command in the blockade of the Acropolis of Athens which was then held by the Turks. But when he arrived at the Athenian camp, Elias was met by an invitation from the Euboeans to aid them in an attack on Karystos and he preferred to command active soldiering in Euboea to the tedious routine of watching the starving Turks at Athens. Unluckily, Mavromichalis was surrounded, with a few of his men, in an old windmill at the village of Stura. After defending himself bravely, he tried to cut his way out, sword in hand, and was shot in the attempt.

Omer Vrioni's task in this campaign was facilitated by the apparent treachery of Odysseus Androutsos who, although he must certainly be reckoned a hero of the War of Independence, proved nevertheless as Homerically devious in his character as his namesake the wily ruler of Ithaca. Soon after the unlucky death of Mavromichalis, Odysseus, whose authority in this theatre of war was now supreme, arrived from Attica with about seven hundred men. Finding the village of Stura evacuated and emptied of stores, the Greeks besieged Karystos; but then, with no warning to anybody, Odysseus upped and marched away with his men. The betrayed and chagrined besiegers raised the siege.

Odysseus the celebrated klepht, who had been trained at the court of Ali Pasha, remains today something of an enigma. With his flowing black locks, glowing eyes, and his bold drooping moustache, neither his fierceness, endurance, nor his dynamism were ever in question. All sorts of legends of his alleged feats of physical strength were current. It was said that he could clear the backs of seven horses standing side by side. But most historians, including Finlay and Gordon, share the belief that it was from the old tyrant Ali at Yannina that Odysseus Androutsos had learned to combine the worst vices of Albanians and Greeks, growing "false as the most deceitful Greek, and vindictive as the most bloodthirsty Albanian".[2] It may be that Odysseus had serious doubts about the ultimate success of the revolution, suspecting that it would end in some form of compromise; also it seems probable that he had little enthusiasm for the cause of liberty. The likeliest key to his conduct at Karystos is a combination of jealousy of his military colleagues, with suspicion of John Kolettis, the then acting Minister of War at Corinth.

The beginning of the year 1822 saw Nemesis finally overtake Ali Pasha, the still formidable, still conspiring "Bear of Pindus", at the ripe age of turned eighty. Mavrocordatos had dangerously extended his lines of communication far north from Missolonghi into Epirus with the object of stiffening the will of the Souliotes not to abandon the Greek cause. After Ali's death, their danger from Kurshid Pasha was both obvious and foreseen, as the Turkish commander would be almost certain to mount a punitive attack before he drove south once more against the Greeks.

The Souliotes were a small patriarchal mountain tribe of Christian Epirots, in all about 4,000 militant men and women, whose rugged territory formed a centre of dedicated fighting resistance to the Moslems. From 1790 until 1803 they had been involved in intermittent successive wars with Ali Pasha, until he had captured their chief mountain fastnesses and they had prudently retired to the Ionian Islands. At the outbreak of the war the majority of Souliotes returned to the mainland to engage once more in harassing the Turks. The mountain fortress of Souli stood on a plateau three thousand feet above the river Acheron and it would be no exaggeration to describe the Souliotes as the most renowned fighters of modern Greece. For they lived only for fighting and had no other occupation, content to exist on the produce of the villages in the valleys, which they both dominated and protected. Like Alexander the Great's Macedonians the Souliotes shaved the front part of their heads, so that no enemy could get a grip on their hair in hand-to-hand fighting. Such was the Souliotes' love of freedom that their example drew to them would-be volunteers from every part of Greece. But before a man could be admitted to this close military caste, or take a Souliote wife, he must first prove himself in battle. Each Souliote was reputed to possess "the eye of an eagle, the speed of a mountain goat and the heart of a lion". And this tiny independent Souli republic had long been a thorn in the flesh of the powerful and vindictive Ali Pasha. Byron, on his first visit to Greece in 1809, had

"Greece Expiring on the Ruins of Missolonghi" by Delacroix

Sultan Mehmet II,
ascribed to Bellini

National Gallery, London

The fall of Constantinople in 1453 by Panayotis Zographo
Reproduced by gracious permission of Her Majesty, Queen Elizabeth II

Ali Pasha

Department of Prints and
Drawings, British Museum

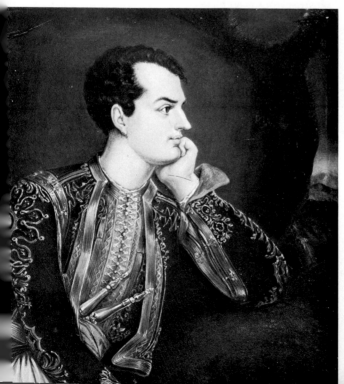

Byron. A hitherto
unpublished portrait

From the collection of
Miss I. Alexander
(Photo: John R. Freeman & Co.)

Count John Capodistrias

*Department of Prints and Drawings,
British Museum*

Prince Alexander Mavrocordatos

*From Harper's Magazine, 1894
(Photo: John R. Freeman & Co.)*

Admiral Sir Edward Codrington
by H. P. Briggs

National Portrait Gallery, London

General Kolokotronis

Ibrahim Pasha

Admiral Miaoulis

The battle of Navarino

much admired the courage and amazing prowess of the colourful Souliotes when he had spent two nights in the monastery at Zitza, and in "Childe Harold" had written:

Oh! who is more brave than a dark Souliote,
In his snowy camese and his shaggy capote?
To the wolf and the vulture he leaves his wild flock,
And descends to the plain like the stream from the rock.

Nobody has ever denied the Souliotes' bravery and endurance, nor questioned the defiant heroism of both their men and women when opposing Ali Pasha in what has fairly been called the "Saga of Souli".

One episode alone from the Saga will illustrate the strength of such stone-hard virtues. Living in a spectacular landscape of almost Dantesque grimness, as might be expected the Souliotes had their own savagery; for instance, like the Turks and the Albanians, they were implacable in their punishment of feminine frailty. A woman even suspected of adultery was likely to be sewn up in a sack and tossed over the cliffs to die on the boulders of the Black River which flowed through a deep gorge of rocks and dark woods. On the other hand, they had a more pastoral side to their lives, tending their flocks of sheep and goats. Like the klephts they were renowned for their love of singing and dancing, for their agility of movement over hard country, their accurate shooting; above all, for their almost incredibly keen eyesight. They were supposed to be able to see in the dark, as cats do.

For thirteen years, since 1790, Ali Pasha had intermittently waged war against the Souliotes, trying by every means he could think of—direct assault, siege warfare, treacherous offers of peace and tempting bribery—to subdue them to his will. But he had had scant success; rather he had suffered a series of humiliating defeats. So he grew more than ever determined to conquer the Souliotes and indulge the bloodthirsty passion for revenge, which was one of his principal pleasures. At last, in December 1803, Souli was starved into submission and a document of capitulation was signed, on generous terms for Ali, promising the Souliotes their safety while they retired to Albania, or to Parga or Preveza on the mainland shore; or from there, if they wished, to Corfu. He assured them that they should go unmolested. But, as so many times before, Ali's most sacred promises proved to be of less worth than the paper they were written on. As soon as the Souliote refugees left their fortress they were attacked by a force of 4,000 men: but a first contingent beat off Ali's troops and managed to fight its way through to Parga. However, a second contingent split up. About a thousand men, women and children had reached the sanctuary of a monastery below a mountain called Zalongos when another division of Ali's army appeared. The gates of the monastery were smashed open and a massacre started. About sixty women, with their children, succeeded in escaping up the mountain, but found themselves to be surrounded on all sides. When they reached the top several young women first threw their children from the rock (as reported by Albanian soldiers on their return to Yannina) and then leaped down themselves. The bodies of four children were found broken below. Another version has it that, after sacrificing their children, the women working themselves up into a veritable frenzy of defiance began to sing the old Souliote folk-songs and to dance in a weaving chain of movement toward the lip of the precipice where, one by one they unlinked their arms, and with cries of triumph leapt into the abyss. Today on the summit of Zalongos a white monument gleams in the sunlight to mark what has been called the most sensational act in the history of Souli. The fifty foot high monument depicts the white stone figures of four women and two children with their arms linked in the dance at the edge of the precipice.

The manner of Ali Pasha's violent death in 1822 was this. Ali—although for purely selfish reasons—had assisted the Greek War of Independence by diverting some twenty thousand Turkish troops from the Peloponnese which was the real centre of the struggle. So the Sultan determined to destroy the arch rebel once and for all. Kurshid Pasha attacked Yannina with a large force and Ali found himself shut up with some four thousand men, closely besieged in the fortress. According to Finlay, "Ali was now living in a bomb-proof cellar, clothed in a bundle of dirty embroidered garments, defending the castle of the lake with a diminished and intimidated garrison. Kurshid was watching his prey with the vigilance of a lynx."³ At last in January 1822, by treachery and surprise, Kurshid forced an entry into the citadel and Ali had only just time to immure himself in the Castro that contained the powder-magazine and his great wealth of treasure. The entrance was guarded by a fanatically devoted young Albanian, Selim Tchami, who was prepared, should the necessity arise, to give up his life for Ali. He sat there waiting with a lighted fuse, ready to blow up the magazine.

Kurshid, through a confidential secretary, invited Ali Pasha to surrender, and eventually Ali replied that he would do so only if he were shown a decree, signed by the Sultan, granting him a full pardon. He promised he would then go to Constantinople. Otherwise, he would blow himself up with his few remaining faithful followers and what was left of his possessions. Kurshid tried a ruse. He let Ali know that the decree was being prepared at Constantinople, and that meanwhile he would like an interview with him. He suggested that they should meet on the little island in the lake, and Ali agreed to this and was rowed over with several of his adherents to the sixteenth-century monastery of St. Panteleimon.

But why did Ali Pasha who had never trusted anybody, friend or foe, or respected a promise, fall into such an obvious trap? Perhaps he thought that since the Sultan was mainly preoccupied with the Greek revolution, he would grant a pardon more easily. Or the aged tyrant could have lost some of his former grip and seemingly ageless lust for living. Perhaps he was tired of fighting and bloodshed. On the island he may have dreamt an old man's dream, living over again his early years in peaceful Albanian Tebeleni.

The Castro was never blown up. After nine days Kurshid informed Ali that the pardon had arrived, but that before it could be made official, he must admit his public submission to the Sultan by commanding Selim Tchami to surrender the "refuge". This Ali did by handing over a string of amber beads to be given to Selim Tchami, the token previously arranged between them. So this paltry gesture sealed the end of Ali's power and deprived him of his last hope of safety.

Lying on a sofa in an upper room of the monastery, all day long Ali had waited anxiously and with gloomy foreboding for the arrival of the decree of pardon. At last in the late afternoon a boatload of thirty armed men, under Mehmet Pasha, arrived from the direction of Kurshid's camp. As soon as Ali saw Mehmet and his escort in the courtyard, he realized that he had been tricked. He shouted from the top of the staircase: "Stay where you are, Mehmet! What's all this?" Then Ali drew out his pistols and fired twice at Mehmet. "Earth's scum!" he cried. "I, Ali Pasha, will show you how hard it is to crack my skull!"

In the fight that followed Mehmet was hit in the hand and Ali was wounded in his left arm. An officer brandished his sabre, but missed slashing off Ali's head. Ali was assisted back to his sofa, bleeding profusely. Now the Turks attacked in force, Mehmet with eight of his men managing to get into the room below Ali's, from where they were ordered to fire through the ceiling. The ceiling was riddled with bullet holes—which can be seen today— and one shot struck Ali in the groin making a hideous wound, so that he collapsed back on the sofa in agony. Before he died, he exhorted his supporters to hold out to the bitter end, almost his last words being a plea that his wife Kyra Vasiliki should be killed rather than allowed to fall into the hands of the Turks. But Mehmet's men rushed up the stairs and took everyone present prisoner, including Vasiliki. They then dragged Ali's corpse to the top of the staircase, cut his head off and carried it to Kurshid. It was reported that when Kurshid saw it, he was so moved that tears ran down his cheeks. The head, wiped clean of blood, was placed on a silver dish and publicly displayed in Yannina for three days in order to prove to everybody that the old Lion of Yannina was indeed dead. Ali's body was taken in a boat over to the Castro with all due ceremony and buried on January the 25th, 1822.

A month later people were flocking to see the notorious head in Constantinople. A dervish named Suleiman, who had been a childhood friend of Ali's, bought it and buried it by the memorial stones of Ali's sons and grandson, Mukhtar, Veli, Sali and Mehmet in the cemetery close to the Silivri gate, beyond the walls of the city. Suleiman composed an epitaph for Ali: "God is the Creator, the Eternal. Here lies the head of the famous Ali Pasha of Tebelini, former governor of Yannina, who, for more than thirty years, made himself independent in Albania."

Vasiliki was not molested, but allowed to retire to an estate near Trikkala that her husband had given her. Still young, she refused all offers of marriage from Greek and Turk alike. "There is no man living," she would say, "for the widow of Ali Pasha." She spent the last years of her life near Missolonghi, but she took to drink and died in 1835. Immense rewards were bestowed upon those who had directly helped in the downfall of the arch-enemy of the Sultan; for Kurshid two and a half million piastres and a jewelled sabre. For the Sultan and those advisers who were closest to him, were confident that now Ali was dead the Greek rebellion could be crushed.

With Ali disposed of, it seemed obvious to all that Kurshid would next attack the Souliotes before driving south once more against the Greeks. So Mavrocordatos's army joined forces with the Souliotes in the very region where Makriyannis described some heroic actions which had taken place the previous year, halfway between Yannina and Missolonghi. But this time the fighting turned out to be on a larger, more important scale. Unfortunately the Souliotes were weakened by a blood-feud between their principal leaders, Marco Botzaris, one of the finest and most disinterested captains of the war, and Bakolas Gogos who, although Makriyannis wrote of him as "that good and noble man", was responsible for the defeat at Peta and surrendered in despair to the Turks.

This decisive battle was fought near the village of Peta, in the burning July sun, under the mountains overlooking Arta and the Ambracian Gulf, and prevented for three generations the inclusion of north-west Greece in the future state. Mohammed Reshid Pasha—or Kiutahi as the Greeks called him—was in command at Arta, and with his Turkish regulars won a complete victory over the Greeks. A gallant corps of philhellenes under Colonel Dania was practically annihilated. Mavrocordatos had set up his headquarters at Komboti fifteen miles away and was not even present. The truth is that Reshid Pasha was as able and experienced an officer in warfare as Mavrocordatos was the reverse. In the absence of the commander-in-chief there was no real authority or unity in the Greek army; and, although the philhellenes fought with great bravery, the treachery of Gogos had allowed them to be attacked both in the front and the rear, so that only a handful escaped at the point of the bayonet. The victory not only left the Turks free to reduce the Souliotes, but had so damaged the prestige of Mavrocordatos that any hope of forming a strong central government under his leadership had to be abandoned. The Souliotes had been forced into a hopeless position; but so esteemed was their reputation for undaunted courage that the Ottoman commander allowed them favourable terms. They accepted the sum of two hundred thousand piastres in compensation for agreeing to quit their impregnable mountain homes and crossed over to the Ionian Islands where, for good or ill, they again threw in their fortunes with the Greeks, to become a most colourful element at least in the War of Liberation.

But while the Souliotes still fought a rearguard action on the mainland, the Greeks had relapsed into internecine feuds, leaving most of the country badly defended. Omer Vrioni, marching southward at the head of six thousand men, found the pass of Makrynoros unguarded, occupied it and was joined by Reshid Pasha who commanded four thousand men. By the autumn of 1822 Omer Vrioni had cleared almost the whole of western Greece and pushed south as far as Missolonghi, whose first historic siege began in November. This unprepossessing and insalubrious little town set on the shore of a shallow and stagnant lagoon could hardly have presented a serious obstacle to Omer had he assaulted it at once. For it was garrisoned by only some six hundred men and some old-fashioned cannon and its fortifications consisted of little else than a low wall of earth and a muddy ditch. However, Omer opted for a conventional siege and encamped before the town.

The size of the Turkish army had been swollen by crowds of Albanian irregulars, brigands greedy to share the expected loot.

The Lapse into Civil War

The defenders led by Mavrocordatos (who by his presence and excellent organization of the defence now regained much of his prestige) were full of courage and high spirits. A Turkish fleet sent from Patras to blockade the town was driven off by seven Greek brigs from Hydra, and the sparse garrison was reinforced by a thousand men from the Peloponnese under the command of Petrobey Mavromichalis and other leaders. The Ottoman bombardment proved ineffective, as the cannon balls topped the roofs of the low houses and many mortar shells sank without exploding in the slime of the unpaved streets and courts. When at last Omer Vrioni decided to assault at earliest dawn on January 6th, 1823, the Greek Christmas day, the garrison had increased to two thousand five hundred men, liberally supplied with ammunition sent from Leghorn. The storming party of Moslems failed to surprise the Christians at their church services, as they had hoped to do, for the garrison had received warning of the attack and were waiting for them. The Albanian brigands were met with a murderous cross-fire as they struggled in the ditch. They broke and fled after losing two hundred men, while only four of the triumphant Greeks were killed. Omer raised the siege, retiring in some disorder back through the pass of Makrynoros, leaving much of his war equipment behind. On hearing the news of the disaster, Kurshid Pasha, who by now was an old man, committed suicide thee days before an order for his execution had been signed at Constantinople.

But previous to this in July 1822 a Turkish parallel drive down the eastern side of Greece had proved less successful. It started from Lamia led by Mahmoud Dramali, who had been appointed an independent commander-in-chief but with a status equal to Kurshid Pasha. His army, consisting of more than twenty thousand men, aimed at eventually clearing the whole of the Peloponnese. Since Admiral Miaoulis's ships were effectively blocking Turkish operations by sea, it was essential to keep the eastern land route to the south open. Ignoring Athens on his left flank—which had capitulated to the Greeks on the 21st of June—Dramali marched straight to the Isthmus of Corinth. He met with little Greek opposition owing to the devious behaviour of Odysseus Androutsos

121

who, uncertain which side was going to win, refused to obey orders from the Areopagus of eastern Greece. At the time Dramali was occupying Corinth and crossing the Isthmus, the Turkish garrison at Nauplia, the most important town in the Peloponnese, was about to surrender. The Greeks had decided to make Nauplia their capital instead of Corinth; but now, with Dramali heading for Argos, the Turks not unnaturally broke off their arrangements for surrender. And it was not until Dramali had actually reached Argos, a few miles distant from Nauplia, that the Peloponnesians abandoned their insensate intrigues and family squabbles and, taking combined military action, fought back. So extended and perilous had Dramali's overland communications become, that the danger to the Greeks collapsed with a dramatic suddenness that might have been foreseen. The sort of harassing action which took place at this time will perhaps be best appreciated by a quotation from the graphic homespun prose of Makriyannis:

> In 1822, the end of June or thereabouts, when the Turks invaded and entered the Peloponnese, they could not get supplies in, because every day we attacked them as guerillas in the passes. . . . We collected all the bands of eastern Greece and we went and bravely fought them, and they too fought like heroes. We beat them; we took their field-kitchens, we killed a number of them, we took such booty, we ousted them from their positions and they entrenched themselves in a strong place. We brought a gun against them and bombarded them. We cut off their water and brought them to great straits. We fought them from mid-day to dawn. Reinforcements came up, we routed them. More reinforcements came from Alamanna, and then they were very strong in foot and horse, and we withdrew of our own accord, without casualties. Each went back to his base, and we to Gravia. And we were attacking them continually, as guerillas.[4]

Makriyannis was fighting with a company of guerillas and had put himself under the command of Odysseus Androutsos; and, although the fighting which Makriyannis so vividly describes was the occasion for much gallantry, it was not strategically effective.

Makriyannis believed that the failure of Odysseus was largely due to the intrigues of the Central Government, especially to the spite of the War Minister, John Kolettis, against him. But this opinion remains controversial. Certainly, like other captains, Odysseus was capable of making truces with the Turks, and he showed no talent for administering a civil population. He liked to withdraw his troops at a critical moment from vanity, to demonstrate that none could do without him.[5] Dramali, on the other hand, had almost ruinously extended his overland lines of communication. In addition Kurshid Pasha was suspected of having lingered and delayed sending Dramali essential supplies through jealousy of his rival's promotion. So Dramali was forced to withdraw from the Argolid and in August he met with a disastrous defeat in an ambush commanded by Kolokotronis in the defile of Devernaki between Argos and Corinth.

When the Turkish army reached the pass they found it already occupied by the Greeks; and, although the vanguard of Albanian mountaineers evaded death by following steep and circuitous paths, the main body of Ottomans was met by a murderous fire which so cluttered the road with the corpses of men and horses that it was impossible for them to advance. The scene of slaughter in the ravine was terrible, more of a holocaust than a battle, as confusion spread along the Turkish line. Only the Greeks' instinct for plunder saved the Turks from total annihilation. The Greeks' purpose was

to cut off the baggage, shoot baggage-mules, and secure the booty. The Turks fled in every direction, leaving their baggage to arrest the pursuit of their enemy. . . . Many abandoned their horses, and succeeded in finding their way to Corinth during the night. Long trains of baggage-mules and camels, and a number of richly-caparisoned horses, were captured. The booty gained was immense.[6]

The remains of Dramali's army, continually harassed and in dire disorder, struggled back to Corinth and to their base at Lamia. Dramali himself, exhausted and in despair, died in December of the same year at Corinth.

The Heroic Struggle

The close of the second year of the war ended with Greek morale raised to a high pitch of aggressiveness by their successes: the capture of Athens, the inspired patriotism of Kolokotronis against Dramali, the raid of Admiral Kanaris in November which had destroyed by means of a fire-ship a Turkish battleship off the Dardanelles. Argos had been recovered by the Greeks and Nauplia had surrendered to Kolokotronis, although the citadel of Corinth still remained in Turkish hands. But for the Turks, with the heavy loss of two commanders-in-chief, Kurshid Pasha and Dramali, it had been a disappointing year, with the balance of forces tipped in favour of the Greeks. True, the Greeks had been territorially restricted, with the loss of Epirus, most of Roumeli and the large island of Euboea. But even their setbacks had shown certain advantages, because Western Europeans had been genuinely moved by the sacrifice of the philhellenes at Peta, by the atrocious massacres on Chios and, perhaps most of all, by the recapture of historic Athens. They would be stirred still more by the long Siege of Missolonghi. This factor of sentiment was something the Turks failed to comprehend, for they had no experience of the classical tradition, nor of the mystical importance of such romantic names to Europe. All they could do, in the face of protest, was to try and soothe outraged European nerves with promises of better behaviour to their rebellious subjects in the future.

Although the Greeks had lost nearly a quarter of the territory which they considered it was their right to rule, they had won strongly fortified Nauplia which, for the present at any rate, would make a natural capital in place of Corinth. The moment was yet distant when Athens would be safe enough to be claimed as the capital city. So Nauplia, the main port of the eastern Peloponnese, was an important prize. But since the early months of the revolution Greek control of civil administration had been hopelessly divided, with a council for western Greece at Missolonghi presided over by Mavrocordatos, the council for eastern Greece, the Areopagus in the Megarid, and the National Assembly which had first met in Argos, but which Kolokotronis now refused to respect. For Kolokotronis, the victor of Dervenaki, had by now thrown in his lot with a few powerful dissident landowners of the

124

Peloponnese, chief of whom was Mavromichalis, overlord of Mani, who were opposed to the National Assembly. When the representatives of the Assembly wanted to hold a second meeting at Nauplia in December, Kolokotronis refused to admit them. So the National Assembly met at a neighbouring village Astros, and passed two important decisions: to send representatives to seek a loan in London, and to decrease the power of Kolokotronis by imposing new rules of government. Kolokotronis's contemptuous reaction was to kidnap four members of the Government and to remove them bodily under armed guard to Nauplia. The remaining members moved to Argos, but finally settled on a southern promontory of the Peloponnese where they benefited from the protection of the near by islands of Hydra and Spetsai. In gratitude for his support, which gave them nominal control of the Greek fleet, they elected a wealthy shipowner from Hydra, George Kondouriotis as their new President. But in 1823 Kolokotronis continued to be the real power in the Peloponnese.[7]

Apart from Dramali's dramatic campaign in the north-east corner, there had been little fighting in the Peloponnese during 1822. The absence of a common enemy proved a fertile breeding-ground for quarrels between the military factions and the rival politicians. Disputes with the central and the provincial governments grew more divisive and out of hand. In the third year of the war this disunity looked irrevocable; by the fourth year it amounted to civil war between the rival congeries for power. Before the end of 1823 civil war had broken out between Kolokotronis and the Central Government, and more personal feuds between some of the Aegean Islands, involving the seamen of Hydra against those of Spetsai, and of Samos against Psara, for example. Under these circumstances it may seem odd that the Turks should not have taken advantage of such disunity to crush the rebellion altogether. But the Sultan's resources were dangerously stretched by war with Persia, by a rebellion of the Druses in Syria, and by the continual fear of war with Russia.

The third Turkish campaign against the Greeks in 1823, which again was to consist of parallel drives south down both flanks of the Pindus mountains, did not even reach the Peloponnese. The intended plan of campaign was for the two forces to make a junction at the Gulf of Corinth, perhaps at Lepanto, the strongest coastal fortress still in Turkish occupation, and then to cross over the gulf and complete the conquest of the Peloponnese. This happened to be too ambitious a project for a single campaigning season and the Ottoman effort was half-hearted, lacking all real conviction of success. Instead, punitive expeditions developed to the east of the Pindus mountains aimed at existing pockets of Greek rebels encamped among the hills of Thessaly; while further south there was a rather aimless and ineffective plundering of east Roumeli, with no serious attempt to capture Athens. When news of the fighting brought Kolokotronis hurrying up from the Peloponnese with an efficient force of guerillas, the Turkish operation in eastern Greece foundered and collapsed.

It was the same thing in western Greece, punitive harrying of their enemies in the central mountains instead of a bold drive south towards the Peloponnese. The Turkish commander, Mustaï Pasha, who should have marched south from Yannina through Arta and Agrinion towards Missolonghi, chose first to move across into the heart of the Pindus country, with an army consisting wholly of Albanian tribesmen. The vanguard of four thousand men, under Djelaleddin Bey, advanced as far as Karpenisi, a village three thousand feet above sea-level, without meeting any serious opposition. But here disaster befell it, chalking up for the Greeks an outstandingly brilliant exploit of the wa :. For the Souliote hero Marco Botzaris, and other guerilla captains, were waiting, and, on the night of the 21st of August Botzaris with three hundred and fifty of his clansmen surprised the Ottomans. The Turks only escaped destruction because a chance bullet tragically killed Botzaris. He had made straight for the tent of the Bey which was pitched in an enclosure surrounded by a wall. Raising his head above the wall to find out how he could effect an entrance, Botzaris received a bullet through his brain. The end of his leadership was a painful loss to the Greeks. Only a few days previously he had corresponded with Lord Byron, the Englishman upon whom Greek hopes were becoming more and more set, who had ⸴rived on the island of Cephallonia in the summer in the role of emissary and financial agent of the Greek Committee in London.

The success of the Souliotes, however, failed to hinder the advance of Mustaï who, at the end of September, linked up at Vrachori with the army of Omer Vrioni. In October, with this combined force, Mustaï laid siege to Anatoliko, a village in the Aetolian lagoons about five miles from Missolonghi, which the Turks surprisingly made no attempt to invest. But it was late in the year when the Ottomans had reached the Gulf of Corinth, too late to mount a campaign in the Peloponnese. The garrison of some six hundred men in unfortified Anatoliko showed such stout resistance that Mustaï Pasha raised the siege on the 11th of December and the Turks retired north to their winter quarters. The Ottoman campaign had failed and the year closed triumphantly for the Greeks.

For Mahmud was short of man-power. What his high command required were two independent armies, one to clear the Peloponnese, the other to consolidate all the territory overrun on the mainland north of the Gulf of Corinth. Large Turkish armies were pinned down in the northern provinces of the Empire throughout most of the war because of the Porte's lasting suspicion of a possible Russian attack. The Sultan now realized that he must look for aid elsewhere, and his thoughts turned to his nominal vassal, the virtually independent Mehemet Ali, Pasha of Egypt. But to invoke Mehemet Ali's help would mean paying a high price and for some time Mahmud remained in two minds about paying it. Since 1822 Crete had been in a state of sympathetic insurrection which had proved partly successful. The insurgents had swept the Moslems from the hilly open country and confined them to the towns. But the Hellenic victories had been followed by the usual dissensions and divisions. The price demanded by Mehemet Ali of the Sultan would include the annexation of Crete to the *pashalik* of Egypt and the appointment of his son Ibrahim as Pasha of the Peloponnese. A preliminary step had been taken in 1822 when operations against Crete had been put under Mehemet Ali's command and a force of Albanians landed there. Yet little occurred until the spring of 1824, when the

Egyptians mounted a violent campaign against the people of Crete, whose transient independence was slowly destroyed. In that same year Ibrahim was appointed Pasha of the Peloponnese.

Byron's Intervention
and Death at Missolonghi

There is good reason to believe that two widely separated events, one more spiritual in its impact, the other decisively material, combined more than all others to settle the War of Independence in favour of the Greeks. These were Byron's death at Missolonghi and, three and a half years later, the sea battle of Navarino. The consequence of Byron's heroic act of free will in choosing to go to the aid of the Greeks at Missolonghi was, especially after his death, to galvanize their souls to continue the struggle; for his name had become the symbol of disinterested patriotism. "All are looking forward to Lord Byron's arrival," Colonel Leicester Stanhope had written, "as they would to the coming of a Messiah." And yet Byron did not go to Greece solely because of his philhellenism; and, it must be admitted, that his sojourn in Missolonghi was on the surface only a succession of failures.

When, in the summer of 1823, Byron had taken his irrevocable decision to leave Italy and his last and deep attachment to Contessa Teresa Guiccioli and go to Greece, he had reached the final crisis of his life. The Tuscan spy Torelli had commented: "It is said that he is already sated or tired of his favourite, the Guiccioli. He has, however, expressed his intention of not remaining in Genoa, but of going on to Athens in order to make himself adored by the Greeks." But Byron tore himself from Teresa's enervating arms reluctantly and their parting was a tragic one. After three years of constancy, Teresa was still only twenty-three and he thirty-five but in experience and health feeling himself seventy. He had told Lady Blessington: "Were the Contessa Guiccioli and I married, we should, I am sure, be cited as an example of conjugal happiness."[1] His constitution at this time had already been somewhat undermined both by his wholesale past dissipations in Venice and by a foolish Draconian system of dieting to correct his ever-present tendency to corpulence. Gone, too, was "that beautiful pale face" which during his youth in London had so captivated and continued to haunt Lady Caroline Lamb. Now the face was fatter, the teeth had deteriorated, and his glossy dark brown curls were streaked with silver and retreating from his temples.

Byron had long been interested in liberty and indeed he had confessed to Lady Blessington: "There are but two sentiments to which I am constant,—a strong love of liberty, and a detestation of cant, and neither is calculated to gain me friends."[2] His liberalism had remained unchanged, from the principles of the French Revolution to schemes of support for the revolutionary Society of the Carbonari in Italy, and sympathy for the success of Simon Bolivar in freeing Columbia and Venezuela from Spanish rule. He had named the schooner which he kept at Leghorn the *Bolivar* in defiance of the Austrian authorities, and would have rejoiced to see the Italians send their "barbarian" oppressors packing. Now, more and more, Byron's mind brooded on ways of escape, even toying with the idea of buying a principality in Chile or Peru, or an island in the Greek Archipelago. For Greece, ever since his first journeyings there with Cam Hobhouse, had remained a latent gleam, a memory of youth and fame and love, a cherished vision of indelible blue skies and waters, of long rides on horseback through violet-shadowed ravines in barren mountains among men and women who spoke a bastard version of the sweet Hellenic tongue.

But now Byron was no longer young and looked and felt much older than his actual years. He knew that his youth had deserted him and suffered from this knowledge with mounting obsession. What, after all, was he now but a spent widower, a soiled dandy with a weakening body; and he was afraid to contemplate what could or would, or might even now, be happening to his mind. He had loved fame and women—the soul had worn out the breast —he had enjoyed his rank as a nobleman, perhaps even his notoriety. He had "squandered his whole summer while 'twas

May"; but now it was time to stop leading the life he had led. All these things so far had only been the means towards some further unseen end—but what end? Byron did not know. But he had an obscure faith that there might be "that within him" which was destined to serve some nobler cause, to grasp a wider horizon in dreamed of deeds. Was it already too late to redeem his honour? Was there still hope of his rehabilitation with his own countrymen? So Byron dreamed and doubted. But at last the moment for ruthless action was approaching, and his way of escape was to be Greece.

On the fatal day July 13th Byron embarked in Genoa harbour upon the *Hercules* which, when he first saw it, Trelawny had dubbed "a collier-built tub of 120 tons, round-bottomed, and bluff-bowed". The parting from Teresa had been harrowing, and Byron limped gloomily on board, with little sign of enthusiasm for the cause to which he was now dedicated. His companions were Trelawny, Count Pietro Gamba (Teresa's brother), Byron's young physician Dr. Bruno and a Greek to whom he had promised a passage home. In addition there were four or five servants to help crowd the small ship, and plenty of livestock as well which included four of Byron's horses and one of Trelawny's, a faithful bulldog Moretto, and Byron's enormous Newfoundland, Lion, to whom he was devoted. At first there were hampering delays due to the weather and the *Hercules* was five days in reaching Leghorn where the commander of an Ionian vessel, Captain George Vitali, greeted Byron with a salute of thirteen guns, and was allowed a passage back to his homeland. A Scotsman, James Hamilton Browne, who on account of his Hellenic sympathies had been dismissed from work in the Ionian islands and was knowledgeable about the English Residents also joined the expedition. It was on his advice that Byron changed his destination from Zante to Cephallonia where Colonel Charles James Napier, a noted philhellene, was in command. On the 24th the weather was fine, and with all on deck, the overcrowded *Hercules* headed south for the Strait of Messina.

In April Byron's interest in the Greek war had been much stimulated by a visit at Genoa from a sea-captain Edward Blaquière (of a Huguenot family settled in Dublin) who was a representative of the London Greek Committee, of which many distinguished Englishmen, including Hobhouse, Bentham, Hume, Lord Erskine and Lord John Russell, were members. Blaquière was accompanied by Andreas Luriottis, a delegate of the Greek government and a man of persuasive eloquence, who had been in London to solicit English help for the crusade. By 1824 Blaquière had become quite the most popular foreigner in Greece, not discounting Byron, for he went further in expressing his admiration for the Greek character, their frugality, soberness, kindness to their families and their industry.

Byron had been elected a member of the Greek Committee in London to which three of his fellow poets Thomas Campbell, Thomas Moore and Samuel Rogers also belonged. Owing to the disruption caused by the suicide of Lord Castlereagh in August 1822 the London Committee was not in fact formed until January 1823 and issued its first circular on the 3rd of March. There were twenty-six variously distinguished members, whose number had been augmented to eighty-five before the end of the year. Out of some forty Members of Parliament nearly all were Whigs or Radicals bemused by Benthamite idealism and lacking in realism, a minority "protest movement". In the spring of 1823 English opinion was split into three main divisions, a Whig pro-Greek active minority, a Tory minority in favour of Turkish legitimacy, who believed that expediency demanded a preservation of the *status quo*, and a large ignorant majority of the uncommitted.

However, one result of the recent Greek successes at sea under Miaoulis and Kanaris, assisted by the spirited philhellene Captain Frank Abney Hastings, was the crucial decision of the British government in March to recognize the Greek naval blockade of the mainland, much to the fury of Sir Thomas Maitland, High Commissioner of the Ionian Islands. The philhellenes had been gradually growing in power; and the arrival on the scene of the pro-Greek George Canning as Foreign Secretary was helping to sway public opinion from the position of questioning the chance of Greek survival, to the hope that in the long run Greece might even prove to be the winning side. England, too, was reacting against the policy of the Holy Alliance dictated from Vienna, with the unpopular hazard of Greece falling under a Russian protectorate. Finally, Byron's engagement had lifted the cause above the sordid reaches of party politics to an enterprise of pith and moment, with all the excitement of a novel and romantic crusade.

Meanwhile Byron himself during the early days of the voyage had sat much apart from his companions, blue-capped and white-trousered, morose, silent and solitary, seemingly disinterested, fidgeting with his lace-fringed handkerchief between his small white hands, as he contemplated the past wreckage of his personal life. He showed no sign at first of any enthusiasm for his high adventure; the other passengers were half afraid of him while he remained in his black mood. Contrariwise, while preparations were being made on shore through the previous weeks, it is recorded that:

Lord Byron gave his personal attention to the design of the uniform and helmets in which he and his immediate staff were to land resplendently upon the shores of Hellas. The uniforms were to be of scarlet and gold. . . . For himself, however, and for Trelawny (he counted on Trelawny) he designed two helmets of homeric proportions, and on the lines of that which, in the sixth book of the *Iliad*, had so dismayed the infant Astyanax. Below the nodding plume figured his own coat of arms, and the motto 'crede Biron', while the whole was secured by a wide chin-strap of a very menacing aspect . . . Byron was delighted with the one he himself had chosen . . . but Trelawny, when he arrived, refused vehemently to put his on. Byron, disconcerted by this refusal, began to have doubts as to the propriety of his own helmet; so that they were all put back in their pink cardboard boxes and did not in the end figure in the disembarkation at Missolonghi; and the order for the three scarlet uniforms was countermanded.[3]

This bad beginning may have been a manifestation of Byron's underlying hatred of cant—the cant of romanticism. He railed inwardly against Trelawny's noisy sham theatricalism, and would have preferred to face his own serious Greek commitment more soberly. To hell then with cant about Causes, Liberty, Adventure! In strong contrast to his other shipmates, who all both loved and venerated their leader, Trelawny never really cared for Byron. But as the empty cloudless days of sailing went on, Byron's confidence and high spirits slowly returned. He fenced with Pietro Gamba. He and Trelawny boxed. He fired at the seagulls, drank grog with his companions, swam, and spent many hours playing with his dogs. Trelawny felt obliged to record: "I never was on ship-board with a better companion than Byron. He was generally cheerful, gave no trouble, assumed no authority, uttered no com-plaints, and did not interfere with the working of the ship; when appealed to he always answered, 'Do as you like'." And yet at other times, Trelawny tells, Byron had interludes of sadness, "his cold fits alternated with hot ones". Byron was not afraid of dying. "If Death," he said, "comes in the shape of a cannon-ball and takes off my head, he is welcome. I have no wish to live, but I can't bear pain."

But now at last the voyage was coming to an end. At sunset on August 2nd the ship hove-to in the channel between the islands of Zante and Cephallonia, in view of the calm mountainous outline of the Peloponnese. The next morning the *Hercules* moved up the inlet and anchored off the capital Argostoli.

The nine months that Byron spent on Greek soil was a time of almost total frustration for him; at the end it must have seemed to himself and to others that he had accomplished nothing except his own death. And yet it is hardly possible to exaggerate the importance of Byron's services to Greece. For one thing he acted as an essential bridge between London and Greece, carrying weight with the Whigs and Radicals because he was Lord Byron; to the philhellenes who were in the field fighting he became a practical inspiration; while to the more emotional Greeks he was a great poet, a courageous hero, almost a god. Without any doubt his contribution to the liberation of Greece was without parallel.

But this legend of Byron as the destined Messiah and hero of

Greek independence has done much to obscure his own modest hesitance and uncertainty, his near reluctance to assume any such heroic or messianic role. During the last months of his life Byron's character underwent a change, a subtle transformation and development which resulted in a more ardent outlook. He never attempted to puff up his own legend nor to the least degree ever denigrated the reputations of other protagonists in the drama.

At the time Byron arrived in Cephallonia the seven Ionian Islands (the Heptaneesa as the Greeks called them) had for eight years been under British protection and were to remain so until 1864 when they were freely ceded to the Kingdom of the Hellenes, surely an act of remarkable generosity from an Empire at the zenith of its power. The Lord High Commissioner, Sir Thomas Maitland, a somewhat alcoholic autocrat known to both friends and enemies as "King Tom of Corfu", ruled with a passionate but generally benevolent despotism in the interest of stability. Although he could be domineering and eccentric, King Tom possessed the virtues of honour allied to a shrewd ability. So far as the outbreak of the War of Independence was concerned, he judged it his duty to enforce the will of the British Government, meaning the intentions of Lord Castlereagh: the Ionian Islands must never become a place of refuge for the Greek rebels, nor be used as a base for their warlike operations. They must be kept strictly neutral. Sir Thomas Maitland, by enforcing stringent regulations to deny all communication between the islands and the mainland, invited the bitter hostility of both Greeks and the foreign philhellenes. Yet Maitland, for all his explosions, was capable of recognizing integrity, honour and ability in others; and this quality he showed by sending his often troublesome, unruly subordinate, Colonel Charles James Napier, to act as British Resident in Cephallonia.

Napier, who much later found glory in India as the conqueror of Scind, was a nephew of Fox whose Christian names he bore and whose Whig politics he had imbibed in his youth from that great statesman of the modern school. But Napier went considerably further in his truculent radicalism, hating the Tory government he was obliged to serve, warring all his life against oppression and injustice. When they met Byron happily discovered a mutual affinity with Napier based upon their admiration for Napoleon and their shared affection for the Greeks. At first Byron lived on the *Hercules* until he took a four-roomed house at Metaxata, a little way inland. He was persistent in refusing the Resident's hospitality, for fear of compromising Napier with the Ionian Government which was ultra-touchy about its neutrality. Byron admired Napier both for his military talents and for his extreme chivalry. Napier found in him, not only a brilliant genius, but a man who had a sane appreciation of the situation, who could judge the Greeks fairly and make allowance for emancipated slaves. What they both respected in one another was that each had a down-to-earth knowledge of the Greeks. Napier, too, had travelled widely in the country, had been on a mission to Ali Pasha at Yannina and could love the Greeks for themselves, apart from "any antiquarian twaddle". One quotation from Napier will suffice written, nearly a year after Byron's death, in March 1825 on returning to Cephallonia:

Now I am once more among the merry Greeks, who are worth all other nations put together. I like to see, to hear them; I like their fun, their good humour, their Paddy ways, for they are very like Irishmen. . . . All their bad habits are Venetian; their wit, their eloquence, their good nature are their own. . . . I am enjoying their good company, their fine climate, their magnificent mountains, their pretty scenery, liking them and all belonging to them, and wishing all belonging to me were here. No, not here in Corfu, but in Cephallonia, which is so dear to me that every hour not employed to do her good seems wasted.

What kept Byron five months in Cephallonia were his diffidence and uncertainty about the role he was expected to play, and which party, if any, he should support. For the internal political dissensions among the opposing Greek factions for power had almost slowed the war to a halt. The Turks were in virtual command of the sea around the mainland, with the Greek fleet mostly bottled up in the harbours of islands off the east coast. The reports

Byron received were all far too confused and biased, it seemed to him, to warrant any action at present. In the meantime Colonel Napier was seeing a lot of his celebrated guest, and paid him every attention, realizing that Byron, as the representative of the London Greek Committee, might have considerable influence both in Greece and London in helping him to obtain a military command. So it was arranged that Napier should be given leave to go to London, furnished with a letter of introduction from Byron to the London Greek Committee. He arrived in January 1824, carrying a letter written on the 10th of December 1823 in which Byron advised that a loan of £500,000 should be raised to provide an army for Greece to be commanded by Napier. "Of his military character it were superfluous to speak; of his personal, I can say from my own knowledge," wrote Byron, "that it is excellent as his military—in short, a better or a braver man is not easily to be found. He is our man to lead a regular force or to organise a national one for the Greeks. Ask the army; ask anybody! He is, besides, the personal friend of Mavrocordato, Colonel Stanhope, and myself; and in such concord with all three that we should pull together, an indispensable as well as a rare point, especially in Greece at present."

Alas, the London Committee was too preoccupied to welcome Napier's services. At the moment they were busy devising acrimoniously the menu for their next public dinner, and were more interested in making plans for the cultural regeneration of Greece than in hearing about Napier's military virtues. Not unnaturally Napier would have none of them. In vain he had tried to explain to them the real existing state of affairs in Greece. "The famous London Committee," Napier had exploded, "from any further connexion with which the Lord deliver me." If only the Greek Committee had accepted Napier's services, it seems probable that the remaining long misery of the war might have been shortened by several years. The man whom Wellington chose later to command the Indian Army would doubtless, with Byron's inspirational and administrative help, have proved more than capable of welding together an efficient army in Greece, as indeed George Finlay believed. Byron had arrived in Cephallonia brooding and irresolute of purpose. In Napier he had found not only a friend and ally but a soldier of outstanding originality and decision, a man who, while no more blind than Byron himself to the faults of the Greeks, never for a moment changed in his affection for them nor doubted their ultimate triumph. It was Napier's infinite energy and resolution that had managed to revitalize the despondent poet during those last months he spent at Metaxata; so that when the historic moment came Byron found his confidence restored and was able, high-hearted and determined, to cross over to the mainland and Missolonghi.

The story of Byron's three and a half months and death at Missolonghi is so well known that here it will not be needlessly elaborated. He sailed from Cephallonia on the 30th of December 1823 and arrived on Sunday the 4th January 1824 after an adventurous voyage; he narrowly escaped capture by the Turks and was twice nearly shipwrecked by being blown by violent squalls onto the rocks close to his destination. The Greeks do not feature very creditably in the first adventure. Although they had looked forward to Byron's arrival as their saviour, they were only too well aware that he would bring with him his personal riches. Both the sailors of the Greek fleet and the Souliote soldiers, whose pay was in arrears, proved inordinately avaricious. But not even the prospect of "much fine gold" could prevent the Greek fleet from cutting their cables and taking flight when several Turkish vessels suddenly appeared from the gulf, thus leaving the enemy free to patrol in front of the port. It appears likely that Byron only evaded capture because of the complete hush kept on his ship, with the added unusual fact, recorded by his servant Fletcher, that the dogs "though they had never ceased to bark during the whole of the night, did not utter, while within reach of the Turkish frigate, a sound." And it is certainly to the credit of Byron's humanity, (also revealing his estimate of the Turks) that, after putting into a creek and landing a boy servant Loukas and a man with a message to Stanhope, he wrote: "I am uneasy at being here: not so much on my own account as on that of a Greek boy with me, for you know what his fate would be; and I would sooner cut him in pieces, and myself too, than have him taken out by those barbarians."4

Byron's actual landing at Missolonghi at 11 a.m. on Monday the 5th was impressive enough. He was clad in scarlet regimentals and was greeted by triumphant salvos of guns, loud musketry fire, and by the wild enthusiastic shouts of the people. He was received on the threshold of the house prepared for him by Mavrocordatos, Colonel Stanhope and a motley collection of Greek and European officers. Pietro Gamba has recorded that contentment and hope shone in his eyes and that he appeared to be emotionally stimulated by the scene.

Byron had hesitated a long time before finally deciding to throw in his lot with Mavrocordatos, simply because he had not known which of the Greek leaders to trust. They seemed quite unable to agree upon either a national policy or a unified command; and one of the best of them, Marco Botzaris the Souliote, regrettably had been killed shortly after writing to welcome Byron's arrival in Cephallonia. Byron had sensibly made all manner of practical enquiries addressed to Kolokotronis and Mavrocordatos's supporters recording their numerical strength, rates of pay, prisoners taken, and communications with the islands. For as Disraeli wrote: "If there was one quality that characterized Byron more than another it was his solid common sense."

His moods, however, were a problem. Previously and during the ensuing weeks they were inconstant. One moment and the whole enterprise would appear to him no more than a fool's errand, next he would gain in courage and determination and write: "I must see this Greek business out (or *it me*)." The truth is that "in Italy as in Greece his historical imagination was fired by the idea of a renascence of the two great nations of the past. 'Only think, a free Italy! Why, 'tis the very poetry of politics.' But although leavened by the practical common sense which he showed again in Greece his was a poet's vision, not a statesman's . . . And beneath all this, there was something more. The motive which underlay the Italian venture and the Greek one was the same: a desire for rehabilitation in the eyes of his fellow-countrymen."5

Probably one of Byron's biggest mistakes was to have trusted to the Souliotes, choosing a hired mob of these people to act as his personal bodyguard. With their brave weather-tanned faces, wearing their characteristic fustanellas, they made an image which carried him back to his youthful and romantic trek with Hobhouse through Epirus in 1809. He was determined to organize a regular corps of infantry, with a nucleus of Souliotes, and to be responsible for the pay of five hundred of them. The trouble was, as Mavrocordatos had warned him in a memorandum, that the Souliotes, besides being brave, were also exceedingly rapacious and venal and rent by internal jealousies. Their family feuds and quarrels among the officers would have been enough to undermine the discipline of any army. Byron's nucleus of Souliotes turned out to be the cause of disruption, blackmail and conspiracy, and were to lead to humiliating disappointments, failure and ultimate despair.

But when he arrived at Missolonghi Byron was in an optimistic frame of mind. He was kept busy during January preparing an attack on the Turkish fortress of Lepanto, a plan which because of its associations with past history appealed to him. He does not seem to have been affected by the melancholy of the ramshackle squalid village in the miasmic lagoon that runs parallel with the Gulf of Patras, behind the indented circles of the Aetolian and Arkananian mountains. Nor did he mind the poor, primitive accommodation provided for him at the three-storeyed house of Capsali which had walls of damp plaster—where he arranged his collection of fire-arms, trumpets and helmets—scant furniture and no drains. His immediate practical concern was to prepare for the attack on Lepanto which he believed would both inaugurate his own military glory and win a glittering prize under the eyes of Europe. Though the Turkish armies were no longer in Western Greece, it was expected that the Sultan would resume his offensive in the spring and try once more to capture Missolonghi, as well as to reinstate his authority in the Peloponnese. The Ottomans were still holding Patras and Lepanto, with the two castles at the entrance to the Gulf of Corinth. The fall of Lepanto before the spring might even induce the Turks to abandon Patras and the castles.

The menace to Missolonghi would be alleviated, the prestige of Mavrocordatos much enhanced, the loan would arrive from London . . . Byron dreamed of a liberated, perhaps solvent, united Greece that might conceivably be recognized by the Great Powers.

Unfortunately, Byron's optimism was little more than a vision. He thought Lepanto should be easy to take; for the Turkish garrison, consisting mostly of Albanian mercenaries, had indicated that, for a trifling monetary consideration, they would put up only a token resistance. Byron and Mavrocordatos were in entire agreement that this action should take precedence over all others. What was needed was some viable disciplined force to march against the unstable broken Venetian walls of the fortress. It would be an advantage too if the remnant of the Greek fleet could assist in this operation. But of the fourteen ships which had been persuaded to leave Hydra nine had already gone home, believing that they would receive no pay. However, five Spetsiot brigs remained, and Byron prevented these from absconding by paying for their maintenance out of his own pocket.

By contrast the organization and equipment of a permanent land force at first looked promising. The London Committee had previously agreed to send out a director of artillery, with a number of expert technicians; so, with the help of Colonel Stanhope and Mavrocordatos, Byron hoped to form an efficient artillery brigade. But difficulties arose and multiplied. There were not enough enthusiastic philhellenes available. The Greeks he enrolled as officers failed to collaborate easily with the Germans and their Prussian etiquette. The problem of the unruly Souliotes remained. And yet the picture still looked encouraging. The artillery brigade practised each morning in the courtyard of Byron's house, the Souliotes also were drilling. The technicians from England were hourly expected. In a few weeks at most they would be in a position to mount a triumphant attack upon Lepanto.

When, on the evening of January 18th, long and frequent discharges of musketry were heard in the town, and news arrived that the Souliotes and the townspeople had come to blows. Byron expected one party or the other to appear demanding help; but the noise of the riot in time abated. Worse news was to follow about an hour later brought by Mavrocordatos's secretary. The Turkish fleet had broken out from Patras and the Spetsiot brigs had fled before them. Two days afterwards Byron and his friends found themselves blockaded. Byron was only with difficulty persuaded from attempting to break the blockade by personally taking command of a manoeuvre to attack the fleet from boats.

On the 22nd of January, which was Byron's thirty-sixth birthday, he emerged from his bedroom to join Colonel Stanhope and his friends, holding the famous verses that were almost the last he wrote. "You were complaining," he smiled, "that I never write any poetry now; this is my birthday, and I have just finished something which I think is better than what I usually write." The poem is too long to quote in full:

> 'Tis time this heart should be unmoved,
>   Since others it hath ceased to move:
> Yet, though I cannot be beloved,
>   Still let me love!
>
> My days are in the yellow leaf;
>   The flowers and fruits of Love are gone;
> The worm, the canker, and the grief
>   Are mine alone!
>
> .   .   .   .   .
>
> But 'tis not thus—and 'tis not here—
>   Such thoughts should shake my soul, nor now
> Where Glory decks the hero's bier,
>   Or binds his brow.
>
> The Sword, the Banner, and the Field,
>   Glory and Greece, around me see!
> The Spartan, borne upon his shield,
>   Was not more free.
>
> Awake! (not Greece—she is awake!)
>   Awake, my spirit! Think through whom

Thy life-blood tracks its parent lake,
    And then strike home!

Tread those reviving passions down,
    Unworthy manhood!—unto thee
Indifferent should the smile or frown
    Of Beauty be.

If thou regret'st thy youth, why live?
    The land of honourable death
Is here:—up to the Field, and give
    Away thy breath!

Seek out—less often sought than found—
    A soldier's grave, for thee the best;
Then look around, and choose thy ground,
    And take thy Rest.

Count Gamba read in these lines (his opinion reinforced by his daily conversations with the poet) that Byron, battered though he was with anxiety and growing ill-health, had a fixed resolution to stay in Greece and "return victorious or return no more". All Byron's hopes and ambition were now concentrated in the single glorious cause of Greece. Yet, in his own self-tormenting destructive way, he must have brooded over a sombre presentiment that he would never leave Greece alive.

The turning point and end of all Byron's hope was approaching; but he managed to keep up his defiant courage until the middle of February. He was plagued with difficulties and disappointment. In the first place, the rift between himself and the Benthamite Colonel Leicester Stanhope, his co-representative of the London Committee, had widened. Byron wanted immediate action, Stanhope, "the typographical colonel", preferred to trust in articles for the *Greek Chronicle*. Byron would limp away in frustrated fury at the sound of the Colonel's voice dictating. The two men's minds were far apart. Byron had fewer illusions than Stanhope; he was sceptical, for example, of any sudden perfectibility of the Greek character, also much more modest in his assessment of his own. Stanhope, for his part, wrote to London slyly voicing his doubt on the purity of Byron's liberalism. Stanhope believed that the propaganda of the press would succeed. Byron did not, pinning his faith on the military attack against Lepanto. Meanwhile at their conferences Mavrocordatos blinked owl-like behind his gold-rimmed glasses, avoiding his face. Was Mavrocordatos guilty of duplicity? Byron wondered. Oh, he was a fool ever to have come to Missolonghi, over-influenced by Hobhouse with his wishy-washy radicalism. But the stimulus of an impending adventure still upheld Byron. The artillery expert would shortly arrive. Then he would show Hobhouse and the world that he could do other things than write poetry. The capture of the fortress of Lepanto would outmatch anything Stanhope was likely to achieve on paper.

When Mr. William Parry, the third representative and delegate of the London Committee, arrived at Missolonghi he proved in the event less of a disappointment than a disaster. Grandiloquently styling himself "Major Parry of Lord Byron's Brigade, Commanding Officer of Artillery and Engineer in the service of the Greeks", he had been first mentioned to Byron in a letter from John Bowring, the honorary secretary of the London Committee, six months previously as "a very intelligent firemaster who was General Congreve's right-hand man, and understands the manufacture of every species of destructive arms and missiles. . . . We understand that large quantities of spoiled powder were found at Nauplia. Now Parry can make it as serviceable as if it had been made yesterday. He will also make Congreve rockets—Greek fire —and a variety of other mischievous things which will inspire terror into the Turks. He is a master of all the improvements in gunnery and of the maritime service of war."[6] Alas, Parry could do few of these things. At first Byron had been much impressed by him, by his energy and practical outlook after the subtleties and indecisions of Mavrocordatos and Stanhope. However, notwithstanding his downrightness and the fact that Byron liked him, Parry turned out to be a hollow reed. For during the eleven weeks he remained at Missolonghi he quarrelled with his own team of technicians, with the German officers of the artillery brigade, with the Greeks and with Byron's entourage. Trelawny described him as "a rough, burly fellow, never quite sober. . . . All he did was to talk and to drink." Moreover, Parry had no idea how to manufacture a Congreve rocket; for it was revealed he had only been a clerk in the Woolwich arsenal and that his sole previous experience in the use of artillery had come from his former service as firemaster in the Navy. Mr. Parry therefore proved as bitter a disappointment to the Greeks as the Greek cause and the situation he found at Missolonghi were to him. From the first all Parry and his staff did was to cause jealousy, disruption and dissension; and when he returned to England in May his mission remained unfulfilled.

Nevertheless, Parry's admiration for Byron solaced the poet's increasing self-tormenting diffidence; for he understood that there was no single person upon whom Byron could positively rely—not Mavrocordatos, Stanhope, Trelawny, Gamba, or Napier—and furthermore he believed that Byron's health was already failing. One man alone, Captain Frank Abney Hastings, the most intelligent, honest English philhellene of them all, had offered cooperation and service in his numerous and enthusiastic letters of advice. But who was this Hastings? The letters were obsessed with a fantastic foreboding of an Egyptian landing on Crete; besides, the fellow would keep trying to persuade him to buy one of these new-fangled steam-driven ships with which to undo to Turks! The project was absurd—the ship would explode. So Hastings's letters remained unanswered. A pity. If only the two men could have met, it is just possible that the story might have ended less tragically.

Accordingly the battle of Lepanto upon which Byron had pinned his cherished hope for victory and personal rehabilitation proved an abortive dream and was never fought. He managed to keep up his defiant courage until the middle of February, still manfully coping with each new vexing problem as it arose. But after the 15th of February his optimism finally deserted him; now he could only drift on, despairing and irritable, towards the inevitable conclusion of his life. The sad details of Byron's vanished health, the leeches and blood-letting, his rage at the ineptness of his doctors during the last embittered weeks and days belong to his familiar biography. Suffice it here to say that by Easter Sunday, April 18th, Byron was so ill that he had abandoned all hope. He said to Dr. Milligen: "Your efforts to preserve my life will be in vain. Die I must: I feel it. Its loss I do not lament; for to terminate my wearisome existence I came to Greece. My wealth, my abilities, I devoted to her cause. Well, there is my life to her. One request let me make to you. Let not my body be hacked, or be sent to England. Here let my bones moulder. Lay me in the first corner without pomp or nonsense." He died at 6.15 p.m. on Monday the 19th of April. The afternoon had been wet and sullen. From the lagoon towards sunset came the grumble of thunder.

Byron had died—though not in military action—full in the public eye, the cynosure of all Europe. And yet the peculiar destiny of his death amounted to action, for he had acted and suffered and shown the world that "it were better to die doing something than nothing". If only he could have lived two years longer to take part in the epic exodus from Missolonghi on Palm Sunday 1826 and lead, with his Souliotes, the counter-attack on the Turks and Egyptians, with the cry *"Elefteria E Thanatos"*—"Freedom or Death":

> Despite of every yoke she bears,
> That land is glory's still and theirs!
> 'Tis still a watchword to the earth:
> When man would do a deed of worth
> He points to Greece, and turns to tread,
> So sanction'd, on the tyrant's head:
> He looks to her, and rushes on
> Where life is lost, or freedom won.

Byron's complete failure at Missolonghi, failure to reconcile the Greek factions, failure to discipline the Souliotes, failure to capture the fortress of Lepanto, provide a variant of the Christian paradox that by losing his life a man will gain it. He (with the philhellenes surrounding him who lost their lives in action) became the phoenix for ever resurrected in youthful freshness from the ashes of his past. For Byron, more than any other single man, by "dying into life" had given to Greece what was noblest and indestructible in himself and made sure her eventual liberty.

Missolonghi did not fall until April 1826 and much happened in the meantime. The feud between Kolokotronis and the legitimate Government under Kondouriotis had been patched up in the early summer of 1824 on the arrival of the first instalment of the loan from London; for Kondouriotis (with Byron and Stanhope) had been named as one of the three commissioners for expending it. This confirmed Kondouriotis as President of the provisional Government. Kolokotronis permitted his son to surrender Nauplia to the Government in return for a share of the money and a promise of amnesty. The delivery of the loan had no sooner halted the civil war than fierce disputes arose about how to spend it, opening up new schisms. The second civil war during the last few months of 1824, initiated by the rebel primates Zaimis and Londos, once again challenged the authority of Kondouriotis's Government. The rebels were joined by Kolokotronis, still smarting under his defeat by the Central Government. Although this final rebellion against the Central Government was quickly crushed by the ruthless determination of John Kolettis, and Kolokotronis was captured and put in prison on Hydra, such divisive dissensions among the Greeks could have proved fatal because they were fighting each other instead of the Turks. Makriyannis, who fought for the Central Government, has described minutely in his *Memoirs* five separate battles, as well as minor incidents, all of them against his fellow Greeks. At first he had refused to join in, saying: "I took oath to fight Turks, not Greeks"; but loyalty to the Central Government eventually overcame his doubts.

The chief objective of the Turks during 1824 was to isolate the Peloponnese both by sea and by land in preparation for the deliverance of a knock-out blow against this heart of the rebellion the following year. At sea overwhelming assaults were launched on the naval islands of Kasos and Psara, each far distant from the mainland, and the two islands were successfully eliminated from the war by methods of extreme brutality. On land the Turks continued to concentrate on the siege of Missolonghi which had stood for three

The Heroic Struggle

years as a bulwark and interruption to their free access between mainland Greece and the Peloponnese. Both sides correctly regarded Missolonghi as a key to the war. Without doubt, in the eyes of Europe the squalid little fishing port had gained an added lustre from Byron's fateful passage across the scene.

Ibrahim Pasha, the mainstay and driving force behind the Sultan's hope of ending the Greek rebellion, perhaps came to his task too late; because by 1824 (albeit unofficially) the idea of Greece as an eventual independent state had taken root in the chancelleries of Europe. In spite of their insensate squabbles the Greeks had shown a considerable tenacity for survival as a political entity. Formal recognition was to come piecemeal and by indecisive stages. The patriotic conception of a new refurbished Hellas was fostered by the moving events of the past and the position in the present. The statesmen of Europe were beginning to take notice. So too was the City of London, as the two foreign loans of 1824 and 1825 attested. Though the financiers received not a penny of interest on their loans and, thanks to the maladroit management of the London Committee, the Greeks much less money than they should have done, the City was induced to back the loans, less from motives of philanthropy, than because of the simple fact that it now expected the Greeks to win. It was against this climate of opinion that Ibrahim Pasha took up the Ottoman cause.

Ibrahim was at the prime age of thirty-five, with ten years of experienced military service behind him, when the Sultan gave him command of the Peloponnese. He had helped his father to suppress the Mamelukes (the Egyptian equivalent of the Janissaries at Constantinople) and had triumphed in the war against the Wahabis in Arabia. He had always shown the utmost energy of purpose, sharing the hardships of his soldiers, never discouraged by failure. He had learned the value of discipline by drilling under Colonel Sève, a veteran of Napoleon's eastern expedition and so knew how to conduct a campaign on the European model. Although his past experience had made him one of the ablest generals in the Mediterranean, Ibrahim was not a prepossessing character. English officers, who were to see him at Navarino, described him as "short, grossly fat and deeply marked with smallpox". He was ferocious towards his enemies and was quite pre-pared, on the principle of Tacitus, to make a wilderness and call it peace and would not have scrupled to annihilate the Greek popula-tion, and re-people the Peloponnese with settlers from Egypt and Africa once it had been incorporated into the swelling Empire of Mehemet Ali. Ibrahim's expedition, which consisted of a squadron and an army of 17,000 men, sailed on July 10th, but for some months could do little more than ply between Rhodes and Crete for fear of the Greek fire-ships opposing his pathway to the Peloponnese. When the Greek sailors mutinied for arrears of pay, the way was open and Ibrahim landed at Modon on the 26th of February 1825. He stayed in the Peloponnese until the end of the war, when capitulation was forced upon him on the 1st October 1828 by the intervention of the Western Powers.

The elimination of Kasos and Psara and some other smaller islands from the war at sea left Ibrahim with the urgent task of neutralizing the bases from which the Greeks could operate their fire-ships. But he was unsuccessful in doing this before the winter. He and the Ottoman fleet commanded by the Capitan Pasha were also worsted in various engagements off the coasts of Asia Minor; and when he tried to force a landing on Samos and visit the island with the evil fates of Kasos and Psara he was completely routed by the fire-ships of Andreas Miaoulis. Ibrahim was once again to be thwarted by the skilled seamanship of Admiral Miaoulis when he attempted to land on Crete in November 1824.

The naval warfare belonging to this year revealed serious deficiencies in each of the rival fleets. Although the battle of Budrun (the ancient Halicarnassus) fought on the 10th of Septem-ber off the coast of Asia Minor was a decided victory for the Greeks and was honoured in a popular song:

> Were there but two like Miaoulis,
>   they had burned the fleet entire:
> were there another ship like his,
>   they had finished off the Armada!

neither side destroyed the other. However, whether Miaoulis

lacked the strategy or the final ounce of determination to press home his advantage, or was hampered by his colleagues, remains an open question. The Greeks withdrew to their respective islands for the winter.

The Ottoman navy had improved since the beginning of the war; but the effectiveness of the united Turkish and Egyptian fleets was impaired by the jealousy existing between Ibrahim and Khosrew, the Capitan Pasha, whose relationship was far from cordial. Ibrahim had noticed that the Egyptians often bore the brunt of the fighting, while the Turks kept out of danger. The Turkish gunners were usually so inefficient that the Greeks suffered small damage. Finlay, writing of an earlier episode at sea, quotes a typical comment from Byron: "These Turks, with so many guns, would prove dangerous enemies if they should happen to fire without taking aim."[8]

What the Greeks underestimated was Ibrahim's brute tenacity of intention; also they failed to realize that he did not regard the winter as a close season for operating at sea. Early in November he had tried once more to reach Crete with an impressive army transported from Alexandria; but Miaoulis had foiled this attempt by attacking the transports which were imprudently sailing ahead of the ships of war. Some of the transports were destroyed, others captured, the rest dispersed; so again the Cretan enterprise had to be postponed. Ibrahim finally achieved his objective in December, landing his troops at Souda Bay in the north-west of Crete, without falling in with a single Greek ship, for the Hydriot seamen had been mutinying because their pay was in arrears. Were they slaves or Turks, they demanded angrily, that they should work for nothing? They believed the sea to have been swept free of the Egyptians and were more interested in money than in glory. Miaoulis, with his unequivocal pure patriotism and his clear perception of the danger to Hellas, had implored his sailors not to return to their homes. They had refused to listen, and Miaoulis was obliged to yield. The Greek fleet had sailed for Nauplia, leaving the sea between the south-western coast of the Peloponnese and Crete unguarded.

With a foothold in Crete, which had been assigned to his

father's *pashalik*, Ibrahim reached the too hasty conclusion that, if he could outmanoeuvre the Greeks at sea, he should be able with less difficulty to crush them on land. He therefore spent two months preparing for the invasion of the Peloponnese which was of first interest to him as being nominally his own *pashalik*. The second phase of his plan of campaign opened when, on February 24th, 1825, he landed at Modon at the extreme south of the Peloponnese with an army of 4,000 infantry and 500 cavalry. The transports returned to Crete to bring back, without meeting any Greek interference, a further 6,000 infantry and 500 cavalry, as well as the necessary ordnance. To an impartial observer it must have appeared as though the tide of war had turned against the Greeks.

CHAPTER IX

Some Devious Fighting.
The Exodus from Missolonghi

The Greeks at first failed to grasp the dire import of Ibrahim's invasion. His unorthodox mid-winter crossing from Crete had taken the much too complacent Central Government completely by surprise. Ibrahim's purpose was to subdue the Peloponnese by a systematic ruthless plan of campaign launched against the forts from south-west to north-east. First Pylos and Navarino, with the historic small island of Sphakteria guarding the entrance to the bay; next Kalamata and Tripolitza and some citadels in the north-east, culminating in a grand finale by the capture of Nauplia itself.

President Kondouriotis's government responded with a dexterous resourcefulness and courage to the desperate peril into which their own complacency had betrayed them. If civil war had weakened them by lowering their prestige, it had enhanced their individual heroism and fighting qualities. The outstanding leaders of the revolution combined in a hastily contrived display of power to try and stem the tide of Ibrahim's advance. Clad in barbaric splendour Kondouriotis, followed by a long train of retainers, took the field in what was to be no more than a bombastic gesture. When he passed through the arched gateway of Nauplia on the 28th of March, the cannon from the ramparts and from the lofty fortress above roared out their salutations, to be answered by the shore batteries and by the shipping in the harbour. Mavrocordatos was present at the unsuccessful defence of Sphakteria where in the classical past Spartans had struggled against Athenians. Petrobey Mavromichalis fought in the Mani but was powerless to save Kalamata. In response to a clamorous public demand Kolokotronis had been released from prison on Hydra and once again made commander-in-chief of the Peloponnese, where his attempt to defend Tripolitza was foiled by the Egyptian forces. Ibrahim in June 1825 approached within sight of Nauplia.

At first it was not surprising that the Greeks' efforts to stop the energetic progress of Ibrahim's disciplined troops, mostly commanded by ex-officers of Napoleon's army, should have met with but scant success. Makriyannis has given a first-hand harsh, though not unjust, account of the battle of Sphakteria:

That day, brother readers, was poison for the country, which lost so many gallant lads and men of position, both soldiers and sailors. For all the country that day was poison, and for us it was like death itself, for we lost our comrades.

The battle now grew fiercer. Our position was extended and we were few. Not a drop of water. Sleepless day and night. And the leading commanders of our country were looking on from the high ground without stirring a finger. Such vast forces were gazing at us unmoved through their glasses as if we were not their brothers and comrades in arms. They saw us, and could hear the death song from the mouths of those very cannon of ours which were cutting us to pieces. The lagoon was full of drowned men like frogs in a marsh; just so they floated in the water. And the island was full of corpses. And the Greek forces looked at us from far off. This is what is wrought by faction, by dissension; and this is the result of constant civil war. Even today our comrades look at us from far off, in our hour of danger: each one of us looks on at the other. And Ibrahim becomes invincible so that History might say his men were brave, not that they were a multitude. In the first years forty men, a hundred, were enough to fill the land with Turkish dead. Then we worked without envy, like brothers, for our faith and country. Our politics were those of the honest, simple village-elder. . . . All this has brought ruin on our country, so that evil persons have been reborn: and the Peloponnesian looks upon the Roumeliot and the Roumeliot upon the Peloponnesian like the Turk in the days that we fought with him.[1]

Within two months of this bitter criticism Makriyannis himself was to be the means of halting Ibrahim's apparently irresistible advance and saving the capital, Nauplia. In early June the Egyptian army annihilated a force under Papaphlessas (the Archimandrite Dikaios, the former renegade and dissolute priest, who was now Minister of the Interior) that was trying to bar the way to Tripolitza. Papaphlessas was killed fighting like a lion. His defence had been in vain; but when his head was discovered among piles of dead Arabs, Ibrahim had it joined to the trunk and the body of the dead leader set upright against a post. For a while he regarded it in silence; then at last he spoke, "that was a brave and honourable man! Better to have spent twice as many lives to have saved his; he would have served us well!" Fired by Papaphlessas's heroic end, the courage of the Greeks had revived.

In the last week of June Ibrahim was encamped in the coastal plain of Argos by a site known as the Mills of Lerna (the scene where aeons ago Hercules had slain the mythic nine-headed hydra) but where now, unknown to Ibrahim, the bulk of the grain which belonged to the Greek Government was stored. Across the bay the town of Nauplia was in panic at the near approach of Ibrahim's army, prepared for evacuation or else surrender. Fortunately, Demetrios Ypsilantis and Constantine Mavromichalis, a brother of Petrobey, had the enterprise to sail over and organize what resistance remained possible with a pitiful two hundred and twenty-seven men. But on the field they found Makriyannis, with a hundred men, already preparing the Mills of Nauplion (as he called them in the *Memoirs*) for defence. They wisely left him in command.

The Egyptian troops fought all through the afternoon of June 25th suffering only comparatively heavy losses; but at nightfall they broke off the engagement to continue their march on Argos, which they destroyed by fire the following day. Although Ibrahim's army nearly reached the walls of Nauplia, with its fortress of Palamidi towering seven hundred and five feet above the sea, the foremost fortress in the Peloponnese, Ibrahim realized the impossibility of taking the capital without a regular protracted siege. He therefore made up his mind to withdraw his troops back in the direction of Tripolitza. On the 6th of July he once more outwitted the tactics of Kolokotronis who, with a hastily levied body of raw recruits, had been harassing his retreat, by simultaneously attacking all the Greek positions and compelling them to withdraw. Various mills, which the Greeks had failed to fortify, fell into his hands, ensuring him abundant supplies. In the autumn he would retire into winter quarters at Modon.

But Ibrahim's initial impulse was exhausted. He had outrun his lines of communication, banking too heavily upon the weakness of his opponents, whose pure patriotic strength of purpose had blunted the edge of his onslaught. Ibrahim's professional Frank-trained soldiers had achieved no decisive result. Though his scorched-earth policy had pulverized the homes and removed the livelihood of countless thousands of unhappy Greeks, all he had succeeded in doing was to have goaded more and more desperately defiant men and women into opposing him, without getting any closer to his objective. Although Ibrahim was still determined to destroy everything and let the inhabitants in the mountains perish of cold or starvation, yet the vital communications of the Peloponnese remained in Greek hands. Ibrahim controlled only such places as his army actually occupied.

In London most welcome reports were already reaching Canning. The statesmen of Europe, who now had their eyes turned towards Greece, were simultaneously outraged by Ibrahim's barbarism and both astonished and gratified by his lack of any obvious success. Ibrahim's commanding success would have to wait until the spring of 1826; but, paradoxically, the fall of Missolonghi at long last made it certain that he would lose both the war and his *pashalik*. Though taken by itself, Lerna had been little more than a skirmish inflicting fairly light casualties on both sides, decisive moral victories need not always depend upon a wholesale carnage. Makriyannis, by his example and courage, had saved Nauplia and encouraged the Greeks by puncturing the prestige for invincibility of the Egyptian army.

A French naval squadron under Admiral de Rigny was cruising in the Argolic Gulf at the time. The English and French fleets sailed close to the scenes of action, partly to protect their own commerce from possible acts of piracy, but also for humanitarian reasons. They were anxious to alleviate the war's horrors whenever they could; sometimes they were able to arbitrate between the contestants; and they reported back to their governments on the war's progress. Nevertheless, they were expected to preserve an Olympian neutrality that often proved less aloof than unpredictable. Greek and Turk alike could never be quite sure which side the fleet of one of the Great Powers would favour next. When Nauplia was threatened, de Rigny, thinking the Greeks' position to be worse than desperate, offered evacuation by sea and was indignantly refused. Makriyannis in his *Memoirs* describes the battle of Lerna, bringing alive whatever incident he touches:

> I sat down to take my meal. There came four French officers with men from the frigate to take aboard the pumps and the other gear which they had to draw water for washing their clothes, lest they be lost when the battle began. I kept the officers back to dine with me. They said "There are few of you, and those Turks, there are a lot of them and regulars too. This station is a weak one; Ibrahim has cannons with him, and you won't hold out." I replied, "When we raised our banner against this tyranny we knew that they were many and schooled in war, with cannons and every wherewithal: we were weak at every point: but God protects the weak: and if we die we die for our country, for our faith, and we shall fight against this tyranny as long as the strength is in us, God be our help. Death in this wise is sweet, for no man is born immortal, and when the angel of death comes, it might be his will to take us in sickness and misery; so it is better for us to die today." One of them kissed me, and I kissed him. Then they left.[2]

Makriyannis had warned his friends that if they were defeated, the Turks "wouldn't leave us even the holes in our nostrils". Of the end, after he had been wounded, he wrote:

> When the battle was ended I was taken off to the French frigate —the Admiral had sent a felucca with officers on board. As we

approached the frigate the band struck up. They wanted to keep me on board of the frigate to give me medical treatment. I refused. The doctors of the frigate bound my arm, and they and half a dozen officers escorted me to Nauplion, as soon as it was fairly dark. I was welcomed by the townsfolk at Nauplion and the Government.[3]

For three and a half years Missolonghi had been intermittently blockaded; though during that time the siege had been variously both pressed and relaxed. As Shelley had foreseen intuitively and Byron sealed by his heroic efforts and death, in the eyes of Europe Missolonghi had grown to be the visible symbol of Greek defiance of the whole might of the Ottoman Empire. Its defence, much assisted by Miaoulis's ships bringing men, supplies and munitions, must always rank, not only in the Greek War of Independence, but in world history as one of those paradoxical "defeats" like Thermopylae or Dunkirk that have unexpectedly helped to change the fate of nations. Here in a small town (new enough not to have existed at the time of the battle of Lepanto in 1571), built on the mud of the estuary of the lagoon, largely as a fishing port, and inhabited by peasants, shopkeepers and simple fishermen, Greek patriotism escaped from the selfish intrigues and broils which elsewhere had marred the cause of freedom.

That Missolonghi was able to hold out for nearly a year until the end of April 1826, was due partly to its better state of defence than during the former seige; to the jealousy existing between Ibrahim and Reshid Pasha; to the help supplied by Miaoulis's fleet, but most of all to the defiant heroism of the besieged. The garrison consisted of four thousand soldiers and one thousand citizens led by Greek captains of first-rate quality. There were also some twelve thousand non-combatants who unwittingly helped to drain the life-blood of the besieged. The defence was conducted by Notis Botsaris, a veteran Souliote; while a Primate from the Peloponnese, the heroic Papadiamantopulos, looked after the civil administration of the town. Since Byron's day, and mainly due to his exertions, the earth wall had been bastioned and much strengthened by other devices; the besieged had more and better artillery than the besiegers, and in the lagoon the islet of Marmora had been fortified.

Reshid Pasha, who had led the Ottoman army at the battle of Peta, had been warned by the Sultan that either Missolonghi or his own head must fall. So he turned to his task with determination, and on the 6th of April 1825 he led an army of wild Albanian troops through the pass of Makrynoros which, with reprehensible negligence, the Greeks had left unguarded. Towards the close of the month Reshid appeared before the town with 15,000 men, and on the 7th of May he opened the siege. Although in June he had received some further ordnance, he was prevented from pressing the siege by a shortage of ammunition—his mortars had to hurl rocks. An attack on the islet of Marmora was beaten off by the Greeks.

And then on the 10th of June a squadron of seven Hydriot ships sailed into the harbour with copious supplies and reinforcements from the Peloponnese, promising the quick arrival of even greater help. A month later a Greek watchman sighted several vessels in the offing and the people of Missolonghi who were then being hard-pressed, concluded with joy and relief that their promised salvation had come. They hoped that Reshid would even be forced to raise the siege. As the fleet drew nearer, however, their confident rejoicings were proved to have been premature. The ships were too numerous and too big to be Greek. The red Ottoman flag was identified both by Turk and Greek. The fleet was that of the Capitan Pasha, Khosrew. Though the spirits of the besieged sank, their constancy of purpose never wavered. Almost at the same time there had arrived from Patras a flotilla of flat-bottomed Turkish gunboats, very serviceable in the shallow waters of the lagoons. Reshid, with their help, was able to capture some of the unfortified off-shore islands and to invest Missolonghi by sea as well as by land.

Yet with each limited success of the besiegers the courage of the defenders seemed to mount. Before July was out the town had been reduced by shot and shell to a conglomeration of ruins. Twice the Turks managed to plant the flag of the Crescent on top of the ruins, but twice they were hurled back into the defensive ditch and obliged to give up. On the first two days of August fresh Turkish attempts to storm the town failed. They had lost five hundred men and Missolonghi remained inviolate. Reshid, in vindictive fury, caused some wretched prisoners to be brought before the walls and beheaded.

But in spite of this apparently triumphant resistance, the plight of those in Missolonghi was serious, even desperate. Hunger was weakening the garrison; their store of ammunition was all but spent. Had Reshid Pasha immediately renewed his attack, the result might well have been disastrous. However, at this critical moment the long-expected Greek fleet of forty sail was signalled as approaching. It was later divulged that the delay had been caused by the venal conduct of the Hydriot seamen in refusing to sail without double payment in advance, and that the Missolonghiots had been saved only by the opportune arrival of a loan from London. When on the 3rd of August the Greek fleet, having manoeuvred to windward of the enemy, sent their fire-ships bearing down on the flag-ship of the Capitan Pasha, Khosrew, who especially feared this form of warfare, stood his whole fleet out to sea. On the pretext that he intended to join up with the Egyptian fleet, he sailed away as fast as possible to Alexandria. Reshid Pasha was abandoned, left without support, the tables entirely turned on him. Miaoulis was now able to destroy the Turkish gunboats and to reprovision the town with plenty of food, powder and shells. The blockade had been lifted. A portion of the garrison under George Karaiskakis succeeded in regaining the islets in the lagoons. The Greek fleet sailed off in pursuit of the Capitan Pasha, leaving eight ships to keep communications open with the Ionian Islands and to deny supplies to the besieging Army.

Although Reshid now found himself in a worse than difficult position, short of ammunition, money, regular provisions, his strength of will did not falter. He sagaciously exchanged the sword for the spade and raised an enormous mound of earth against one of the bastions. The Greeks greeted this operation with shouts of derision. Nevertheless, the bastion Franklin was taken, only to be at once recaptured and three weeks of work wasted. In September sorties were made by the garrison, in conjunction with many citizens armed with pickaxes and spades to demolish the Ottoman earthworks, while the soldiers drove back the Turks. Then came the autumn rains to complete what the Greeks had begun, and Reshid watched the work of a year destroyed. No immediate further action against Missolonghi was possible. Reshid's army, reduced by death and desertion, was down to some three thousand men; so all he could do was to wait for help to arrive.

On account of the unwholesome and malodorous malarial swamps, Reshid Pasha withdrew his army to the more healthy foot of Mount Zygos where he entrenched himself defensively. Behind the Turkish camp the mountain passes were held by virile bands of Greek Armatoli; in front of the Turks lay Missolonghi. Only the foolish *laissez faire* of the too complacent Greeks probably saved the Ottoman army from destruction; for had the garrison combined with the Armatoli in a joint simultaneous attack the Turks would no doubt have been annihilated. But the Armatoli chieftains were either too preoccupied with jealous quarrels among themselves or too ignorant of military matters to sieze the opportune moment. The Greeks, for their part, were too satisfied to make the necessary effort of offensive action, no doubt expecting the Turks to retire to the Peloponnese for the winter. In this they were mistaken; for Reshid knew that he must either conquer Missolonghi or die before its walls. However, on the 18th of November the Capitan Pasha's fleet reappeared in the nick of time to save the Turks from starvation and, meeting only a token Greek squadron, took command of the sea.

And now Ibrahim, who had been ordered by the Sultan to combine with Reshid at Missolonghi, was advancing by forced marches from Navarino; after seizing some stores of grain intended for the beleaguered town on the way, he appeared on the 27th of November and held an immediate war council with Reshid and Yussuf Pasha. The three men agreed to support one another as much as lay in their power and to press the siege with the utmost vigour. But there was bad feeling between Ibrahim and Reshid, who resented the mere presence of the Egyptian commander, particularly when Ibrahim failed to ask for his help and advice. Ibrahim boastfully exacerbated the situation: "What! Were you kept out eight months by this fence? Why, I took Navarino in eight *days*!" The boast, in the event, would not be justified. Yet Reshid revealed himself as a bloodthirsty monster, venting his suppressed rage by a ferocious act of cruelty. He caused a priest, three boys and two women to be impaled as spies in front of the walls of the town. The boys must have been above twelve years old; for had they been less, they would have been spared but compelled to embrace Mohammedanism.

The Greek Government was seriously alarmed by Ibrahim's threat to the town; for now the fate of Missolonghi and Greece seemed to be one. How were they to relieve the besieged? The treasury was empty and all attempts failed to float a new loan. The answer was given by personal patriotism. Sufficient money was raised by private subscription to allow Miaoulis to equip a fleet for the relief of Missolonghi, and on the 21st of January he landed some stores on the island of Vasiladi. But then, attacked by the dual Turco-Egyptian fleet, he was forced to retire. The Greeks, however, by means of a fire-ship destroyed an Ottoman corvette; and on the 28th of January they were victorious in a sea-battle; so that before February Miaoulis had been able to supply the town with two months' provisions. Then, unfortunately, contrary to their usual brave and buccaneering spirits, his Hydriot sailors had refused to continue fighting without receiving their payment in advance. Miaoulis was obliged to sail home. So once more the Turks took command of the sea.

Ibrahim was unable to put into effect any active operations while the winter rains flooded the marshes around the town, rendering them impassable. During the final three days of February his batteries, mounting forty pieces of artillery, bombarded Missolonghi with a hail of iron and two unsuccessful attempts were made by his drilled regiments of united Turks and Egyptians to storm the walls. Three times, after gaining a foothold on the walls, the Arab guard was hurled back by the gallant determination of the Greeks. Ibrahim was furiously aware that he stood small chance of taking the town unless he could invest it both by sea and land. One may believe that Reshid unkindly demanded to know what he thought of "the fence" now. However, with a flotilla of thirty-two flat-bottomed boats Ibrahim was soon in control of the lagoon. The fort of Vasiladi, which commanded the entrance to the lagoon leading by sea straight to Missolonghi, was taken by storm on March the 9th and the town of Anatoliko capitulated on March the 13th. Its three thousand inhabitants were spared by the honourable terms of the capitulation and sent in transports to Arta.

Both Greek and Turk—as well as Sir Frederic Adam, the Lord High Commissioner of the Ionian Islands—had by now perceived that this was the beginning of the end, that the fall of Vasiladi and Anatoliko had rendered the fate of Missolonghi inevitable. The Greeks enjoyed one final gleam of brilliant success. The islet of Klissova, about a mile to the south-east of Missolonghi, was still in their possession and was magnificently defended by the garrison of a hundred and fifty soldiers led by the brave Kitzo Djavellas. On the 6th of April an attack by some two thousand of Reshid's Albanians was repulsed by the Greeks' lethal fire power. The Albanians, leaping from the flat-bottomed boats, tried to scramble ashore through water and mud soon to be cumbered with dead. Though Ibrahim's much more disciplined troops made a second attack, the Egyptians were no more successful than the Albanians. Three separate assaults were driven back by the Greeks, and in the third Hussein Bey Djeritlee, the conqueror of Kasos, Crete, Sphakteria and Vasiladi, fell mortally wounded by a musket-ball. The Greeks lost only thirty-five men and held the island. Of the Turks five hundred men were killed or wounded in vain.

Perhaps if at this point the Greeks had made a mass sortie against the temporarily discouraged besiegers, they might have succeeded in cutting their way through the enemy ranks. But though the Missolonghiots were hard pressed for provisions and rations were now being doled out only to those who were performing some useful service, as each hour passed the Missolonghiots, still confidently expected Miaoulis to arrive and bring them relief. So they did nothing but wait. When Miaoulis's fleet had at last appeared at the end of March, it was found to be disappointingly small and poorly armed. The combined Turco-Egyptian navy had the overwhelming advantage. After the failure of a weak attempt by the Hydriots to penetrate the lagoon and revictual the unfortunate town, there was nothing Miaoulis could do except abandon Missolonghi to its fate.

Ibrahim had seized his opportunity to offer Missolonghi respectable terms of surrender. The garrison would be permitted to withdraw in safety and the people allowed either to follow or to remain in their battered homes under the protection of the Sultan. But the heroic defenders, with nothing to believe in except the imminent near-certainty of disaster, decided to hold out. They would face every danger and privation rather than agree to surrender. This "undaunted mettle" was in the true spirit of Greek patriotism, past or present, and was to earn the admiration of the world. As for the terms, however honourable, the people would have none of them. The Missolonghiots had made their choice. They had chosen to live, or to die, as free men and women.

The climax could no longer be delayed. The conditions in the town had grown pitiable:

The starved inhabitants wandered amid the ruins of their homes, looking more like ghosts than living men. For days they had been reduced to subsisting upon the most loathsome food; and now even rats and mice were luxuries no longer obtainable. The sick and wounded, for whose care it was impossible to make provision, lay in neglect and filth, rotting in a living death. The brave defenders of the shattered walls, weakened by hunger, could scarcely any longer bear the weight of their arms. And now, even of the most miserable food, rations remained for only two more days. Yet no voice was raised in favour of surrender.[4]

The Missolonghiots in a consultative assembly decided that there was but one remaining chance: to cut a passage to freedom for the entire population through the lines of the enemy. Hopefully, it was thought that in the confusion and surprise of this unexpected attack, though many would be slaughtered, a fair proportion of the besieged might well escape to a life of liberty; but dead or living they would all be alike free.

The plan for evacuating the town on the night of the 22nd of April 1826 was well conceived by the Souliote, Notis Botsaris. Contact was established with the chieftain Karaiskakis, who agreed to send a strong force of Armatoli to Mount Zygos to make a feint attack behind the Turkish camp which would divert the attention of the besiegers. The sound of gun-fire would be the signal for the mass sortie. The Missolonghiots would be divided; one band would attack Reshid's camp, the other, with the women and children, would attempt to force its way through Ibrahim's Egyptians. Once they had broken through, they could join up with the Armatoli on Mount Zygos and find security in the mountains. But tragically the plan was betrayed to Ibrahim by a Bulgarian deserter. And Karaiskakis failed to carry out his part of the programme: Botsaris's messenger discovered him stretched out ill in his tent; while the other Armatoli chieftains seemed too involved in their selfish private disputes to care much what happened to the heroic Missolonghiots. On the afternoon of the 22nd Botsaris, with only about two hundred men, marched to Mount Zygos, but fell into a trap laid for him by Ibrahim when he met two thousand Albanians posted there to cut him off. The sound of the firing which followed was taken by the besieged to mean that the Armatoli had reached the agreed rendezvous. Unhappily, it also warned Ibrahim and Reshid—though they probably never anticipated a mass exodus of the whole population—that a sortie by the garrison might be expected that night. They had therefore taken every precaution to repulse the Greeks.

At about sunset a discharge of musketry on the ridge of Zygos was taken by the Missolonghiots as the signal for the exodus to begin. The garrison, divided into three divisions, were lying in the shallow moat in front of the walls. Bridges were thrown across this moat and breeches opened in the walls.

There were still nine thousand persons in the town, of whom only three thousand were capable of bearing arms. Nearly two thousand men, women, and children were so feeble from age, disease, or starvation, that they were unable to join the sortie. Some of the relations of these helpless individuals voluntarily remained to share their fate. The non-combatants, who were to join the sortie, were drawn up in several bodies. . . . Most of the women who took part in the sortie dressed themselves in the fustinello, like the Albanians and armatoli, and carried arms like soldiers; most of the children had also loaded pistols in their belts, which many had already learned to use.[5]

Near midnight the moon rose. Now, with impatient shouts, the excited soldiers, their nerves stretched to breaking-point, sprang out of the moat and hurled themselves against the enemy; simultaneously men, women and children started to crowd across the bridges. The Turks reacted with a savage fusillade from their trenches, while the Ottoman guns caused havoc among the packed non-combatants on the bridges. In the vast confusion of shot and shell, amid the shrieks of the wounded and the splash of bodies thrown into the water, the larger part of the inhabitants miraculously managed to cross in reasonably good order. Yet it was hard for the Missolonghiots to abandon their homes and many had still lingered behind. As soon as the first body of Missolonghiots had reached the other side, the garrison had rushed with drawn swords on the Turks. But presently one or two non-combatants caught in the crush on the bridge suddenly cried out in terror "Back! back!" and panic spread. In the belief that all was lost, obeying a blind impulse of fear, many turned and fled back into the Town. The Turks, uttering blood-curdling cries of "Allah! Allah", jumped from their trenches and pursued the wretched fugitives into Missolonghi.

There was a grim slaughter. In a "night of cloudless climes and starry skies" the indifferent moon looked down on an awful spectacle of carnage which needs no elaboration. Yet this night of lurid horror had its redeeming aspects of cool courage and sublime heroism. Two examples must suffice. In one of the bastions (named after Botsaris) of the fortifications a lame man sat waiting, lin-stock in hand, for the Turks to arrive. When they surged over the battlements he put his lighted match to the powder-magazine and blew both himself and his enemies to kingdom come. The Primate Papadiamantopulos of Patras, a pre-eminent Hetairist who was one of the executive commission responsible for the administration of Western Greece, had been living in Zante to procure supplies for the besieged and had been urged by his friends to stay there. But when matters were at their most critical the devoted old gentleman had returned through many dangers to Missolonghi to die a hero's death with his fellows in the final sortie. "He silenced every entreaty by the simple observation: 'I invited my countrymen to take up arms against the Turks, and I swore to live and die with them. This is the hour to keep my promise'."6

Those Greeks who had not panicked back into the town, led by Botsaris, by Makris, by Djavellas, thrusting and slashing with their long sharp yataghans in the Turkish trenches, succeeded with a comparatively small loss of life in cutting their way through the Ottoman lines. Doubtless the confusion and lack of light helped them; also the inclination of the brutalized Turkish soldiers to prefer the more rewarding pleasures of rapine in the town. The Greeks now supposed themselves to be safe, but how mistakenly! Once in the open, Ibrahim's cavalry charged and scattered their already broken ranks; for foot soldiers were powerless against cavalry. Escape was made still more difficult by the fitful moonlight which betrayed the movements of the fugitives. It was only a sorry residue of men and women who managed to reach the steep slopes of Mount Zygos where the rugged quality of the ground checkmated the horses. Gordon records an individual act of bravery of one of the Roumeliote women: "A young girl, and her brother in delicate health, being overtaken by an Ottoman horseman, she, seeing that the youth was spent with fatigue, carried him on her back to a neighbouring hillock, seized his gun, received the fire of the Turk, and returning it, shot him dead."7

Here at last the fugitive army expected to be safe, for here Karaiskakis was to have met them with his Armatoli. But there were no Greeks; nor could they elicit any response to their signals. Utterly exhausted by marching and fighting, the vagrant army halted to rest in the deep shadowy cool of the forest and to collect up their dispersed forces. Suddenly a destructive volley rang out and the whole undergrowth round them seemed lit up by the flashes of muskets. Instead of the anticipated help from friendly Armatoli, they had fallen into an ambush planned by Reshid and were being attacked by a large body of his Albanians. Many fell at the first volley; and any worthwhile resistance was impossible. Makris launched a brisk counter-attack, and, belatedly, about three hundred of Karaiskakis's troops came to the rescue, gaining the Greeks a breathing-space. But it was a pitiful remnant of fugitives who under cover of darkness struggled on up the mountain to eventual safety in Amphissa. A great number died of starvation and exposure on the roads. Rocks and forest paths were strewn with dead bodies. In Missolonghi itself Ibrahim boasted of his war trophy: a ghastly pile of three thousand heads. According to Gordon, of the original nine thousand inhabitants of Missolonghi, "500 perished in the sortie, 600 subsequently starved to death, and perhaps 1800 escaped, near 200 of the latter being females . . . and from 3000 to 4000 women and children were made slaves."

If Missolonghi held out to the end of April 1826, the honour was due to the skill and boldness of Admiral Miaoulis's fleet in thrice relieving it; to the jealous relationship existing between Ibrahim and Reshid Pasha; but above everything to the valour and unshaken tenacity of the garrison. Of these Greek soldiers even their foes admitted that their courage and constancy could have gone no further; so the Missolonghiots kept true to their word and, whether in life or in death, had remained free.

Today Missolonghi is entered through the Venetian walls by the restored "Gate of the Sortie", out of which the exodus was made. Within the gate is the agreeable Garden of Heroes, shady with yew-trees, pine, palm and eucalyptus, where only the tireless chirping of innumerable cicadas breaks the summer silence. By the old ditched earthen walls stand four British cannon, survivors of the forty-eight cannon that defended Missolonghi in 1825–1826 through 366 sanguinary days. Perhaps most moving of all is the tumulus, the common burial mound beneath which lie the bones of countless unknown Greek men and women, beside those of the foreign philhellenes from many different countries, who fell in the fight for freedom during the three separate sieges. To the right is the tomb of Notis Botsaris—"The Son of Greece". Close by in the centre of the garden stands a full length statue of Byron, curly-headed, his shoulders cloaked in a military cape, his eyes turned towards the sea and the grey limestone mountains of the Peloponnese, the centre of the revolution. On the base is the following inscription:

Stranger, stop in front of this English Lord Byron upon whom the Muses have bestowed their love. For all the great deeds which Byron did for Greece, the Greeks have erected this statue because at a time when Greece needed encouragement and help, he gave fully of himself to those who were beseiged.

The fall of Missolonghi added a powerful impetus to the wave of philhellenic enthusiasm which afterwards swept over Europe. International public opinion forgot the follies, and often selfish conduct of the Greeks and could see only a small and gallant country fighting for its existence "against fearful odds". In France and Germany, even in Austria, societies were formed to help the Greeks, much to the chagrin of Metternich who rightly felt his reactionary policy to be threatened. Even the Crown Prince of Prussia and Ludwig of Bavaria appeared to be against him. If the coffers of the Greek Government grew empty, they were quickly replenished with foreign gold. Also the Greek armies were continually being reinforced by European volunteers, until Reshid Pasha himself was heard to exclaim with bitterness and disillusion, "We are no longer fighting the Greeks, but all Europe!"

CHAPTER X

The Siege of Athens.
The Battle of Navarino

The fall of Missolonghi, ostensibly a triumph for Ibrahim, was to
have unforeseen paradoxical consequences. Clearly it had removed
a barrier which had kept the Ottoman armies confined in that
north-west corner of Greece and the tide of war now flooded
eastwards. But Ibrahim—not entirely to Reshid's disappointment—soon showed that he had no intention of taking part in the
invasion of Eastern Greece. Instead, he returned to his own *pashalik*
of the Peloponnese where he proposed to resume his bloodthirsty
methods of pacification. Yet the event proved that in 1826
Ibrahim not only wasted the Peloponnese but wasted his time.
He was short of funds and reinforcements and squandered the
summer in relative inactivity.

Not so Reshid Pasha. As soon as he was free of his hated rival,
he was so successful in quickly pacifying Western Greece that in
July, before the harvest, he was ready to advance into Eastern
Greece. He had occupied the mountain passes without meeting
with too serious resistance; he was able to reinforce the garrison
at Thebes and effect a junction with Omer Vrioni's forces in
Euboea. Then the united Ottoman army of some 8,000 men, with
a full complement of guns and cavalry, marched into Attica.
Reshid's objective, of course, was Athens, the final stronghold
north of the Isthmus of Corinth to remain in Greek hands. He laid
seige to the town. The historic Acropolis, with its immortal
memories, was now, as Missolonghi had been, the cynosure of all
Europe. The holy Parthenon shone in European eyes, for it seemed
to be the last bulwark of Hellenic freedom. If it fell, there would
be collapse in the Peloponnese. But so long as the Acropolis

remained impregnable, the Peloponnese was secure. Reshid would not dare to advance, leaving such a symbolic fortress unconquered in his rear.

Odysseus Androutsos by this time was dead and Yannis Gouras, his former lieutenant, ruled Eastern Greece for the Government in his place. But Gouras was much less a civil administrator than a hardened and avaricious brigand chief, whose tyrannical exactions and general misrule struck the poor peasantry of Attica as worse than the persecution of the Turks. Reshid had been swift to take advantage of this state of affairs by making concessions to the peasants and by granting them portions of public lands; thus by a politic generosity he transformed the atmosphere of Attica from hostile to friendly. So Reshid was able to advance quickly on Athens and lay siege to it. Gouras and his followers took shelter in the Acropolis, brutally repulsing those townspeople who tried to follow him. Left to their fate, they were in no position to make a protracted resistance, and on August the 25th the Turks took the town by storm. A fresh stream of terrified fugitives arrived at the Acropolis whom Gouras admitted this time. But Reshid was to be baffled for more than a year in his efforts to bring about the surrender of the Acropolis.

If the Acropolis fell . . . the totality of this possible disaster braced the supine Government of Greece faced by a common peril to close ranks and put aside their divisions. There was one man who might yet, if he wished, save Greece, George Karaiskakis. The son of a nun by a klepht chieftain, Karaiskakis, associated previously with Ali Pasha, had been appointed commander-in-chief in central Greece after the fall of Missolonghi. He was an extraordinary man whose career and character reveal a duality of black and white, a contrast of shamelessness and nobility that lends such dramatic colour to many of the actors in the Greek revolution. Bred among the brigands of Epirus, he had never lacked a reputation for absolute courage, combined with a crafty wit, qualities which had endeared him to the old Lion of Yannina. Although after the death of Ali, Karaiskakis, living as a klephtic chieftain in the mountains, had eventually identified himself with the Greek cause, his patriotism was far from being above suspicion. He was known to have bargained with the Turks and was suspected of having on more than one occasion acted with the same selfish interest as Odysseus had done. However, both his courage and his skill as a leader were exemplary, and among the Armatoli his name had become a legend. "Why are you running, fool," they would cry out when any one fled, "as though Karaiskakis were after you?" Karaiskakis was the only captain of whom the Albanians of Reshid's army were afraid. He knew he was distrusted with reason by Zaimis the Greek President who had agreed to forget old scores and had embraced him in public. What in effect Karaiskakis now said was: "Hitherto I know I have often been a bad boy—now I will be a good boy!" And he kept true to his word, translating himself from an untrustworthy minor partisan chieftain into a great national commander who surrendered his selfish interests to the dedicated service of his country and sealed this devotion by his death.

Karaiskakis's plan was to advance by way of Eleusis in the direction of Athens and raise the siege of the Acropolis. Although he proved at first successful in harassing the Turkish communications spread over the countryside, with the support of the French Colonel Fabvier at the head of a thousand well trained troops (hired by the Greeks to stiffen their own more undisciplined troops, as Colonel Sève had done for Ibrahim's), his advance was halted at Chaidari by a rapid attacking movement from the Ottoman cavalry and had to be abandoned. Later on, in 1827 two foreign notables, the English commanders-in-chief on land and at sea, General Sir Richard Church and Lord Cochrane arrived on the scene to strengthen Greek resistance. These were unofficial appointments so far as the British Government was concerned, privately negotiated by the Greek Government who here showed an instinctive, shrewd flair for signs of a swelling foreign interest in their cause.

Of the Greeks' varying ill-fortunes during the more than year-long siege of Athens, perhaps the most significant phenomenon is how misfortune enabled them to unite. Pouqueville, who had once been French consul-general at the court of Ali Pasha and was a familiar figure in Greece, wrote in his *Histoire de la Régénération de la Grèce* the simple truth, "Les Grèces sont étonnants dans l'adversité." There came a moment of crucial danger when it looked as though Ibrahim intended to occupy the strategically important island of Spetsai. The islanders, rather than risk being forced to surrender, approached their neighbour Hydra, asking if they might transfer the whole population to that island. They received a noble reply, passed unanimously by the people of Hydra in brotherly love and concord in the interests of their common safety:

> So you shall have all the accommodation you need . . . without paying a farthing rent, so long as you stay here. Any differences that exist between your citizens and our citizens are forgotten and shall not be mentioned so long as we live together. Hasten your coming then, brethren, every family of you, so that the whole expedition may the sooner take place; and your families will find their houses empty and ready when they arrive here; and you will find the most brotherly greeting from all of us.

But the barbarians never came. . . . There was no need for an evacuation of Spetsai because Ibrahim, for whatever reasons, relapsed into comparative inertia. All the same, Hydra had sent a splendid reply.

In the summer the defence of the Acropolis looked in danger of collapsing. Much of the garrison was made up of mercenaries and brigands who were no Missolonghiots prepared to stake all for love of their country. The conditions within the narrow citadel as the siege continued grew ever grimmer and more intolerable; for the rock of the Acropolis was only a hundred and fifty yards wide and some three hundred yards long. The interior "was densely built up, and earth and debris was thick enough upon it for trees to grow. The gutted Parthenon still harboured a mosque within its columns, and the Erectheum, then half underground, became Gouras's command post. The old town, the modern Plaka, lay to the North."[1] And so desertions became more frequent and on more than one occasion there had been outbreaks of mutiny. Gouras kept up a constant fusillade against the enemy so that they would remain on the alert and his men be unable to escape through the Turkish ranks in the darkness. Then at last Gouras himself was killed on the 13th of October. It seemed as if the fortress must now fall; but Gouras's heroic wife stood in front of the soldiers, first upbraiding them for faint-heartedness and then exhorting them to a renewal of courage; and, helped by Makriyannis, she persuaded them to carry on with the defence.

Late in 1825 Makriyannis, who had just recovered from a serious wound that nearly cost him an arm, had joined the regulars under the admirable French philhellene, Colonel Fabvier, who helped to stiffen the Greek resistance. Makriyannis had meanwhile married, with Gouras as best man at his wedding. There is an episode (immediately preceding the death of Gouras in the autumn of 1826) which shines with a certain quality, both lyrical and tragic, typical of the siege. Gouras was suffering from deep sadness over some comrades who wished to save their skins and desert in the hour of danger for their country:

When I beheld his grief I spoke with some Athenians of high place and they went and told him, "Do not take it too hard that these men want to quit. This citadel will be guarded by us who won it from the Turks. And we shall not give it them back now unless they kill us."

So Gouras and the others sat down and we took our meal. We sang and made merry. Gouras and Papakostas asked me to sing, for we had gone so long without singing, so long since the self-seekers set us to quarrelling so they might accomplish their evil plans. I sang well, and I gave them this song:

The Sun had set (ah, men of Greece, a Sunset for you!)
And the Moon was no more to be seen,
No more to be seen the clear Morning Star,
Nor the Star of Eve that shines in its place,
For these four held council, and spoke in secret,
The Sun spins round and tells them, spins round and says
"Last night when I set I hid myself behind a little rock,

And I heard the weeping of women, and the mourning of
  men
For those slain heroes lying in the field,
And all the earth soaked in their blood—
Poor souls all gone below in their country's cause."

Gouras groaned in his misery and said, "Brother Makriyannis, may God grant a good end to this: you have never sung
with such feeling before. May this song bode well for us." "I
was in the mood," I said, "for we have not sung for so long."
For formerly in our camps we were always making merry.

The fighting started and a fierce firing flared up. I took my
men and went to our appointed post. I stayed there some time
while we fought. I made a tour round the posts outside. I went
to my quarters to send out the messenger to the Government,
as the moon had begun to set. Men came up and said, "Come
quick, Gouras has been killed at his post. He fired at the Turks,
they shot back at the flash and hit him in the temple, and he
never spoke a word." I went, and we took him on our shoulders
and put him inside a dungeon; his family laid him out and we
buried him.[2]

By July 1827 it looked as though the Turks had won the war.
Indeed, this too confident claim was made by Ottoman writers
at the time. For disaster had befallen the Greeks in the last remaining free corner of the mainland. In May Karaiskakis fell mortally
wounded at Munychia near Athens; and on the 5th of June Sir
Richard Church had advised the Greeks to surrender the Acropolis. Earlier in the summer Ibrahim was again terrorizing across
the Peloponnese where the Greeks, instead of returning to aid
Karaiskakis in trying to save Athens, were disputing amongst
themselves. In July they even fought each other in the streets of
Nauplia, where only the intervention of a British naval force
commanded by Admiral Sir Edward Codrington put an end to
this private war. The Sultan's armies had by now reduced the
land-revolt to the area of the Peloponnese and appeared to have
every chance of finally crushing the rebellion. The Greek mastery

at sea, Hellenic political rhetoric, the philhellenes and the Greeks' financial supporters—even the English commanders-in-chief—all seemed to have failed them. Yet at the eleventh hour the Turks were denied their anticipated total victory by the intervention of a timely external event.

This was an agreement reached on the 6th of July at the Conference of the Powers in London on the terms of the Treaty of London, which derived directly from the Protocol of St. Petersburg that had been signed in April 1826. The main architect of the Treaty, ratified in the nick of time, was the liberal-minded Tory, George Canning, who had succeeded Lord Liverpool as Prime Minister on the 10th of April and died only four months later on the 8th of August, leaving behind this progressive legacy of his short premiership. As members of the Holy Alliance, Austria and Prussia had abstained from supporting the decisions of the Conference and so were out of the running as "Protecting Powers". Though the freedom and independence of Greece was by no means yet guaranteed, Canning had taken an important step forward when he "was happily inspired to put up a barrier to Russian aggression in the Levant by erecting an independent Greek nation, rather than by supporting the continued abominations of Turkish misrule."[3]

But Canning had moved only gradually towards perceiving and backing the case for Greek freedom, through slow separate stages such as initially the recognition of the Greek naval blockade as far back as March 1823, and the liquidation of the Levant Company in the summer of 1825, which while it existed had strongly biased British diplomacy in favour of the Turks. By the Treaty of London the three contracting parties, Britain, France and Russia, bound themselves to secure the autonomy of Greece under the suzerainty of the Sultan, without rupturing friendly relations with the Porte. To this end—a far from easy objective—the fleets of the three allied Powers under Admirals Sir Edward Codrington, de Rigny, and Count von Heyden, were to blockade the Peloponnese against Turkish and Egyptian ships, with the hope of compelling Ibrahim Pasha to return to Egypt. However, in its published clauses the terms of the Treaty were vague, if not obscure. In addition secret clauses had been attached to the original Protocol providing that, if the Sultan declined to mediate, the powers were to enter into commercial relations with the Greeks, suggest an armistice to both sides, and "jointly exert all their efforts to accomplish the object of such armistice, without, however, taking any part in the hostilities between the two contending parties." It will be noticed that, although the intention of using force had been disclaimed—and without force the object of the blockade seemed at least dubious—an equivocal and perhaps unfairly wide discretion had been left to the admirals.

Both luck and personal credit belong largely to Mavrocordatos who, throughout the war, was responsible for the direction of Greek foreign policy and for bringing England over to the Greek side. Much depended upon England's attitude. The Greeks' luck lay in the astonishing fact that during the year which succeeded the opening of the Conference of London in 1827, Britain had no less than four prime ministers and in a remarkably advantageous order: Lord Liverpool until April, Canning until August, Lord Goderich until December, and Wellington in the first month of 1828. Like Lord Castlereagh—Metternich's henchman—Wellington was pro-Turk; had he followed Lord Liverpool as prime minister, there might have been no Treaty of London. The effect of this on the Battle of Navarino was to be crucial. Meanwhile, the British public, influenced by Byron's self-sacrifice and death, and at that time profoundly pro-classical in its culture, idealized the Greek Chieftains as if they had been the heroes of Thermopylae.

When Lord Stratford de Radcliffe (formerly Stratford Canning, Canning's cousin) was transferred from St. Petersburg to become British Ambassador at Constantinople, he had been authorized to visit Greece on the way. In January 1826 he conferred with Mavrocordatos on Hydra; and, although their meeting proved to be something of a non-event, it did serve to raise Greek hopes of Britain and enabled Mavrocordatos to commit the fate of Greece more fully to British protection. On the mainland the bitter factional disputes continued throughout the year with rival presidents of rival Assemblies. This quarrel was resolved for the time being when, early in 1827, General Sir Richard Church and Lord Cochrane arrived on the scene and made it plain that they could not serve under two divisive authorities. They had been privately invited to come to Greece by the previous government of Kondouriotis. So the rival presidents resigned. A reconvened session of the third National Assembly met in March near the ancient classical site of Troezene and ratified the appointments of the English philhellenes as commanders-in-chief.

Although these two paladins of fortune arrived too late in Greece to have much serious effect on the fighting, they rendered a conspicuous service to the moral cause of freedom and the grateful Greeks adored General Sir Richard Church. But as soon as Church and Cochrane assumed command of land and sea operations to bring relief to besieged Athens, they met with serious difficulties over coming to an agreement with those commanders already in power, such as Karaiskakis, and Colonel Fabvier who naturally took a pride in his position. After Church and Cochrane had departed, the third National Assembly at Troezene resumed its work. The most notable decision was to elect Capodistrias, then in exile at Geneva, President of Greece; but being uncertain whether or not Capodistrias would accept this office, the Assembly appointed a committee of three to carry out the presidential duties.

The surrender of the fortress of the Acropolis on the 5th of June, which followed on the advice of Sir Richard Church, did more honour to the Turks than to the Greeks. Church had moved his base from Piraeus to the eastern part of the bay of Phalerum, and a month earlier had landed there his main offensive force. It was an unfortunate choice of terrain because the open downs in front of him provided no cover at all for infantry but offered a handy manoeuvring ground for the Turkish cavalry. And Church had caused a good deal of dissatisfaction by chartering a splendid armed schooner to use as a yacht, and establishing his headquarters in this unmilitary vessel. These Greek troops, uncheered by Church's presence, without any eagerness or order straggled forward across the open space. Suddenly, from a ravine in which they had stayed hidden, a large force of Ottoman cavalry flashed down upon them. After no more than a token resistance, the

Greeks broke and fled. Cochrane and Church, who had just landed from their yachts, were met by a throng of hard-pressed fugitives rushing panic-stricken to the shore. The English commanders had scarcely time to wade into the sea and climb into their boats before the defeated soldiers were almost upon them. There was nothing to be done now but train the ships' guns on the Turks and hold them back until as many fugitives as possible could be taken off in the boats. Though many were saved, some 1,500 Greeks died in this shocking rout.

It was only natural that Church and Cochrane should have forfeited some credit in Greek eyes, although the battle itself was not of major importance. They were blamed for failure to have grasped the true tactical situation. The army of irregulars now melted away and any hope of driving Reshid Pasha from Attica or relieving the Acropolis had to be relinquished. Church held on to his position at Munychia for three weeks longer, more for the sake of "face" than for any practical good it could do the Greeks. When he abandoned the post and ordered the garrison of the Acropolis to yield the fortress up to the Turks, he met at first with a scornful refusal. "We are Greeks," they answered "and determined to live or die free. If Reshid wants our arms, let him come and fetch them!" Such heroics of course were unavailing. Negotiations were opened with the Ottoman commander-in-chief through Admiral de Rigny who happened to be in the harbour. A rumour that his rival Ibrahim was on his way from the Peloponnese made Reshid more prepared to offer moderate terms; his conduct in carrying them out with notable straightforwardness gained him immortal renown. On the 5th of June the garrison of the Acropolis marched out with the full honours of war, while Reshid Pasha himself patrolled the ground at the head of a disciplined body of horsemen to see that his troops, who were escorting the Greeks to the place of embarkation, observed the terms of the capitulation.

The Battle of Navarino has been copiously documented and illustrated, pictorially for example in the imaginative interpretation of the Greek primitive painter, Panayiotis Zographos, under the inspiration of General Makriyannis; and by the depictions of various phases of the battle by other artists such as H. P. Reinagle, the Frenchman A. L. Garneray, and by W. Daniell, some of them now in the National Maritime Museum at Greenwich. Since, therefore, on all the evidence Navarino rests securely as one of the most important and remarkable of British naval engagements, it remains something of a puzzle why it is so little known and finds so small a place in our history books. For like Trafalgar, Navarino was a decisive battle which determined the result of a war and settled the destiny of a nation. To understand the tortuous complication of events which led up to it, it is necessary to hark back.

During the early summer of 1826 Sultan Mahmud, fuming at fresh pressure from Russia that had followed the Protocol of St. Petersburg, began to push forward with his long-cherished plans for the reform and training of a new modern army. On the 14th of June the Janissaries, whose ancient privileges were drastically affected by these reforms, rose in open mutiny. However, this had been anticipated and the Janissaries, so long tyrants of the capital and masters of the Harēm, were overwhelmed by Anatolian soldiers brought to Constantinople for the purpose. They were driven back to their barracks and massacred to a man, mown down by Mahmud's new field guns in the *At Meidan*, the Hippodrome or Horse Parade. Although Mahmud had thus freed himself at a stroke from his mutinous "Praetorian guard" and could press on unhampered with his military reforms, the strength of his available forces was now much diminished. Therefore he was compelled in the autumn to accede to an ultimatum from Nicholas I and send his representatives to meet those of Russia at Akkerman, where on the 26th of October Turkey assented to all the demands imposed by Russia, such as free navigation in the Black Sea and the Bosphorus, the surrender of some Circassian fortresses, and certain changes of administration in the Danubian principalities of Servia and Roumania. For the Turks concurrence with the Russian demands was the only alternative to war. Though humiliating, acceptance of the terms of the Convention of Akkerman offered at least a breathing space.

At sea the Greek position for two-thirds of the year 1827

remained complicated and indecisive. Lord Cochrane had done nothing to redeem the fiasco before Athens. He had formerly distinguished himself by his mastery of naval tactics in the South American wars of independence; but now, for all his wayward brilliance, he was much less successful in the Mediterranean. He had failed in May to prevent a Turkish fleet of twenty-eight sail from uniting with the Egyptian fleet at Navarino in the southwestern Peloponnese. He might have chosen a naval diversion off Patras to support the land actions of Kolokotronis. Instead, he decided on a far bolder, more risky move. At the beginning of June he sailed with a squadron of twenty-two men of war and six fireships to a secret destination. Not until he had passed Crete did he reveal to his captains that his objective was Alexandria and his intention an attempt to destroy the fleet which Mehemet Ali was fitting out in the harbour to help Ibrahim to demolish the remnants of Greek sea-power. When on the 17th of June Cochrane appeared off Alexandria, the Egyptians were caught napping and the guard-ship at the mouth of the port was destroyed before it could escape. Had Cochrane then sailed straight through the narrow entrance to the harbour, he might have triumphed over the ill-equipped and unprepared Egyptian fleet. On the other hand, failure would have meant his own entire destruction. Cochrane hovered outside. He hesitated and lost. Mehmet, enraged at the threat to his city, went on speedily arming his ships; then, as soon as they were ready, put out to sea to punish the presumptuous Greeks. But the Greeks, fearing to engage Mehemet's now superior force, set all sail for home. This second fiasco for the present destroyed what little was left of Cochrane's prestige.

Furthermore, the Greek seamen, now thoroughly disillusioned by their obvious naval failure, returned with some zest to the more lucrative hazards of wholesale piracy. Of course a minority of them, obeying the high examples of Kanaris and Miaoulis, went on serving their country with an indefatigable patriotism. Yet more of the best ships of the three naval islands ranged the sea as pirates than cruised with the fighting fleet, though Hydra was certainly the least guilty. Piracy had reached its period of widest extent by the autumn of 1827, and perhaps about a quarter of the male population of Greece was directly or indirectly involved in it.

On the first day of August Lord Cochrane scored a minor victory off Cape Papas. The high admiral in the *Hellas* and Captain Thomas in the *Soter* fell in with an Egyptian corvette and a fine Tunisian schooner; after a short sharp engagement, they took and brought these prizes in safety to Poros, though pursued by the entire Egyptian fleet. This was to be the last success won by the Greeks before the Powers intervened in the war. On the 11th of August came the good news of the Treaty of London which was conveyed to the French and English admirals at Smyrna. De Rigny and Codrington were authorized to intervene between the combatants if possible peaceably, if necessary by force. The island of Melos had been chosen as the meeting-place for the allied fleets. Meanwhile, at Nauplia Codrington had informed the Greek Government of the decision of the Powers. The Greeks, in the present state of their fortunes, were only too glad to accept the armistice. On Codrington's advice the Government transferred its seat of power to the more faction-free island of Aegina.

But the armistice, which had been wildly welcomed by the Greeks, was rejected with contumely by the Turks. The Porte in fact doubted whether the Powers as a final expedient would ever resort to force, and continued with preparations for the subjugation of Hydra and Spetsai. Early in August Admiral Codrington had written to Stratford Canning, the British ambassador in Constantinople, that his instructions from London made hostilities inevitable if the Turks decided to take any action which he was instructed to oppose. He had already had one reasonably satisfactory interview with the French Admiral de Rigny at Smyrna and they met again on August the 12th to co-ordinate their plans. They both felt uneasy about the vagueness of their joint directives in the Treaty, which de Rigny characterized as "bien peu précis". On the other hand, they shared the view that the Treaty of London, however imprecise its terms, would lead eventually to the independence of Greece.

In the meantime the Greeks, having accepted the armistice, had no intention of remaining passive so long as the Ottomans continued to wage war. They could reap the benefit of the combined coercion of the Powers against the refractory side. The most important enterprise of this renewed Greek activity was an expedition sent, under Church and Cochrane, to try to recapture Missolonghi and perhaps establish a footing in Albania. Important, because it led to the intervention of the allied fleet. Church was to advance with a small army from the Isthmus of Corinth along the southern shore of the Gulf. During this time Cochrane would have sailed round the Peloponnese with a squadron of twenty-three ships to unite with him and transport his army over into Western Greece. On the 18th of September Cochrane's fleet anchored off Missolonghi; but Admiral Codrington had sailed north from Navarino and was present to observe his movements. With rigid punctilio Codrington forbade him to disembark his troops in Albania; so the original plan had to be abandoned. All Cochrane could do was to bombard the fort of Vasiladi—fruitlessly. He then sailed away to the island of Syra in the Cyclades, leaving the staunch Captain Hastings in charge of a small squadron to join Church in the Gulf of Corinth.

Captain Frank Abney Hastings, the idealistic philhellene adventurer now in the Greek service, had entered the British Navy and taken part in the battle of Trafalgar at the age of eleven on board the *Neptune*. He had been unfairly dismissed the Service on account of an involved misunderstanding with the Admiralty which affected his honour. So he had first sought foreign service in Greece in 1822, with a brilliant career behind him. For nearly fifteen years following Trafalgar he had served with distinction in many actions on almost every sea, and so was capable of fighting an orthodox naval action. He had been to France and, besides learning to speak an easy and precise French, had also acquired a professional interest in the latest theories of naval gunnery. As well as his own vessel, the steam-corvette *Karteria*, Hastings's squadron included the brig *Soter*, commanded by Captain Thomas, a couple of schooners and two gunboats each mounting a long 32-pounder. On the 29th of September—a few weeks before Navarino— Hastings in the *Karteria* had followed the *Soter* into the Bay of Salona to attack the Turkish squadron which was lying at anchor under the protection of several shore batteries and a body of troops.

The Ottoman complement was composed of an Algerian schooner, mounting twenty long brass guns, six brigs and schooners and two transports. The Turks were confident that they would capture the whole Greek force. Hastings had anchored the *Karteria* about five hundred yards from the enemy's vessels, while the rest of his flotilla, with the *Soter* and gunboats, were compelled to anchor about three hundred yards farther out. Hastings now came under a fierce fire from the Turkish ships and batteries:

> He proceeded with the greatest coolness and deliberation. Some rounds of cold shot were first fired from the small cannon, in order to discover the exact range. This having been done, Hastings loaded the long guns and carronades with bombs and red-hot balls, and poured in a murderous fire on the Turks. The effect was instantaneous. A shot entered the magazine of the Turkish commodore, and blew him into the air; a brig was sunk, one schooner burnt, and another driven ashore; and within half an hour the Ottoman fleet was completely destroyed. The gunboats now ran in shore and silenced the Turkish batteries; and an attempt was made to haul off the stranded schooner. This, however, had to be abandoned, as the woods near the shore were occupied by Albanian sharp-shooters, who prevented anyone from approaching the vessel. It was thereupon bombarded from a distance; and the work of destruction was complete.[4]

This rewarding—though relatively small—victory gave the Greeks control of the Gulf of Corinth and re-opened their communications between the Peloponnese and the northern mainland, with the possibility of penetrating Epirus and Thessaly. Yet in the event it proved of less importance from a military point of view than in its ultimate political effects. For it was the startling success of Captain Hastings in destroying nine Turkish ships that exacerbated the fatal quarrel between Ibrahim and the three allied admirals and so led on to the Ottoman catastrophe of Navarino.

Ibrahim, feeling himself now no longer restrained by verbal

agreement, was determined to avenge Salona and to put a stop to any further actions by Hastings, Cochrane and Church. On the 1st of October the frigate *Dartmouth*, commanded by Captain Fellowes, that was acting as watch-dog over the Turkish fleet in Navarino, signalled to report that a Turco-Egyptian squadron was leaving the bay. From the hills of the island of Zakynthos thirty Turkish warships which had been observed sailing in a north-westerly direction, left small room for doubt that Ibrahim's objective was to save the Turkish garrison of Patras. Though high seas were running, Codrington aboard the *Asia* immediately put out from Zakynthos in pursuit and intercepted Ibrahim's ships about midnight in the strait between Zakynthos and the mainland. But he allowed them to pass northwards, the British fleet following the Turco-Egyptian squadron, losing contact for a time, but recovering it at dawn, when the British ships were able to position themselves between the enemy and the entrance to the Gulf of Corinth. Codrington, after issuing orders to prepare for battle, sent a message to the Ottoman admiral accusing him of acting in breach of the armistice and forbidding him to proceed. He would fire on the first ship trying to pass. After further exchanges and argument, the Turkish admiral insisted in writing that there had been no breach of the armistice since the agreement concerned only action against Hydra, with no mention of Patras. Nevertheless, he agreed to return to Navarino.

Codrington accompanied the enemy fleet back as far as the southern point of the island of Zakynthos, hoping on the way to make contact with the French admiral who would help him to prevent the Turks from entering the harbour at Navarino. On the evening of the 2nd of October, just before twilight, thirteen unidentifiable ships were sighted approaching from the north. The next day they were recognized as Turco-Egyptian reinforcements, two frigates, four corvettes and seven brigs that must have slipped out of Navarino. Ibrahim himself commanded one of the frigates; the other two senior enemy commanders were his brother-in-law, Moharrem Bey and the Turkish admiral Tahir Pasha. Codrington, who found himself outnumbered and outgunned, acted with resolution. Suspecting that the larger fleet might renew the attempt to reach Patras, he stationed the *Asia* across their path and waited patiently, watching signals exchanged between the flag-ships of the Ottoman commanders for nearly two hours. The signals ended towards 6 p.m., when the Turco-Egyptian fleet set their sails for Navarino, though the wind would have aided them more towards Patras. Both fleets were scattered in the night when the wind blew to a hurricane. But Codrington, much relieved, had decided against any more interference.

On his arrival at Navarino, Ibrahim received instructions from the Porte ordering him to redouble his efforts to reduce the already thrice devastated Peloponnese. He was promised the quick support of Reshid Pasha. Powerless to act against the three hated admirals, nothing could have better suited the mood of the furious Egyptian commander-in-chief. Ibrahim straightway practised this ruthless policy without compassion, killing and burning along the coast, while the British officers watched from their warships the columns of flame and smoke signifying to the Powers the Ottoman defiance.

Admiral Codrington resolutely accepted this defiance as a fact; on the 13th of October the three admirals had met off Navarino for a momentary council of war. Born of a family of country gentry distinguished for public service, Codrington was a dedicated fighting sailor, with excellent personal qualities, such as a blameless private life, who combined a professional red-hot pugnacity when in action with a humane concern for the interests of his men in the true Nelson tradition. He lacked, however, any diplomatic finesse, a quality he was perhaps too ready to grant, with a shrug of contempt, to his French colleague, Admiral de Rigny. After all, he had spent the greater part of his life fighting the French, "as a Lieutenant, he had served in Admiral Howe's flag-ship at the battle off Brest on the 'Glorious First of June' of 1794, and the Admiral had commended his gunnery. As a Captain, he had commanded the *Orion* under Nelson at Trafalgar in 1805."[5] It was hardly surprising therefore that his relationship with de Rigny was at first troubled by uneasy suspicions. From the beginning Codrington had viewed the prospect of having to work closely with his foreign colleagues with a characteristic distaste.

On the 7th of August he had written to Sir Frederic Adam at
Corfu: "It is true I cannot confide in the conduct of de Rigny, nor
perhaps should I do so in any other of his nation: and what the
deuce shall I do with a set of tallow-eating Russians! . . . But
what then? I *cannot* help it: and I will therefore make the best of
it . . ."[6] Yet from the start Codrington's relations with Count von
Heyden, the admiral of the Russian fleet, were excellent—"all I
could wish", and later "a plain-sailing, open-hearted man". And
when it came to hostilities de Rigny showed tact and restraint in
his dealings with Codrington; in fact the relationships between the
admirals turned out to be wholly satisfactory and co-operative.
Curiously, Codrington, when he first met Count Capodistrias
who was now the provisional President of Greece, had disavowed
his rightful claim to be a philhellene warning him: "I am no
philanthropist, nor am I the least of a Philhellenist; I set no particular value upon either Greeks or Turks, and I have no personal
feeling towards either. I am guided solely by my duty as an
English officer . . ."[7] This was true so far as it went; and yet the
tone of Codrington's correspondence with the Greek authorities,
though peremptory, had never been devoid of sympathy. The
Greeks, using the inward eye of visionary faith, believed that they
knew better, and that Codrington's destiny was to be their salvation; that he would save them from destruction by standing
between them and the Turks.

Codrington could not have done without his reinforcements; and
by the 13th of October outside the bay the allied fleet stood off
complete. The British squadron included three line-of-battle ships
and four frigates, the French three line-of-battle ships and two
frigates, the Russian four line-of-battle ships and two frigates. The
total number of guns amounted to one thousand two hundred and
seventy. Ibrahim had by now fatalistically accepted that the allied
Powers favoured the Greeks and that, if the imperial Turco-
Egyptian fleet opposed them, there would be war. He had estimated with near accuracy the combined strength of the allied
fleet at twenty-eight ships; and although his own total armada
greatly exceeded this number, he was conscious of its inferiority in

quality and seamanship. The ultimatum he had received demanded the return home of the Turkish and Egyptian fleets, a prompt end to land hostilities and the evacuation of the Peloponnese. At Constantinople a conflict was regarded as inevitable; and on the 20th of October (eve of the twenty-second anniversary of Trafalgar) a Turkish official had exclaimed to a British interpreter "We shall have war! You believe it, and so do I! At this very moment, it has perhaps already begun!" He was right; yet it was only the Russians who really wanted war.

The allied admirals had been granted a wide margin for using their own discretion; and fortunately Codrington, the senior of them, was not afraid of responsibility. On the 18th a further council of war was held to make a final decision. The blockade from outside, Codrington decided, had failed. Therefore he would mount a stronger demonstration by sailing into the harbour in the hope that, together with conciliatory representations to the Ottoman commander, the Turks could be persuaded to yield. But he had no illusions on this score. He was too well informed of both the number and disposition of Ibrahim's fleet and, as a result of exact reconnaissance, about the possibilities of the harbour and the surrounding locality.

A point of some technical interest is that Codrington, a keen student of history during his leisure hours, was fascinated by the coincidence that he found himself poised for action on the very scene of one of the most celebrated naval engagements of the Peloponnesian War between Athens and Sparta in the fifth century B.C. Codrington was aware from Thucydides that the Athenians had sailed round the island of Sphakteria, which formed the western arm of the Bay of Navarino, and that the Spartans had surrendered there to an Athenian fleet and army in 425 B.C., with important consequences for the war. The account given in Thucydides of Sphakteria had been a rewarding study, because Ibrahim's camp and one of the shore batteries defending the entrance to the Bay were upon that same island. Of the Athenian attack on Sphakteria Codrington would have read: "The Spartan plan was to block up the harbour entrances with lines of ships placed close together with their prows facing the sea . . .".

Thycydides then describes how the Athenians set out prepared for battle:

> Their intention was to fight in the open sea, if the enemy would sail out to meet them: if he would not, they would sail in themselves and attack him in the harbour. The Spartans, on their side, did not put out to sea, nor had they blocked the entrances to the harbour, as they had meant to do.
>
> Seeing this, the Athenians sailed in to attack by both entrances. The main body of the enemy's fleet was already at sea and in line, and the Athenians fell upon it and put it to flight. They pursued it as far as they could in the limited space, disabled a number of ships and captured five, one of them complete with its crew. They then began to ram the ships which had fled back to the shore and to put out of action others that were still getting their crews aboard, before they could put to sea. Others they took in tow with their own ships and dragged off empty, since the crews had fled.[8]

Without pressing similarities too far between battles fought in the same waters, but divided by twenty-two centuries, it is true that the Battle of Navarino had a closer similarity with that of the Athenian commander than with a modern naval battle of today. Codrington was fully justified therefore in studying the unchanging factors recorded by Thucydides. Most important was the weather hazard, the shelter available as winter advanced, off the west coast of the Peloponnese.

The harbour of Navarino lies within a large bay. Protected on the west by the wooded, hilly island of Sphakteria, which is about a mile and a half long and stretches across close in to the shore, it is vulnerable from the sea at its south-western point through a channel less than a mile wide. Since the northern end of Sphakteria is only separated from the mainland by a narrow shallow channel, the bay is virtually land-locked. Codrington, anticipating the near certainty of a fight, had made his arrangements, disposing each ship suitably in the line of battle, and on the 19th of October had concluded his operation orders to his colleagues and senior captains aboard the *Asia* with the practical words of Lord Nelson: "No captain can do very wrong who places his ship alongside that of an enemy."

The Ottoman fleet was anchored in the bay, facing the entrance in a huge half-circle. The eighty-two ships were disposed in a triple line, so that the gaps in the front line were filled by the ships immediately behind. On either side of the front line, which consisted of twenty-two of the biggest warships, three fireships stood in readiness for action. Although the Capitan Bey's fleet by far surpassed the allied squadrons in the number of vessels and guns, it was inferior in the size of its ships with a mere three line-of-battle ships compared with ten of the allies.

There was early active preparation in the allied fleet on October the 20th. The day which had begun with "light airs and cloudy weather" had improved and it was fine all through the morning. At mid-day, as the breeze flagged, the *Asia*, followed by the *Genoa*, the *Albion* and the *Dartmouth* were making directly for the entrance to the harbour. Then came the French squadron, and a little behind to the leeward, the Russians. There were twenty-seven allied ships manned in all by 17,500 men, as against the Turco-Egyptian fleet of sixty-five ships manned by almost 22,000 men. At about half-past one o'clock in the afternoon Codrington signalled to prepare for action; then his flag-ship the *Asia* sailed safely into the harbour followed by the rest of the allied fleet. Because the entrance was so narrow, the ships were obliged to pass singly in line ahead by the shore batteries on either side; but no gun was fired, except for a blank round from one of the forts; the Turks just sat on the battlements and smoked their pipes. It looked almost as if the affair might finish peacefully. With no resistance offered, the British, French and Russian warships took up their assigned positions, anchoring, turning their broadsides towards the enemy. The Russians, though a little delayed by a sudden fall of the breeze, had ample time to take up their positions in the line.

Both sides were now in an equivocally dangerous situation. The battle virtually started by accident. At 2 p.m. Codrington in the *Asia* had anchored close to Moharrem Bey's flag-ship at the eastern end of the Turco-Egyptian horseshoe formation and within range of two Turkish frigates. The *Dartmouth* had received orders to request the removal of a fire-ship lying dangerously to windward near the *Asia*. But so far there had been no sign at all of any hostile intent by the Ottoman fleet. It was simply a more than unlucky act of folly which occurred within reach of the *Dartmouth* that thwarted Codrington's own amicable intentions. Fortunately, Captain Fellowes of the *Dartmouth* recorded the exact details of this incident in a report written for Codrington, though regrettably nearly two months after the battle:

Sir,—Having been called upon by you to furnish a statement of the immediate causes which led to the commencement of the action of Navarin, on 20th October, 1827, I have the honour to state for your information, that, in pursuance of your instructions of the 19th October, I anchored H.M.'s ship under my command betwixt the brûlot and the first ship (double-banked) on the eastern side of the harbour. While in the act of furling sails, a Turkish boat pulled past the 'Dartmouth', in the greatest hurry, and went on board the brûlot. On perceiving them occupied in preparing their train, and from our being so very near, I felt it absolutely necessary that immediate steps should be taken to prevent the destruction of the fleet, which, from their manner of proceeding, seemed inevitable. I accordingly sent the pinnace with the first lieutenant, directing him to explain to them that if they remained quiet no harm was intended; but, as their position was one of great danger to us, I wished them to quit the vessel in their boats, or to remove her further in shore out of our way. As our boat left the ship, perceiving one of our midshipmen with his sword drawn, I desired him to sheath it; and that the men in the boat might perfectly understand, I called out from the gangway, in the hearing of the ship's company, "Recollect, Sir, that no act of hostility is to be attempted by us *on any account.*" When the boat reached the quarter of the vessel, and was in the act of laying in the oars, the coxwain was shot dead, although the first lieutenant had made signs to the Turkish commander that no violence was intended, which he even repeated after the man had been shot close by him. This shot was followed up by several others, fired through the after ports, killing and wounding others of the boat's crew. At the same moment we observed part of the Turkish crew ignite the train forward; upon which I despatched Lieutenant Fitzroy in the cutter for the purpose of towing her clear of this ship; in executing of which he met a boat conveying the crew of the burning fire-vessel towards the shore, who immediately opened a fire of musketry upon him by which he was killed. On observing this, I ordered the marines to cover the retreat of the boats, which were again sent to tow the vessel, then in flames, clear of us. Almost at the same instant, two shots were fired from an Egyptian corvette in shore, one of which passed close over the gangway, and the other we observed strike the 'Sirène', bearing the flag of Rear-Admiral de Rigny, then in the act of anchoring. Thus, from the aggression on the part of the Turks, commenced the action; nor could forbearance on ours have been exceeded, or your particular instruction to avoid hostility more fully complied with.[9]

What is sure is that the irresponsibility of the Turkish ship in firing on Fitzroy's boat started the battle of Navarino at precisely 2.25 p.m. Confirmation came from de Rigny who wrote to his wife: "C'est un malheureux coup tiré par les Turcs qui a engagé l'affaire." Records confirm also that the fateful incident occurred against the intentions of the commanders of the Turco-Egyptian fleet, Tahir Pasha and Moharrem Bey, who both withheld their own ships from joining in the battle until the fighting had passed beyond control. The opposing fleets, bottled up close together in the comparatively narrow bay, had no room to manoeuvre and could only go on pounding one another in a cannonade that went on for two hours. From the surrounding amphitheatre of hills twenty thousand of Ibrahim's troops watched the progress of the struggle.

The battle continued until about 6 p.m. when darkness intervened on scenes of terrible carnage. Codrington need not have worried about hostility among the French and the Russians; for the allies co-operated with an unshaken determination in a long stubborn slogging match between almost immobile targets at point-blank range. The battle was very one-sided and by nightfall the Ottoman fleet was completely destroyed. The allies lost no ships, and their casualties amounted to no more than 174 killed and 475 wounded. The losses in the Turco-Egyptian fleet were naturally vastly more severe. Apart from the fact that the enemy had been ruinously defeated, their casualties were augmented by the circumstance that their facilities for treating the wounded were much inferior. Also, according to eye-witnesses, many of the wretched Turco-Egyptian sailors were inhumanely chained to their posts.

All through the night the allied commanders remained in the bay, now lurid with corpses and wreckage, engaged in the hard task of saving their own ships from the burning hulks of the enemy. Six thousand Turks and Egyptians, as well as impressed men of many other nationalities, had perished, and sixty ships had been destroyed. In the morning only twenty-nine Ottoman vessels were found to be still afloat. The whole bay appeared as one horrid tangle of blackened and blood-stained wreckage in which floated the mutilated corpses of the poor men who had died in the explosions and fire on the Turkish ships; the entire sea was incarnadined with human gore. But the guns of Navarino had proclaimed a message to all the world: that Europe had at last decided on the right of the heroic Greek people to be free.

CHAPTER XI

The Making of a Nation

But the making of the Greek nation remained a tortuous and prolonged process. The consequences of Navarino proved to be less
decisive than might have been supposed; the battle, indeed, was
important rather for its diplomatic effect than for any immediate
military advantage. Sir Edward Codrington, after being awarded
a G.C.B., was recalled on the unfair charge of having mis-
construed his much too vague directives from the Admiralty. The
Speech from the Throne at the opening of Parliament in January
1828 spoke of Sultan Mahmud as "an ancient ally" and referred to
the battle as "this untoward event", although Lord John Russell
had called it "a glorious victory and as honest a victory as was ever
won". The truth was that since Canning's death, Britain had lost
confidence in her own judgement on the Greek question and
lacked a strong government to help her make up her mind. But
here the Greeks were in luck. As C. M. Woodhouse pin-points the
crux of the situation:

If Wellington had succeeded Liverpool as prime minister in
April 1827, there might have been no Treaty of London. If he
had succeeded Canning in August, the instructions to Codrington would have been precise and soldierly instead of vague and
puzzling; and they would hardly have admitted misconstruc-
tion in favour of the Greeks, for whom Wellington had neither
admiration nor sympathy. As it was Goderich who succeeded
Canning, there was in effect no government at all worthy of the
name in the weeks preceding Navarino, and the Admirals were
free to present a *fait accompli* according to their understanding of

orders which could have meant anything. As it was Wellington who succeeded Goderich in January 1828, there would at least be no going back on the outcome of the great action, even if for many months there was no going forward either.[1]

For Wellington was in no hurry to resolve the problem, which enabled the Russians to regain the initiative in the Middle East.

Ibrahim is reported to have merely laughed grimly as he contemplated the smoking wreckage of his fleet. But now that the battle was over, his resolution continued as unshaken as before and he refused to evacuate the Peloponnese until ordered to do so by the Sultan. The allied Admirals had been left in no position to issue or enforce any fresh ultimatum since the battered allied fleet required to be refitted: for this purpose the British and Russian squadrons sailed off to Malta, the French squadron to Toulon. Paradoxically, Ibrahim may even have felt a certain relief following the destruction of his fleet, because he would now be far less bound and hampered by the obscure cross-currents of international policy. So he made his arrangements to winter in the Peloponnese, determined to serve the Ottoman cause with redoubled vigour. He embarked his sick and wounded for Alexandria, and sent several thousands of captured Greeks to the slave markets of Egypt.

The news of Navarino had been received by the Sultan with a burning animosity. All Moslems were exhorted to rise up in defence of Islam which the Christian Powers had perfidiously betrayed. Had they not, while professing friendship and in peacetime, done to death six thousand true believers? Mahmud's vituperation bitterly singled out Russia for blame; the Convention of Akkerman, recently concluded with her, was denounced and declared void. This suited Russia because the repudiation gave her the pretext of going to war with Turkey. In the Mediterranean, where military operations could have been too complicated, Russia agreed to be bound by the Treaty of London. In return France, and England (with some misgiving), allowed her a free hand elsewhere. Metternich's nightmare of Russian aggrandizement in the east of Europe had come true. Soon Russia established herself in the Danubian principalities; and, having complete control now of the Black Sea, was able to revive by subsidies the low-flickering flame of the Greek revolt. Russia had at last come to Greece's rescue.

Metternich, who as the characteristic statesman and the *beau ideal* of the reactionary European chanceries, was more interested in diplomatic protocol than in any national aspiration, had made the enormous blunder of remaining deaf to the idealistic voices of the peoples of Europe, to whom the Greeks were ultimatly to owe their liberty. Navarino had cut the Gordian knot of Greece's helplessness; yet the curious thing was that not one of the leaders of the Powers—not even Tsar Nicholas—was prepared to order his admiral to fight. Philhellenism had revealed itself as an active power, and shown that the forceful sentiment of public opinion in Greece's favour was more potent than the haverings of weak Cabinets. And the people of all Christendom rejoiced.

After Count John Capodistrias had been elected in April 1827, at the assembly of Troezene, the first President of independent Greece, he was slow to take up his onerous duties. However, when he arrived nearly a year later in February 1828 at the island of Aegina, which was then the seat of the Hellenic Government, to assume the Presidency he was welcomed with wild demonstrations of enthusiasm by the Greek people. The British frigate *Warspite* had conveyed him to Greece, with French and Russian frigates in attendance as honouring escorts. On his landing, the three ships fired a salute, and raised aloft the Greek ensign, this being the first recognition by any of the Powers of the Greek flag. All the grumbling at his long delay was forgotten in the joy and satisfaction of his arrival. To the Greeks he represented both their national will and the guarantee of support from Europe.

But Capodistrias, whose long career in the Russian Diplomatic Service had begun as far back as 1809 and had culminated in his being Joint Russian Secretary of State, had acquired in considerable measure the rigid viewpoint of a bureaucrat; and he was at first hardly looked upon as a Greek. He was still sometimes to be seen in Russian uniform. On his voyage he had been detained at Nauplia; his general impression of the country he had come to govern was an unfavourable one of feckless misery and chaos, enough to make him almost regret the burden he had undertaken. Ibrahim's cavalry roamed the country and there was famine and disease inside the town; everywhere an unending war of factions. And yet, backed by the authority of the Powers, Capodistrias was temporarily able to quell the civil strife. Forces were put at his disposal, and the ministers furnished him with a report on the condition of the Government and the state of the country. In the Peloponnese and in continental Greece conditions were well beyond the control of any organized government; and there was anarchy in the islands. Furthermore, there was no money in the treasury.

Probably what Greece needed was a spell of enlightened dictatorship; but Capodistrias, although he was a man of lofty moral character, had neither the strength nor sufficient resilience to lead it. His experience hitherto had been limited to the "corrupt school of Russian statecraft"; and there persisted in his nature a vein of bureaucratic obstinacy. So he decided without delay to substitute for constitutional government a centralized régime based on the Russian model, with himself behind it as the sole motive power. To help him fulfil this portentous task of restoring order Capodistrias had to rely on his reputation, his experience, and about 300,000 fr. in money subscribed by European philhellenes for the ransom of captives. He possessed also the prestige of legitimacy, with the support of the Powers, which earned him from the beginning universal recognition, and caused even the most anarchic spirits to submit to his authority. Capodistrias was able to effect the changes he wanted without much serious opposition by the disingenuous method of threatening to resign if his demands were refused, thereby forcing the Senate to annul the Constitution of Troezene. He carried through a *coup d'état* by abolishing the Senate and replacing it with the Panhellenium, a council of twenty-seven members which he himself nominated, ostensibly to advise him on policy but for practical purposes solely to record his decrees. He had adroitly parried any likely trouble from the old leaders by incorporating the most important of them into the Government; thus he appointed Kondouriotis, Zaimis, and Petrobey Mavromichalis presidents of the three committees of the Pan-hellenium, while attaching Mavrocordatos to himself as financial adviser. The potential disruptive threat of the powerful Koloko-tronis had been neutralized in 1825 when he had been released from prison to command the army and organize resistance to Ibrahim Pasha in the Peloponnese.

Capodistrias, however, was not sufficiently far-sighted, nor tactful enough in his methods to achieve his reforms and keep for long the love and trust of the people. As his difficulties multiplied an opposition arose which grew in strength and bitterness; for it seemed to many that the President was imposing his drastic will upon the country. His government was developing into a tyranny, almost a police state, with all the centralized machinery of spies, secret police, arbitrary imprisonment and censorship of the press. To be sure the difficulties that faced Capodistrias were tremendous. He had to restore a country devastated by the war; and in every-thing he was hampered by a shortage of money. The war, though dormant because the belligerents were temporarily exhausted, was not yet over. Ibrahim, who was in the south of the Peloponnese with an army of 20,000 infantry and 4,000 cavalry, marched north in February and ravaged Tripolitza with fire and sword, blowing up buildings and sowing the ruins with salt. Capodistrias tried to negotiate with him to leave the country. "If I go," he said grimly, "it will be by way of the Isthmus, and my course shall be like that of the simoon, which overthrows cities, buries the inhabitants in the ruins, and dries up the trees to the roots!"[2] Had he done so, the demoralized Greek armies would have been in no condition to fight back.

Therefore it was urgently necessary that the Hellenic forces should be brought under good discipline and made once more militarily efficient. The French Colonel Fabvier could have done this, but Capodistrias had dismissed him from the Greek service out of jealousy. Capodistrias knew nothing about soldiering, and Goethe was shrewd in his judgement of the President in what he afterwards said in a conversation with Eckermann: "We have no example of a man trained in cabinet government being able to organize a revolutionary State and subjugate the military and the

Commanders-in-Chief. Sword in hand, at the head of an army, a man is in a position to command and make laws, he can be certain of being obeyed, but without this it is a precarious business."[3] Demetrios Ypsilantis was appointed the commander-in-chief of the Greek armies.

At sea a major problem was still the suppression of piracy; and reform was as urgently needed in the Greek fleet as in the armies. The Powers had for some while been turning a blind eye on the continuance of piracy because it offered them a pretext to meddle in the Mediterranean. Nests of corsairs had become strong in various islands of the Aegean. Soon after Capodistrias became president Hydra sent a somewhat high-handed deputation with offers of help, coupling this with an airing of their grievances and a demand for financial compensation on account of losses sustained in the cause of Greece. But because his coffers were empty Capodistrias met the arrogance of the Hydriotes with a snub. He replied that he could do without them; either they obeyed his orders or they would be excluded from the eventual peace treaty declaring Greek independence. He had tried, without success, to establish on Aegina a national bank to which he brought pressure on wealthy Greeks to subscribe. But in spite of a few handsome deposits contributed by such enthusiastic philhellenes as the mad King Ludwig of Bavaria, the project never got off the ground. The friction with Hydra was the first of several *contretemps* which eventually led the islands into armed intervention against Capodistrias.

By January 1828 piracy had grown so rife and troublesome that there could be no question of not suppressing the corsairs. Accordingly, the allied admirals had received their instructions to sweep the seas clean. On Grabusa off the coast of Crete there existed a flourishing town, living solely on the riches of piracy, which was demolished by an Anglo-French squadron. Capodistrias had despatched the Greek fleet in other directions to hunt down the pirates; at the islands of Skopelos and Skiathos Admiral Miaoulis destroyed in all seventy-nine pirate ships. Then he was sent to assist in the blockade of Ibrahim in Navarino where the Egyptian commander was receiving intermittent supplies from Crete and also from the Ionian Islands. Ibrahim had organized yet another brutally destructive but futile campaign in 1828; however he was induced to evacuate the Peloponnese in October of that year.

On the financial front it was not until Russia had declared war on Turkey that Capodistrias acquired big enough subsidies to relieve some of his difficulties. Yet this advantage was impaired by the distrust he felt for some of the Greeks in his government with whom he was obliged to work. The unruly chieftains of the revolution, who at first had been won over by their inclusion in the government, were increasingly alienated by Capodistrias's European airs and obvious preference for the educated semi-Venetian Corfiot aristocracy of the Phanar to which he himself belonged. Such people, they grumbled, had played no part in the War of Liberation and were out of step with the democratic ideals of the Greek people.

This partial distrust of his colleagues led Capodistrias to commit what was probably his greatest blunder. For many Greeks were much offended when he promoted his brothers, Viaro and Agostino, to high commands for which they were both totally unfitted. Viaro, a lawyer who was lacking both in brain and heart, was made the administrator of the Sporades group of islands, where his arrogance and contempt for law and justice caused the unfortunate islanders to want the Turkish cadis back again. And then shortly after Lord Cochrane arrived to resign his naval command, Capodistrias had appointed Viaro High Admiral. Similarly he had promoted, over the heads of such true heroes as Demetrios Ypsilantis and Sir Richard Church, his younger brother Agostino (who had no qualification whatsoever for the high office, unless it were an imposing presence) the supreme commander of the Army. Such flagrant nepotism of course alienated so proud and jealous a people as the Greeks. For a while yet the reign of Capodistrias remained unshaken and was supported because the Greeks believed that his Presidency guaranteed the goodwill of Russia and the Triple Alliance where lay their best hopes for the future. On the other hand, these foolish promotions of his corrupt and incompetent brothers were already damaging in many eyes the personal reputation of Capodistrias. Makriyannis for one, who was not a man to stay silent, spoke out fearlessly against his policy both in the National Assembly and to the President's face. And this dissatisfaction in the end was to lead to open rebellion.

Events grew complicated, with much desultory fighting, during the closing years of the war. Battles continued in the north-west of mainland Greece under Sir Richard Church and in the east under Demetrios Ypsilantis with the object of advancing and enlarging as far as possible the boundaries of Greece before a peace treaty should settle them permanently. The last engagement of the war was fought on the 25th of September 1829. But the Turks held out on the Acropolis of Athens until peace was finally declared in 1830.

Certainly Metternich was right when, referring to the current dubious position of the Triple Alliance, he said, "Europe has never experienced such an imbroglio." The Russian war with Turkey had produced a real diplomatic tangle which appeared almost impossible to unravel. The British Cabinet viewed with considerable alarm and despondency the threatened break up of Ottoman power in Europe, the maintenance of which it was part of their policy to support. Wellington declared bluntly that he would have no Russian aggrandizement. But England's alarm over Russia proved to be premature. The "Sick Man of Europe" in the face of danger showed remarkable recuperative powers; the Tsar's expected easy victories did not materialize. After crossing the Pruth, so far from marching in triumph on Constantinople, the Russian armies became bogged down fighting two hard campaigns before they succeeded in bringing the Turks to accept the Peace of Adrianople.

After Ibrahim's evacuation of the Peloponnese in October 1828, not only were Hellenic forces set free for service elsewhere but, because of the Russian invasion, the greater part of the Turkish troops had been withdrawn from continental Greece. Therefore it seemed to Capodistrias that it should be more than feasible to reconquer all the land that had been previously won from the Greeks by Reshid Pasha. He suggested to the French General Maison, who with his army had been filling the vacuum left by Ibrahim in the Peloponnese, that he should now march north, cross the Isthmus and compel the Turks to retire into Macedonia. But this the French

General was unable to do without further authority from his Government in Paris. Much to their chagrin, the French forces, disappointed in the hope of military glory, withdrew from Greece, leaving only a battalion or two in the fortresses of Modon and Navarino to guarantee the preservation of peace and order.

Capodistrias's decision to press the war more vigorously both in the north-west and the north-east came in November with the publication of a Protocol of the Conference of London declaring the Peloponnese, with its adjacent islands and also the Cyclades, under the protection of Europe. For by implication this excluded continental Greece from benefiting by any territorial advantages already won in the war. This had aroused furious popular resentment, which Capodistrias shared. He was firmly resolved to secure the natural frontiers of Greece.

In October Ypsilantis felt free to move from his camp at Megara and marched with quick strides into Attica, which he soon overran. Levadia, the capital of Boeotia, and Salona fell to his arms and it looked as though Eastern Hellas had been won for the Greeks. With winter coming on, he concentrated his army near Thebes. In Western Hellas for most of the past year military operations had been quiescent; the Greek troops were demoralized, with many of the peasants hostile to them. At the turn of the year Captain Frank Abney Hastings, commanding his steamship the *Karteria* had captured the fort of Vasiladi, the key to Missolonghi. Owing to shallow water the *Karteria* could approach no closer than a mile to the low fort, whose man-high walls rose above the surface of the lagoon; but the gunnery was excellent and the third shot, aimed by Hastings himself, put a shell into the powder magazine. The *Karteria's* boats arrived before the Turks had time to organize any resistance. Twelve men were found killed by the explosion, the rest were taken prisoner. But Hastings retired in disgust for a while when he discovered that the Greek chiefs were trading their rations (supplied to them by the philhellenes) with the Turks at Patras! However, with the arrival of Capodistrias, Hastings had been persuaded to resume his command under General Church and on the 25th of May 1828 he attacked the fortress-town of Aitolikon, where he was mortally wounded:

The draught of the "Karteria" did not allow her to approach. The two gunboats were winding slowly through the intricate channels between the shoals. Captain Andrea, who commanded the first, was killed, and the crew were thrown into disorder. Hastings hurried forward in his gig to put heart into the men and take the place of their lost commander. As he drew near he was struck, and fell. This was the signal for a general retreat. By a mischance there was no regular surgeon on the "Karteria" at the time. A doctor was obtained from shore. He dressed the wound, which was in the arm, and pronounced it not dangerous. But alarming symptoms developed and amputation became necessary. The "Karteria" made for Zante with all the speed of which she was capable, to obtain skilled surgical aid. But it was too late. Tetanus set in and the patient died on board, in Zante harbour, on the 1st June.[4]

Captain Hastings is important in the saga of Greek liberation because, as Finlay testifies, "No man served a foreign cause more disinterestedly . . . Frank Hastings was perhaps, the only foreigner in whose character and deeds there were elements of true glory." And Gordon confirms this estimate: "If ever there was a disinterested and useful Philhellene, it was Hastings; he received no pay and had expended most of his slender fortune in keeping the 'Karteria' afloat for the last six months." In fact, Gordon himself, Fabvier and Hastings were all three volunteers indifferent to titular rank and pecuniary rewards. Moreover, in addition Hastings had initiated a revolution in naval warfare by the use of steam and by his expertise in modern heavy gunnery. When Hastings died his body was taken to Aegina where Finlay took charge of it, until a year later it was transferred in the *Karteria* to Poros where the funeral was held. Thirty-seven salutes were fired, as for Byron, but Hastings was only thirty-four years old.

Before the end of June Capodistrias had visited the camp of Sir Richard Church and, finding the troops in bad condition, had rudely refused to be introduced to the officers. Church, however, ignored the President's biting tongue and gladly took advantage of the incentive of his visit to renew active operations. In September the Greeks had advanced to the Gulf of Arta and taken Loutraki. After a preliminary failure under the command of a Corsican naval adventurer, Passano, to force an entrance into the Gulf, the Greek officers ran the gauntlet of the guns of Prevesa and secured control of the Gulf. A capable Hydriot admiral, Kriezes, had been appointed to succeed Passano. On the 29th of December Vonitsa fell to the Greeks, but its vulnerable Venetian castle held out until March, 1829.

The long war was now moving sluggishly to its close. The initial fervent rapture of the revolt had been almost forgotten in eight exhausting years of laborious campaigning. But the stubborn Ottoman opposition was at last crushed. It remained only for the Greeks to clear the mainland of the final remnants of their Turkish oppressors. Lepanto had surrendered on the 30th of April; and the Turks had evacuated Missolonghi and Anatoliko on the 14th of May. Capodistrias's brother Agostino had conducted the land operations from the safe quarterdeck of the *Hellas* and gained much undeserved credit; for a cunning Greek called Paparri-gopulos had previously been undermining the morale of the Turkish garrisons. The Turks made one last expiring effort in Eastern Hellas before ceasing all hostilities.

A body of Albanians under Aslan Bey marched south by Thermopylae, Levadia and Thebes. The army of Ypsilantis, taken by surprise, panicked and scattered, and Aslan reached Athens without meeting any opposition. After leaving behind a small select garrison in the Acropolis, he collected up all the Turks he found left in Attica and Boeotia and began his return march. In the meantime the army of Ypsilantis had re-grouped as quickly as it had dispersed. So when Aslan Bey reached the Pass of Petra, between Thebes and Levadia, he was confronted by a strongly posted Greek force. Unable to advance, he was compelled on the 25th of September 1829 to conclude a capitulation by which the Turks agreed to evacuate all Eastern Greece, except the Acropolis of Athens and the fort of Karababa on the Euripus. Thus Prince Demetrios Ypsilantis in this last engagement had the honour of terminating the War of Greek Independence which his brother

Alexander had opened eight years before on the banks of the river Pruth.

Politically, in the same month the future of Greece was decided by a weightier and more dramatic event, the sudden ending of the Russo-Turkish conflict in the Balkan peninsula and the signing on the 14th of September of the Peace of Adrianople. The Ottomans had revealed a surprising strength, the Russias an unsuspected weakness; and it was only by the boldness of his troop movements and the sheer bluff of self-assurance that the Russian General Diebitsch, with his 13,000 men at Adrianople in the centre of enemy country, prevailed upon the alarmed Ottoman Government to submit. For General Diebitsch's modest force was in fact threatened by the armies of the Grand Vizier and the Pasha of Scutari behind him, while before him he was confronted by the powerful city of Constantinople, which contained at least a hundred thousand men ready to bear arms.

The terms of the Treaty of Adrianople accepted by the Porte included increased Russian influence in the Danubian principalities; provisions tabling Russian trade rights, with the free navigation of the Bosphorus; and, concerning Grecian affairs, agreement on the principles of the London Protocol of the 22nd of March, establishing the boundaries of the new Hellenic State. The frontier would be drawn from the Gulf of Arta to the Gulf of Volos and, among the islands, Euboea would be included and the Cyclades. Greece would pay a yearly tribute of about £30,000 to the Porte; but she would enjoy complete autonomy under the suzerainty of Sultan Mahmud and be ruled by an hereditary prince chosen by the Porte and the Conference of the Powers. Prince Leopold of Saxe-Coburg, afterwards King of the Belgians, had been tentatively proposed as a candidate for the sovereignty as long ago as 1825. But now Leopold's nomination by the Conference of London both disappointed the hopes and irritated the feelings of Capodistrias, who considered that he alone was capable of organizing a state in Greece.

The publication of the Protocol had been received in Greece with bitter indignation. What was this "autonomy" worth? The Hydriots and Spezziots had been "autonomous" before the war.

Were they now, after eight years of bloody fighting, to be cheated of their freedom? And what of the boundaries—were Samos, Crete, above all Chios, to be abandoned to the Turk, cut off from the body of a new Hellas by the cynical self-interest of Europe? The Maniot tribesmen protested angrily at the yearly lump-sum payment for the right to exist which was no better than the blood-tax that the *rayah* had previously paid to their Ottoman oppressors. And some of this hostile criticism rubbed off on Capodistrias as a representative of the Powers.

Capodistrias was now at the zenith of his power. He had ulti-mately persuaded Prince Leopold to resign his candidature for sovereign on the grounds that acceptance would necessitate Leo-pold embracing the Greek Orthodox religion. By harsh sup-pression of the least sign from the political classes of constitutional opposition, he had brought the administration of Greece com-pletely under the control of his own will; so that he was virtually a reigning monarch. He still retained his popularity with the masses and his reputation throughout Europe was unimpaired. As Metternich had observed, "Greece is Capodistrias." The Presi-dent's position seemed more assured than ever.

And yet in the summer of 1829 the first warning shadow of dissent heralded the coming storm. On the 23rd of July Capodis-trias, wearing a much be-medalled Russian uniform, inaugurated the new Congress of the National Assembly in the ruins of the old theatre of Argos; no criticism was allowed to make itself heard and a vote of confidence in the President was passed with-out one hostile voice. But the Assembly had created a fresh Senate which had overruled the democratic principles of previous congresses. It was when Capodistrias had offered places to Miaoulis, Kondouriotis and Mavrocordatos and they had refused that the storm-cone, in the guise of a possible nucleus of influential opposi-tion, first revealed itself darkly above the horizon.

The revolution of July 1830 in France which resulted in the popular monarchy of Louis Philippe was bound to react upon the fortunes of Greece; for the new liberal government in Paris had moved away from Russian influence and drawn closer to English policy.

The forces of discontent against Metternich and the Holy Alliance were generally gaining ground; and the reborn republican cry from the Parisian barricades of "Liberty! Equality! Fraternity!" reached Greece and awoke echoes among her mountains and on the islands. The bureaucratic wooden government of Capodistrias —who had already begun to be referred to as the "Russian proconsul"—grew increasingly odious to public opinion until dissatisfaction ended in open rebellion when the islands revolted.

By law the Constitution had established the liberty of the press, though in the past there had been some interference by Capodistrias. Now a young Greek lawyer from Paris named Polyzoides launched a political and literary newspaper, the *Apollo*, as a platform for liberal opinions opposed to the administration. This was too much for the "official mind" of the *régime* which feared the likely influence of the newspaper's propaganda. So, although Polyzoides was within his legal rights, there was a Government-inspired police raid on the Nauplia office on the morning of publication and the first issue of the *Apollo* was confiscated, with the machinery and plant on the premises. While a law limiting the liberty of the press was being rushed through the Senate, Polyzoides removed the *Apollo* to Hydra where it appeared on the 31st of March, 1831 and flourished twice weekly under the protection of the independent Hydriot government. Hydra thus became a rallying-point for the forces of discontent, a focus of conspiracy that spread over the archipelago.

Capodistrias confronted the intrigues around him with his customary stern tenacity, but his grip on affairs was slipping. When he sounded the representatives of the Powers on the degree of their support, the liberal Western Powers barely concealed their sympathy with the opposition. Only the Russians advised that he should "stamp on the head of the viper of revolution", promising naval support if he did so. Capodistrias acted by refusing the Hydriots their ships' papers, without which they could be treated as pirates. He then "applied to the admirals of the three to support him, by preventing the Hydriot ships from keeping the sea without their legal warranty. Admiral Ricord, who commanded the Russian squadron, at once acceded to this request. The French and

English admirals, on the other hand, said that they had no authority to prevent the Hydriot vessels from sailing."[5] Now the crisis drew near, with Hydra as the storm-centre. Mavrocordatos was already there, and Kondouriotis and Miaoulis were among the members of a "Constitutional Committee".

The national Greek fleet, including the frigate *Hellas* and Hastings's steamer *Karteria*, lay anchored in the harbour at Poros, where the arsenal also stood. Another island, Syra, had defected from the Government. Capodistrias had promptly ordered the fleet to be prepared to go to sea to coerce the rebel islands. But Miaoulis anticipated this danger by a bold *coup d'état*. On the 26th of July, 1831 he sailed, with as few as fifty men, to Poros and seized both the Greek fleet and the arsenal. The grand old Admiral Kanaris, hero of Chios, who was aboard the corvette *Spezzia* and believed in the mission of Russia, refused to be disloyal to the established Government, and was placed for a while under arrest.

Enraged by Miaoulis's exploit, Capodistrias called in the aid of the Russian admiral Ricord to compel the Hydriots to leave the island and surrender the fleet. However, Ricord's ultimatum from Poros was scornfully refused by the intrepid Miaoulis, who was now an old man of sixty-three and within four years of his death. He replied that he would obey only the government of Hydra, or the combined orders of the three Powers; and that, if attacked, he would destroy the fleet sooner than let it fall into Government hands. So the Russian waited, watching the outlets of the harbour to obstruct the chance of Miaoulis absconding with the fleet. Meanwhile, an army led by Nikitas (the nephew of Kolokotronis, nicknamed "the Turk-eater") had been despatched to attack Poros from the land where only a narrow channel divided it from the Peloponnese.

While the situation simmered, Capodistrias had sent an express letter overland to Admiral Ricord commanding him to strike. The frightened people of Poros had already agreed to surrender the town and arsenal to the Russians. But fighting had now broken out between Ricord and Miaoulis; the Russians, while ostensibly quiescent, had blockaded the Greek fleet in the narrow strait. A Hydriot brig loaded with provisions for Miaoulis was fired on;

the Russians in turn were attacked by Greek ships and by the fort which controlled the entrance to the channel. During this skirmish the *Spezzia* was dismasted and the Hydriot brig was captured by the Russians. Miaoulis threatened Ricord that unless hostilities ceased he would blow up the Greek fleet, and the Russian admiral wavered. However, the letter from the President had tipped the balance and Ricord began moving his ships, intending to put them into line of battle. But the keen resolute eye of Miaoulis had seen and accepted this manoeuvre.

> As the Russian ships sailed toward their new quarters, two explosions were heard, and over the brow of the island great columns of smoke ascended. Admiral Miaoulis had carried out his threat, and rather than suffer them to be used to coerce the freedom of the islands, had blown up with his own hands the magnificent frigate *Hellas* and the corvette *Hydra*. He himself escaped with his men in the ships' boats, to Poros, and thence to Hydra.[6]

The very same day Nikitas and his troops entered Poros which they treated as a hostile city, despite the fact that it had capitulated freely. For many hours the unhappy town was given up to the lust and cruelty of the mercenaries who, at last tired of outrage and looting, had returned to Nauplia stuffed with booty. Though they were innocent of any honest fighting, Capodistrias welcomed them back as the saviours of their country.

After the Poros affair, the differing attitudes of the allied Powers crystallized clearly: while the opposition knew that they could rely on France and England, Capodistrias made no bones about his dependence upon Russia. Admiral Ricord sailed to blockade Hydra and Syra; English and French frigates followed to prevent open warfare. The Greek islanders, once happy to serve under the Russian flag, had hoisted in its place the revolutionary tricolour. Capodistrias tried to regain some popularity by dismissing his brother Viaro and his hated chief of police; but this gesture was made too late to affect public opinion. All those who had dreamed that he would now inaugurate a more constitutional government lost hope when he postponed the meeting of Congress. Was liberty in Greece to be abandoned? Among the more ruthless men of the revolution there were even dark whispers abroad about the virtues of tyrannicide.

But Count Capodistrias was by no means the conventional tyrant, though some of his methods may have bordered on tyranny. After all, he had quite unselfishly sacrificed his lofty position in Russia in order to accept the Presidency of Greece; and for Greece he had toiled without respite, rising early and working the whole day in his office which was furnished only with a sofa and a plain writing-desk. The normal pleasures of tyrants never tempted him; his sobriety in his youth, he had declared, had left him in old age "like winter, cold but healthy". Far from accepting any income from the national funds, he had used his own small fortune to help replenish the Greek treasury. He was, it is clear, a man of high moral virtue, whose great gift for government unfortunately fell short of genius.

There existed therefore a fundamental clash of temperament between the civilized Capodistrias and the more primitive chieftains of the revolution whom he was endeavouring to wean away from their more brutal instincts, such as revenge and blood-feuds, which they had inherited from the barbarous past. Some of the robber tribes boasted their descent from the ancient Spartans, and hated the President's Russian airs and preference for the educated Greeks of the Phanar. The climax of tension was reached when Capodistrias tried to coerce the powerful Mavromichalis clan from the province of Mani, bravest and most arrogant of mountain clans whose chief Petrobey Mavromichalis—"King of the Mani" —had first raised the standard of revolt in the southern Peloponnese.

The result of the growing pressure of Capodistrias's coercive policy was that at Eastertide 1830 Djami Mavromichalis, Petrobey's brother, headed an insurrection in the Mani against the prefect who had been instructed to curb all unruliness. Capodistrias acted now with Machiavellian subtlety. He interviewed Petrobey's son George, treating him with such respect and kindly consideration that the flattered young man was induced to go to the Mani and persuade his uncle Djami to come to Nauplia to air his grievances with the President. But once in the town, Djami was arrested, tried on a past murder charge, and put in prison where he was confined for eighteen months. The other members of his family were placed under police control and forbidden to leave Nauplia. However, in January 1831 Katzakos, the son of Djami, escaped to the Mani with the news that Capodistrias was bent upon destroying the Mavromichalis clan. Joined by his uncle Constantine, between them they roused the wrath of the rampageous clansmen. The Maniots flew to arms, threatening that unless the Government released their chiefs, they would march on Nauplia with 5,000 "Spartans".

Against the will of Capodistrias, Petrobey had left Nauplia to return to the Mani. He sailed in General Gordon's yacht which was bound for Zante; but owing to a contrary wind the yacht was unable to anchor at Mani and landed Petrobey at the small port of Katakolo, where he was at once arrested by Kanaris and sent back to Nauplia as a state prisoner. Almost at the same time Constantine Mavromichalis was decoyed by Kanaris on board ship and carried to Nauplia; and both he and George were also imprisoned in the fortress. Public sympathy ran strongly in favour of the Mavromichalis clan. It was generally held that Petrobey was hardly treated, Constantine unfairly beguiled, and George unjustly detained. Petrobey's mother, a venerable old lady of nearly ninety, pleaded with Admiral Ricord to petition with the President for her son's release. It appears certain that Capodistrias allowed the prisoner to dine aboard the Russian flag-ship, implying forgiveness for past offences. He had, in fact, promised to release Petrobey on condition that the old chieftain should admit his errors. The proud and dignified veteran of so much fighting at first rejected any thought of an apology; but, weary of eight months imprisonment, he was reluctantly persuaded to submit. An interview with Capodistrias was arranged for five o'clock on the 8th of October. Unfortunately, since the affair of Poros, Capodistrias had become more peevish and changeable, overwrought with the cares and anxieties of his office, and when Petrobey arrived under guard to keep his appointment, he refused to see him.

At this insult the haughty old chieftain became speechless, livid with rage and mortification. He, the Bey of the Mani, forty-nine of whose kinsmen had already died for Greece, had demeaned himself in vain before a cold Corfiot aristocrat who had never struck one soldier's blow against the Turk. As he was led through the streets back to prison, he passed by the house where his brother Constantine and his son George were staying and called out to them. Leaning from the window, they asked him how he fared. Petrobey, his voice hoarse with passion, pointed to his guards. "You see how I fare!" It was enough, they had understood. There was only one possible course of action. The head of their family had suffered a wrong which must be paid for in blood.

At dawn on Sunday Morning, the 9th of October, Capodistrias walked as usual with his one-armed servant, Kokonis, to hear mass in the church of St. Spiridion. He had risen, as was his habit, at five o'clock and had already put in an hour's work. As he approached the low door of the church, he saw Constantine and George Mavromichalis standing one on each side of the porch and hesitated, as he wished to avoid speaking to them. He had been warned of danger to his life but had taken no precautions, though he was aware of the customs of the Mani. "Providence," he said, "watches over the President of Greece. They will reverence my white hairs!" When Capodistrias moved on into the church, Constantine fired a pistol, and he collapsed mortally wounded with a double charge in the back of his head; as he fell down on the pavement George thrust a dagger through his lungs and he died without uttering a word.

The two assassins turned and fled. Constantine had been wounded in the leg by a shot fired by Kokonis who had rushed after him. He was quickly overtaken, dragged to the ground and manhandled by an infuriated cursing mob. But his native courage remained. "Don't dishonour me, boys!" he cried; "Is there no pallikari who will end me with a pistol-ball?" His corpse was taken to the square, where it was exposed naked to the insults of the people for several hours, after which it was thrown into the sea.

The whole population was in the streets; yet George had managed to take refuge in the French consulate, some distance from the scene of the murder. The crowd clamoured for his blood. He was given up, marched off to the fortress under a guard of soldiers, tried by court-martial and condemned to be shot. He too was a brave and handsome man and the people were divided between sympathy for his character and loathing of his crime. He was executed on the 22nd of October and faced death with a calm courage for a murder inspired by the law of retaliation inherited from an age of barbarism.

Greece was now left utterly demoralized by the removal of her strong but equivocal leader. As Finlay acidly comments, "she had exchanged the sufferings of illegality for the tortures of anarchy."

After the death of Capodistrias there is not much more to tell. Anarchy? Greece had suffered it before and it wears the same face. Yet, with the collapse of the late President's administration, the liberals at the close of 1831 saw Hellas relapse into a confusion and disorder not paralleled since 1824.

At first the Senate had chosen a triumvirate of Agostino Capodistrias, Kolokotronis and Kolettis to assume authority; but in December Agostino convened a fifth National Assembly at Argos to elect himself sole President and was supported by Kolokotronis. Then Kolettis set up a rival Assembly in the same town; while yet a third Constitutionalist Assembly was held on Hydra to which Kolettis soon added his faction. In Nauplia the foreign Residents made confusion worse confounded, the Russians backing Agostino, the British and French united in their support of Kolettis and the Constitutionalists. The quarrel was still further exacerbated by the territorial division of loyalties between the parties, the Peloponnesians loyal to Kolokotronis, the Roumeliotes at the service of Kolettis with his early connexion with Yannina and Ali Pasha. So, by the beginning of 1832, there were once more rival governments in Greece. It now behoved the protecting Powers to be less dilatory and to take some definite action to halt the civil war.

While the Greeks may justly be accused of irresponsible and fratricidal behaviour, a balanced judgement must admit that blameworthy fumbling expedients were being authorized from London. The Conference of London had issued a spate of Protocols which in turn cancelled one another. As the fire of civil war continued to rage through the Peloponnese, yet another Protocol dated March the 7th arrived, authorizing the allies—meaning primarily the French troops stationed there—to restore order and the three allied Residents to establish a representative government by force. But no sooner was each step taken than it seemed out of date. And the strange thing was that not even the important news which reached Nauplia on the 11th of March that the young Prince Otto, second son of Ludwig of Bavaria, was about to be elected King of Greece, had for the moment any calming effect upon the hostilities. On the contrary, each faction fought harder than ever, hoping to be in possession of the Greek capital before the new King's arrival to enjoy such benefits as might accrue.

Only armed intervention by the Powers could have restored order. While intermittent skirmishes continued between the Roumeliotes of Kolettis and the Peloponnesians of Kolokotronis, the Conference of London had arrived hesitantly at their final decision. In the Convention of the 7th of May, 1832, the Kingdom of Bavaria had joined with Britain, France and Russia when Ludwig I had accepted the crown of Greece for his seventeen-year-old son, under a regency of Bavarian courtiers. The fact that Otto was so young was considered by many people to be a positive advantage, as it should enable him to be more easily adaptable to the ways of the foreign country he had been called upon to govern. His father Ludwig had wanted some modifications of former Protocols; but he had not succeeded in getting the islands of Samos and Crete included in the new kingdom. Nor was the northern boundary allowed to be extended beyond the Arta-Volos line. But Otto was to be King of the Hellenes, no mere "Sovereign Prince" of Greece, and the stability of his throne was guaranteed by a more than adequate international loan, so that the new Government would start unhampered by lack of funds. The naval squadrons of the allied Powers, together with the promise of 3,500 Bavarian troops to replace the French and maintain order, were put at the disposal of the Regency.

In August the civil war raged daily with rising ferocity and violence in the Peloponnese, as the power of Kolokotronis increased. The Maniots were plundering independently in the south, with Niketas endeavouring to bring them to order. From the north the fires of war had crossed the Gulf of Corinth, while the Armatoles of Gardikiotis Grivas, a staunch Othonian royalist, had captured Missolonghi. From East Hellas united forces were marching south for the invasion of the Peloponnese. Alone in Greece Nauplia was peaceful under the protection of the French garrison. And then, in the middle of all this confusion, on the 15th of August Stratford Canning brought news from Constantinople of confirmation by the Porte of the Treaty of London. The Ottoman Government had formally accepted in July the terms imposed by the protecting Powers and had acquiesced in ceding to the Greeks, with the compensation of an indemnity to be paid before the end of December, some districts in Greece, which included Athens, that were still held by Turkish forces. The Greek question would seem to have been settled for ever.

When the young King Otto reached Nauplia on the 6th of February, 1833, he was welcomed with much jubilation by the population. The watchmen on the hills round Navarino had reported the advance of a squadron of men-of-war, with the leading battleship flying the blue and white Greek ensign, as it sailed along the coast. The fleet entered the harbour at Nauplia to the roar of artillery and the joyful cries of the people, as the first King of the Hellenes stepped upon the sacred shores of Greece. To begin with his youthful elegance and charm, coupled with his palpable anxiety to please his subjects, won all hearts; for he had adopted the Greek form of his name, Otho, and dressed himself in Greek costume.

Unhappily, the arrival of the Bavarian boy-king failed to usher in the golden age which had been so hopefully looked for; nor could Otho ever have acted as a *deus ex machina* to round off the long-protracted agony of the Hellenic drama. For one thing he had brought with him in his blood a German authoritarian tradition; and Capodistrias had transmitted, most acceptably to the regents, his own type of autocratic government. It was to take more than a generation before open conspiracy and active insurrection, led by men like Kolokotronis and Makriyannis, were at last quelled under another dynasty and the Greeks were able to realize a truly free democracy. At the commencement of the revolution Shelley had written in *Hellas* "The world's great age begins anew," but how long the new age was in coming! However, the events of these after-years do not properly belong to the story of the Greek War of Independence.

There is a somewhat foolish slogan, which doubtless springs partly from idealistic wishful-thinking, to the effect that war settles nothing. For present purposes it is sufficient to note what none may deny, that the War of Independence settled a great deal and altered the map of Europe by giving it a new Christian State which, by its mere existence, affected the relative importance of the other nations. Chronologically and territorially the boundaries of the Greece of today came into being in a piecemeal fashion throughout the remainder of the nineteenth and into the twentieth centuries. If the four dark centuries of bondage under the Turks are to be regarded as a period of preparation for the renaissance of liberty, the century and more following formal independence was a time of conditioning and consolidation. For the conception of liberty and independence, since it is something dynamic and not static, becomes a habit of mind, also an appetite that grows with what it feeds on. The generous return by the British Crown under Lord Palmerston of the Ionian Islands to Greece in 1864 had just this effect. Greek irredentism required still more territory, and Thessaly was ceded to Greece by the Turks in 1881. Lesbos, Chios and Samos were liberated in 1912; Crete and the Greek districts of Macedonia and Epirus in 1913; and the Dodecanese islands not until 1947.

Looking back over those heroic agonizing war-years of dreams and bloodshed, then back beyond them to the long centuries of protracted Ottoman oppression, it becomes clear that Greece was able to preserve her national identity by means of the unchanging heritage of her superb language and the Byzantine tradition and strength of her enduring Orthodox faith. Makriyannis was perhaps in a class apart because his standards were set higher than most of his contemporaries and the colleagues whom he outlived, as when he wrote in his *Memoirs*:

Thou, oh Lord, shalt set upon their feet these long dead Greeks, the descendants of those famous men, who gave mankind the fair raiment of virtue. And by Thy power and Thy righteousness Thou shalt bring back life to the dead, and it is Thy just will that the name of Greece shall be spoken once more, that she shall shine forth, and the worship of Christ too, and that the honest and the good, those who are the defenders of justice, shall live on.[7]

But in the ultimate judgement of history it will not be the Phanariotes, the world-renowed philhellenes, nor the celebrated chieftains and politicians, who achieved what most of the countries of Europe would have liked to prevent. Rather victory belongs to the genius of the ordinary Greek people upon whom the divine spark had fallen and who had poured "out the fire of Hellas, the everlasting fire!"

> Yet still victorious Hellas, thou hast heard
> Those ancient voices thundering to arms,
> Thou nation of an older younger day,
> Thou hast gone forth as with the poet's song.[8]

There was much that was Homeric in the Greek War of Independence, both in the noble and brutal incidents of the fighting, in its astonishing bravery and frequent moods of discouragement and often devious betrayals. For, although Homer's heroes used different weapons, he has told for all time with complete naturalism the universal realities of warfare. Many of the participants in the War of Independence were men of honour, some were less so, full "of many devices". And in this sense there was never any old Greece or new Greece; for in Greece, more than anywhere else, past and present merge in a timeless continuum.

So from their realm of misty Cimmerian darkness the multitudinous ghostly dead of the war, *klutea ethnea nekron*, "the glorious tribes of the dead" rise up again to proclaim their ancestry and their hard-won victory in the fight for freedom and their faith in perpetuity for the future.

Notes and Sources

Notes and Sources

CHAPTER I

1. Alexander Kinglake, *Eothen*, Chapter III.
2. Edwin Pears, *The Destruction of the Greek Empire*, pp. 208–9.
3. Edward Gibbon, *The Decline and Fall of the Roman Empire*, Everyman's Library, Vol. VI, p. 422.
4. Edwin Pears, *The Destruction of the Greek Empire* (Quoted), p. 216.
5. Edward Gibbon, *The Decline and Fall of the Roman Empire*, Everyman's Library, Vol. VI, p. 438.
6. Edward Gibbon, *The Decline and Fall of the Roman Empire*, Everyman's Library, Vol. VI, p. 442.

CHAPTER II

1. Khodja Sa'ad ed-Din, *The Capture of Constantinople, from the Taj-ut-Tevarikh*. Translated by E. J. W. Gibb, p. 29.
2. Edward Gibbon, *The Decline and Fall of the Roman Empire*, Everyman's Library. Vol. VI, p. 451.
3. Alexander Pallis, *In the Days of the Janissaries*, p. 185.
4. N. M. Penzer, *The Ḥarēm*, pp. 17 and 82.
5. Kenneth Young, *The Greek Passion*, p. 123.
6. Sir Steven Runciman, *The Fall of Constantinople 1453*, p. 189.

CHAPTER III

1. Patrick Leigh Fermor, *Roumeli*, p. 99.
2. Alexander Pallis, *In the Days of the Janissaries*, p. 174.

Notes and Sources

3. Alexander Pallis, *In the Days of the Janissaries*, pp. 175–6.
4. Terence Spencer, *Fair Greece, Sad Relic*, p. 22.
5. George Manwaring, *The Three Brothers; or, The Travels and Adventures of Sir Anthony, Sir Robert and Sir Thomas Sherley*, p. 29.
6. Sir Thomas Sherley, *Discours of the Turkes*, p. 9.
7. John W. Baggally, *The Klephtic Ballads in Relation to Greek History (1715–1821)*, pp. 18 and 19. (Quoted Fawrey 1, p. 156.)
8. Sir Harold Nicolson, *Byron: The Last Journey, April 1823–April 1824*, Preface.
9. C. M. Woodhouse, *The Philhellenes*, Preface, p. 11.

CHAPTER IV

1. William Plomer, *The Diamond of Yannina*, p. 31.
2. William Plomer, *The Diamond of Yannina*, p. 47.
3. Hilary Pym, *Songs of Greece*, pp. 60 and 61.
4. Lord Byron, *Letters and Journals*, Vol. I, p. 246.

CHAPTER V

1. W. Alison Phillips, *The War of Greek Independence*, p. 48.
2. Thomas Gordon, *History of the Greek Revolution*, Vol. I, pp. 148–149.
3. Patrick Leigh Fermor, *Mani: Travels in the Southern Peloponnese*, p. 51.
4. John W. Baggally, *The Klephtic Ballads in Relation to Greek History (1715–1821)*, pp. 92–95.
5. George Finlay, *History of the Greek Revolution*, Vol. I, pp. 214, 215.
6. George Finlay, *History of the Greek Revolution*, Vol. I, p. 220.
7. Aristodimos N. Sofianos, *Hydra*, pp. 30, 31.

CHAPTER VI

1. Makriyannis, *The Memoirs of General Makriyannis 1797–1864*, pp. 13–14.
2. Makriyannis, *The Memoirs of General Makriyannis 1797–1864*, pp. 21 and 22.
3. Makriyannis, *The Memoirs of General Makriyannis 1797–1864*, pp. 58 and 59.

4. Harold Nicolson, *Byron: The Last Journey, April 1823–April 1824*, p. 62.
5. C. M. Woodhouse, *The Greek War of Independence* (Quoted), p. 23.

CHAPTER VII

1. T. F. Higham, *The Oxford Book of Greek Verse*, "The Blind Old Man", p. 160.
2. George Finlay, *History of the Greek Revolution*, Vol. I, p. 305.
3. George Finlay, *History of the Greek Revolution*, Vol. I, p. 115.
4. C. M. Woodhouse, *The Greek War of Independence* (Quotation), pp. 91–92.
5. *The Memoirs of General Makriyannis, 1797–1864*, p. 42.
6. George Finlay, *History of the Greek Revolution*, Vol. I, p. 362.

CHAPTER VIII

1. Lady Blessington, *Conversations of Lord Byron*, p. 49.
2. Lady Blessington, *Conversations of Lord Byron*, p. 220.
3. Sir Harold Nicolson, *Byron: The Last Journey, April 1823–April 1824*, pp. 82 and 83.
4. Leslie A. Marchand, *Byron: A Portrait* (Quoted), p. 429.
5. Iris Origo, *The Last Attachment: The Story of Byron and Teresa Guiccioli*, pp. 16 and 17.
6. Sir Harold Nicolson, *Byron: The Last Journey April 1823–April 1824*, p. 209.
7. C. M. Woodhouse, *The Greek War of Independence* (Quoted), p. 108.
8. George Finlay, *History of the Greek Revolution*, Vol. II, p. 70.

CHAPTER IX

1. Makriyannis, *The Memoirs of General Makriyannis 1797–1864*, pp. 72, 73.
2. Makriyannis, *The Memoirs of General Makriyannis 1797–1864*, pp. 88 and 89.
3. Makriyannis, *The Memoirs of General Makriyannis 1797–1864*, p. 91.

4. W. Alison Phillips, *The War of Greek Independence 1821–1833*, p. 195.
5. George Finlay, *History of the Greek Revolution*, Vol. II, p. 106.
6. George Finlay, *History of the Greek Revolution*, Vol. II, p. 111.
7. Thomas Gordon, *History of the Greek Revolution*, Vol. II, p. 265, note.

CHAPTER X

1. Makriyannis, *The Memoirs of General Makriyannis 1797–1864*, p. 94.
2. Makriyannis, *The Memoirs of General Makriyannis 1797–1864*, pp. 111, 112.
3. George Macaulay Trevelyan, *History of England*, p. 629.
4. W. Alison Phillips, *The War of Greek Independence 1821–1833*, pp. 259–260.
5. C. M. Woodhouse, *The Battle of Navarino*, p. 32.
6. *National Maritime Museum*, COD/8/6.
7. Lady Bourchier, *Memoir of the Life of Admiral Sir Edward Codrington*, Vol. II, p. 169.
8. Thucydides, *The Peloponnesian War* (tr. Rex Warner), Book Four, pp. 233 and 237.
9. Lady Bourchier, *Memoir of the Life of Admiral Sir Edward Codrington*, Vol. II, pp. 135–6.

CHAPTER XI

1. C. M. Woodhouse, *The Greek War of Independence*, p. 125.
2. W. Alison Phillips, *The War of Greek Independence 1821–1833*, pp. 290 and 291.
3. Richard Friedenthal, *Goethe his Life and Times*, p. 484.
4. Z. D. Ferriman, *Some English Philhellenes*, p. 9.
5. W. Alison Phillips, *The Greek War of Independence 1821–1833*, pp. 350–351.
6. W. Alison Phillips, *The Greek War of Independence 1821–1833*, p. 356.
7. Makriyannis, *The Memoirs of General Makriyannis 1797–1864*, p. 148.
8. James Elroy Flecker, "Ode to the Glory of Greece."

Select Bibliography

Select Bibliography

ALLEN, W. E. D., *The Turks in Europe* (John Murray, 1919).

BAGGALLY, JOHN W., *The Klephtic Ballads in Relation to Greek History (1715–1821)* (Basil Blackwell, 1936).

BLESSINGTON, LADY, *Conversations of Lord Byron* (ed. Ernest J. Lovell Jr., Princeton, N.J., 1969).

BOURCHIER, LADY, *Memoir of the Life of Admiral Sir Edward Codrington* (London, 1873).

BRADFORD, ERNLE, *The Sultan's Admiral. The Life of Barbarossa* (Hodder and Stoughton, 1968).

BYRON, LORD GEORGE GORDON, *Letters and Journals* (ed. Rowland E. Prothero, John Murray, 1898).

CAMPBELL, JOHN, and SHERRARD, PHILIP, *Modern Greece* (Ernest Benn, 1968).

DAKIN, DOUGLAS, "The Origins of the Greek Revolution of 1821" (*The Journal of the Historical Association,* no. CXIX. George Philip, 1952).

— *The British and American Philhellenes During The War of Greek Independence, 1821–1833* (Thessaloniki, 1955).

FERRIMAN, Z. D., *Some English Philhellenes* (The Anglo-Hellenic League, 1917).

FINLAY, GEORGE, *History of the Greek Revolution* (William Blackwood, 1861).

FOSS, ARTHUR, *The Ionian Islands: Zakynthos to Corfu* (Faber and Faber, 1969).

FRIEDENTHAL, RICHARD, *Goethe his Life and Times* (Weidenfeld and Nicolson, 1965).

GIBBON, EDWARD, *The Decline and Fall of the Roman Empire* (J. M. Dent, 1910).

GORDON, THOMAS, *History of the Greek Revolution* (William Blackwood, 1832).

KEIGHTLEY, THOMAS, *History of the War of Independence in Greece* (London, 1930).

KINGLAKE, ALEXANDER WILLIAM, *Eothen* (J. M. Dent, 1908).

KNIGHT, G. WILSON, *Lord Byron: Christian Virtues* (Routledge & Kegan Paul, 1952).

— *Neglected Powers: Essays on Nineteenth and Twentieth Century Literature* (Routledge & Kegan Paul, 1971).

LEIGH FERMOR, PATRICK, *Mani: Travels in the Southern Peloponnese* (John Murray, 1958).

— *Roumeli: Travels in Northern Greece* (John Murray, 1966).

LYTTON, H. BULWER, *An Autumn in Greece* (London, 1826).

MARCHAND, LESLIE A., *Byron: A Portrait* (John Murray, 1971).

MAKRIYANNIS, *The Memoirs of General Makriyannis 1797-1864* (ed. and trans. H. A. Lidderdale, Oxford University Press, 1966).

MANWARING, GEORGE, *The Three Brothers: or, the Travels and Adventures of Sir Anthony, Sir Robert and Sir Thomas Sherley* (1825).

NICOLSON, SIR HAROLD, *Byron: The Last Journey April 1823-April 1824* (Constable, 1924).

ORIGO, IRIS, *The Last Attachment: The Story of Byron and Teresa Guiccioli* (John Murray, reissued 1971).

PALLIS, ALEXANDER, *In the Days of the Janissaries* (Hutchinson, 1951).

PEARS, EDWIN, *The Destruction of the Greek Empire* (Longmans, 1903).

PENZER, N. M., *The Harēm* (George Harrap, 1936).

PHILLIPS, W. ALISON, *The War of Greek Independence 1821-1833* (Smith Elder, 1897).

PLOMER, WILLIAM, *The Diamond of Yannina (Ali Pasha 1741-1822)* (Jonathan Cape, 1970).

POUQUEVILLE, F. C. H. L., *Histoire de la Régénération de la Grèce* (Paris 1824).

POWYS, JOHN COWPER, *Homer and the Aether* (Macdonald, 1959).

PYM, HILARY, *Songs of Greece* (The Sunday Times, 1968).

RAINE, KATHLEEN, *William Blake* (Thames and Hudson, The World of Art Library, 1970).

RUNCIMAN, SIR STEVEN, *The Fall of Constantinople 1453* (Cambridge University Press, 1965).

SA'AD ED-DIN, KHODJA, *The Capture of Constantinople from the Taj ut-Tevarikh* (trans. E. J. W. Gibb, Glasgow, 1879).

SHERLEY, SIR THOMAS, *Discours of the Turkes* (Camden Miscellany

1936, ed. E. Denison Ross).

SOFIANOS, ARISTODIMOS N., *Hydra* (Hydra, 1965).

SPENCER, TERENCE, *Fair Greece, Sad Relic* (Weidenfeld and Nicolson, 1954).

SPENDER, HAROLD, *Byron and Greece* (John Murray, 1924).

TRELAWNY, EDWARD JOHN, *Recollections of the Last Days of Shelley and Byron* (London, 1858).

TRYPANIS, CONSTANTINE A., *The Penguin Book of Greek Verse* (Penguin Books, 1971).

TREVELYAN, GEORGE MACAULAY, *History of England* (Longmans, Green, 1926).

WARNER, REX (tr.), *Thucydides: History of the Peloponnesian War* (Penguin Books, 1954).

WARD, AILEEN, *John Keats: The Making of a Poet* (Secker & Warburg, 1963).

WOODHOUSE, C. M., *The Battle of Navarino* (Hodder & Stoughton, 1965).

— *The Philhellenes* (Hodder & Stoughton, 1969).

— *The Story of Modern Greece* (Faber & Faber, 1968).

— *The Greek War of Independence* (Hutchinson's University Library, 1952).

YOUNG, KENNETH, *The Greek Passion* (J. M. Dent, 1969).

Index

Index

Index

Diebitsch, 204

Dimitrios, 67

Discours of the Turkes, 42

Disraeli, 139

Djavellas, Kitzo, 162, 166

Djeritlee, Hussein Bey, 162

Dramali, Mahmoud, 121–3, 124, 125

Drayton, Michael, 36

Eckermann, 197–8

Emerson, James, 95

Eminé, wife of Ali Pasha, 65

England, and the Levant Company, 38–9

  attitude towards Turks, 39–40, 42

  attitude towards Greeks, 40–1, 55–6

  conflict with Russia, 51, 52

  European policy in 1815, 74–5

  occupation of Ionian Islands, 75–6, 108–9, 135, 215

  support for Greek War of Independence, 78, 83, 103, 108–9, 111, 132–3, 134, 137, 144–5, 148, 155, 171, 174

  and battle of Navarino, 178–92

  and Treaty of London, 175–6, 193, 212–13

  and Hydra crisis, 206–7

Epirus, 45, 52, 61, 65, 66

Erasmus, 40

Erskine, Lord, 132

Fabvier, Colonel, 171, 173, 177, 197, 202

Fellowes, Captain, 184, 190–1

Femlario, 72

Ferdinand I of Belgium, 40

da Ferrara, Constanza, 9

Finlay, George, 46–7, 56, 116–17, 137, 150, 212

  judgment of Androutsos, 86, 113

  description of Greek atrocities, 90–1

  description of battle of Eressos, 92–3

  comments on Hastings, 202

Fitzroy, Lieutenant, 191

Fletcher, 138

Fox, Charles James, 135

France, 57, 78, 83, 156–7, 208, 212

  impact on Greeks, 51–2

  French Revolution, 51, 74, 130

  clash with Ali Pasha, 73, 74

  occupation of Ionian Islands, 75

  support for Greek War of Independence, 168, 186–7, 189, 191–2, 194, 200–1

  and Treaty of London, 175–6

  revolution of 1830, 205–6

Francis I, Emperor of Austria, 103

Frosyni, Kyra, 68–70

Gamba, Count Pietro, 131, 134, 139, 143, 145

Garnery, A. L., 179

Gateluzzi, family, 38

Gennadius, George Scholarius, 25, 28

Genoese, 4, 12, 15, 16, 21, 22

Germanos, Archbishop, 81–3, 104–5

Gibbon, Edward, 5, 8, 15, 31

Goderich, Lord, 176, 193–4

Goethe, 197–8

Gogos, Bakolas, 99, 119, 120

Golden Horn, the, 4, 22, 23, 29

Gordon, General, 113, 166, 167, 202, 210

Gouras, Yannis, 86, 170, 172–4

Grand Seraglio, the, 25, 28

Greece, origins of, 33, 34–5

  conquest by Turks, 37–8

  the Levant Company, 38–9

  Byron's discovery of, 54–5

  signs of national renaissance, 56–7

  position at beginning of 19th century, 74–7

  civil war, 125, 136, 147, 152, 212–14

  election of first President, 195–200

  autonomy, 204–5

227

impact of revolution in France,
205–6
disputes under Capodistrias, 206–12
Otto of Bavaria as first King, 214
see also Greek War of Independence
Greek War of Independence, 23, 30,
33, 35, 46, 47, 77
English support for, 78
conflicting aims, 78–9
outbreak of war (1821), 79–81
rising under Germanos, 81–3
rebellion in the Peloponnese, 80,
81–3, 83–5
in Eastern Roumeli, 85–8
war at sea, 88–92
under Makriyannis, 98–101
martyrdom of Gregorios, 101–3
efforts at national government,
103–7
massacre of Chiots, 108–12
position in 1822, 112–14
attack on Souliotes, 119–20
Dramali's attack on Eastern Greece,
121–3
siege of Missolonghi, 120–1, 124,
147–8, 155, 157–68
Turkish campaign of 1823, 125–8
Byron's planned attack on Lepanto,
140–2, 145
Ibrahim Pasha's invasion, 148–51,
152–5
siege of Athens, 169–78
battle of Navarino, 178–92, 193,
194, 195
end of the war, 200–4
effects of the war, 215–16
Greeks, character of, 4, 40, 88, 89
Greek Orthodox faith, 3, 4–5, 7–8,
18
during siege of Constantinople, 12,
13, 14, 15, 19–21
superstitions, 13, 16–17
massacre by Turks, 22–3
under Mehmet's rule, 27–31

origins, 33, 34–5
the "Dark Age", 35, 37, 45–6, 50
"bad image" of, 37, 38–9, 40
philhellenism, 40–2, 53–6
maritime power, 49–50
support for Catherine the Great, 51,
52
influence of France, 51–2
the "Eastern Question", 52–3
see also Greece, Greek War of
Independence
Gregorios, Patriarch of Constantinople,
101–3
Grivas, Gardikiotis, 214
Guiccioli, Contessa Teresa, 129–30,
131
Giustiniani, 12, 16, 20–1

Hagia Sophia, 18, 24
Halil, Vizier, 11
Hastings, Captain Frank Abney, 56,
111, 132, 145, 207
at battle of Salona, 182–4
death, 201–2
Hercules, the, 131, 134, 136
von Heyden, Count, 175, 186
Histoire de la Régénération de la Grèce,
171, 172
Hobhouse, John Cam, 54, 61, 66–7,
130, 132, 140, 144
Holy See, 12
Homer, 33, 109, 216
Hume, 132
Hydra, 172, 180, 181, 198, 206–8, 212

Ibrahim Pasha, 71
marriage, 64–5
background and character, 148–9
capture of Crete, 149–50
invasion of Peloponnese, 151, 152–5,
169, 172, 174, 175, 196, 197
jealousy of Reshid Pasha, 157,
160–1, 167, 178

Index

But Greece and her foundations are
Built below the tide of war,
Based on the crystalline sea
Of thought and its eternity.

From "Hellas" by Shelley